A Field Manual for the Amateur Geologist

Tools and Activities for Exploring Our Planet

Revised Edition

Alan M. Cvancara

John Wiley & Sons, Inc.

New York ▪ Chichester ▪ Brisbane ▪ Toronto ▪ Singapore

To Ella:
wife, mother, listener, provider of a suitable environment
for one who desired to write, writing critic,
and trusted friend.

Copyright © 1985, 1995 by Alan M. Cvancara
Published by John Wiley & Sons, Inc.

Library of Congress Cataloging-in-Publication Data:

Cvancara, Alan M.
   A field manual for the amateur geologist : tools and activities for exploring our planet / Alan M. Cvancara. —Rev. ed.
     p.   cm.
   Includes bibliographical references.
   ISBN 0-471-04430-X (pbk. : acid-free)
   1. Geology—Guidebooks.   I. Title.
QE45.C83 1995
550—dc20   94-18496

PREFACE TO THE REVISED EDITION

This book is for the lover of the outdoors, the amateur geologist, or anyone who wishes to acquire a better understanding of his or her natural, physical environment. It will be of special use to you, the traveler, whether you wander by automobile, bus, train, plane, bicycle, or on foot. To learn geology "on the run" is to learn geology best with the least effort. A week in the field with this manual is worth at least several weeks in the classroom. Bear in mind, this field manual can be applied wherever you may be because it doesn't restrict you to a specific region.

Part I, "The Lay of the Land: Landforms," helps you to identify landforms from a distance and explains how they form and change with time. Part II, "Contemplating the Past," emphasizes geology from a chronological distance. For greatest perception, digest this part when you are stationary: by a campfire at day's end or as you wait out the rain or a snowstorm.

Parts III and IV encourage you to become a sojourner at times, in order to gain an intimate experience of geology. "Minerals, Rocks, and Fossils: The Stuff of Geology" allows you to identify the most common Earth materials and learn their features. "How to Do Geology" explains the way a geologist operates and how you can participate in several geological activities. You will also learn some of the tools of the geological trade. The appendixes condense much information useful to the geological traveler.

If you wish to learn geology with relative ease—from a distance or close-up—this book is for you. May it also help you enjoy and appreciate your natural, physical environment.

Now a few points concerning my approach. I have included a list of suggested reading at the end of most chapters; I selected material for its readability. Technical terms in this book are emphasized by boldface where they are defined and informal pronunciation follows words likely to be unfamiliar; stressed syllables are shown in capital letters. For instance, the pronunciation of my surname would appear as Cvancara (SWUHN-shuh-ruh).

A Field Manual for the Amateur Geologist: Tools and Activities for Exploring Our Planet was originally published by Prentice-Hall, Inc. in 1985. I rewrote and updated much of the text for this revised edition, including many of the suggested readings. Appendixes D and E and 21 illustrations are new.

A Strategy for Geologic Excursions

If you are a novice at geology, skim this book, especially Part I, before you leave on a trip. For a quick introduction to the regional geology in your area of travel, check Appendix D. Consult pertinent roadside geology guides to specific regions listed in Appendix E. If you have time to plan a route in some detail, acquire geologic maps in addition to general highway maps. I especially recommend the regional geological highway maps listed in Appendix C. Should you desire to cover less ground in more detail, topographic maps (see chapter 1) will prove useful.

Visit parks and museums (Appendix A). Stop at state or provincial geological survey offices (Appendix B). Better still, inquire beforehand about geological features to visit and geological maps and publications they may have available.

With continued exposure to geological information, you may wish to carry a pocket-sized geological dictionary. One is *Dictionary of Geological Terms* edited by R. L. Bates and J. A. Jackson. Another, in which many geological features are illustrated in color, is Alec Watt's *Barnes and Noble Thesaurus of Geology*.

Assemble a few items of equipment. To collect minerals, rocks, or fossils, take along a geologist's or mason's hammer, hand lens, acid bottle, and collecting supplies (see chapter 21), most of which will fit into a backpack. Include binoculars and a camera, and, of course, don't forget a notebook in which to record observations and any specimens collected. If you intend to collect specimens, bear in mind the ethics of collecting (see chapter 21).

As you travel, observe with care and write down your observations. Analyze, question, interpret. This is the way geologists learn. With this same strategy, *you* will also learn.

Acknowledgments

My parents, Charles and Lillian Cvancara, long deceased, provided me with the means, stimulus, and encouragement to acquire a formal education—much beyond their own—that led me to write this book and others. Mary E. Kennan Herbert provided useful criticism, editorial incentive, and encouragement for writing the original version of this book and encouraged me to write a revision. Providers of illustrations are acknowledged in the figure captions. Unacknowledged illustrations are my own.

CONTENTS

The Lay of the Land: Landforms

Introduction to Landforms

Construction Versus Destruction

Earth's surface is the scene of ongoing geological battles. Barely noticeable at times, escalated to minor skirmishes at others, they occasionally flare into a major confrontation, as when a volcano erupts. Combatants assemble into two camps: **destructional processes**, which tear down the land, and **constructional processes**, which build it up.

Destructional processes include **weathering**, the in-place breakup of rocks by physical or chemical means, and **erosion**, (ih-ROW-zhun), which encompasses weathering and the wearing away and transport of Earth materials from one place to another by stream water, seawater, lake water, groundwater, wind, glacial ice, and gravity.

Solar energy and gravity drive destructional processes to accomplish their geologic work. Solar energy evaporates seawater and lake water; the evaporated water later falls and collects into streams or precipitates as snow and, in time, compacts to glacial ice. Gravity drives streams and glaciers to cause erosion, and impels Earth materials down slopes via landslides. When caused by the pull of the sun and moon on Earth, gravity also creates tides that allow waves and currents to erode Earth materials at more than one level. And tidal currents themselves may erode. Solar energy also generates wind, which erodes materials directly, or indirectly by the action of waves and currents along shorelines.

Constructional processes are **volcanism**, the formation of volcanoes and lava flows; Earth movements, in particular those that raise the land to provide, with volcanism, more fuel for destruction; and **deposition**, the laying down of cool, nonmolten Earth material by stream water, seawater, lake water, groundwater, wind, and glacial ice. You can see that stream water, groundwater, seawater, lake water, wind, and glacial ice construct as well as destroy.

OVERLEAF. A stack framed by a sea arch. (Chapter 4 explains how these features are formed.) Rocky shore near La Push, northwestern Washington.

Destructional and constructional processes sculpt the myriad **landforms**, the major and minor features we see at Earth's surface that make up the landscape, and are the subjects of chapters 2 through 10. Erosional landforms, formed by the effects of erosion, are the most conspicuous and owe their identity mainly to the differing resistance to erosion of Earth materials of which they are made. Depositional landforms are nearly always found in low-lying areas, below the source of the materials that constitute them.

Using Topographic Maps and Aerial Photographs to Identify Landforms

Landforms are characterized by their setting or surroundings, ground plan and profile, internal makeup, and surface features. Setting, ground plan, and profile are well displayed on topographic maps and aerial photographs. Use these tools to help you identify landforms, especially from the air.

Topographic maps (Figure 1-1) show topography, the lay of the land or the configuration of Earth's surface, by means of **contours** or lines connecting points at the same elevation. Contours wrap horizontally around hills, curve outward around ridges, and bend up valleys before crossing streams. The main point to remember about them is this: Closely spaced contours mean steep slopes, widely spaced contours signify gentle slopes. A vertical cliff appears on a topographic map as many contours drawn on top of one another. Generally, every fifth contour is a heavier line labeled with its elevation above (or below) average sea level.

If reading contours seems unclear to you, imagine a volcanic island isolated in the Pacific. The shoreline corresponds to the zero contour that circumscribes the island. If sea level should drop 20 feet (6 m), remain for a time for a beach to form, and then drop 20 feet (6 m) two more times, two beach lines will encircle the island high and dry above present sea level. The two beach lines would represent contours at 20 feet (6 m) and 40 feet (12 m) above sea level.

To find the height of a landform, you need to know the **contour interval** or difference in elevation between adjacent contours, which is given at the bottom of a map. If a hill on a map is encircled by five contours and the contour interval is 20 feet (6 m), the hill is at least 80 feet (24 m) high. To be more precise, suppose the lowest encircling contour has an elevation of 2,000 feet (610 m). A spot elevation at the top of the hill reads 2,093

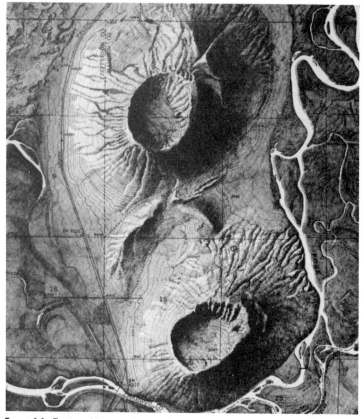

FIGURE 1-1. Topographic map of two volcanic cinder cones (Menan Buttes) near Menan, southeastern Idaho, showing relief by shading as well as by contours; the cones project about 770 feet (235 m) above the surrounding lava plain, incised by the meandering Snake River. Squares of the grid are one mile (1.6 km) on a side. (From the U.S. Geological Survey Menan Buttes Quadrangle, 1954.)

feet (638 m); the exact height of the hill, therefore, is 93 feet (2,093 minus 2,000), or 28 meters (638 minus 610). Encircling contours may also depict enclosed depressions if they are set with short lines at right angles to them, and point inward and downslope as they would if they define a volcanic crater. Count these contours to determine the crater's depth. Contours also portray the **relief** of a region or the difference in elevation between the high and low points. A region may have low or high relief. Some topographic maps also show relief by shading (Figure 1-1).

To find the ground plan dimensions of a landform you must

know the map's **scale**, or the relationship of distance on the map to that on the ground. Scale, which is most usable if depicted as a divided bar or line (see Figure 20-3), is given at the bottom of the map. On a strip of paper, mark off the dimensions of a land-form and measure them with the scale for specific values. Maps come with various scales: Small-scale maps show large areas smaller and in less detail; large-scale maps show small areas larger and in more detail. Both types of maps are useful for the same landform, because small-scale maps portray setting and patterns and large-scale maps show details.

Consult topographic maps before you visit a region to help spot landforms and review them again after a visit to check your observations or measure landform dimensions. To help sharpen your identification eye, examine compilations of maps selected for their good portrayal of landforms. Two, Debruin's *100 Topographic Maps Illustrating Physiographic Features* and Upton's *Landforms and Topographic Maps Illustrating Landforms of the Continental United States*, are useful for this purpose.

How can you locate topographic maps of any region in the United States? The most likely places to search are libraries of universities or state geological surveys. Other libraries may house a collection of maps for your state. If these or similar sources are unavailable, you might be able to purchase maps through a local or national outlet.

For the national source, request an index to topographic maps for your state and an order form from the U.S. Geological Survey (USGS): USGS Map Distribution, Box 25286, Denver, CO 80225 (Phone: 303-236-7477). (You may also request a map index from any Earth Science Information Center [ESIC] located in Anchorage, AK; Denver, CO; Menlo Park, CA; Reston, VA; Rolla, MO; Salt Lake City, UT; San Francisco, CA; Sioux Falls, SD; Spokane, WA; Stennis Space Center, MS; or Washington, DC. For information on any ESIC or USGS products, call 800-USA-MAPS.) From the map index, select your **quadrangle maps**, which cover areas bounded by lines of latitude and longitude, by name and scale. The area covered by the quadrangle depends on the scale. Order maps according to the instructions of the USGS.

Aerial photographs are either vertical (most common, Figure 1-2) or oblique (see Figure 2-2), in which case the view is at some angle to the vertical. Lower altitude photographs, of course, show the most detail. Oblique photographs allow for rapid identification of landforms but vertical photographs are useful for a detailed look at landforms.

To identify landforms on vertical photographs, look for dif-

FIGURE 1-2. Vertical aerial photograph of the area shown in Figure 1-1. Part of a lava flow is visible in the upper left, and fields are evident on the Snake River floodplain (see chapter 2). (U.S. Geological Survey photograph Idaho 7B.)

ferences in tone—the relative amount of light a feature reflects; the degree of erosion of a surface (see chapter 2); and patterns as they relate to deformed (and eroded) rocks and stream drainages (see chapter 9). Since most aerial photographs are taken in black and white, you must concentrate on the shades of gray. Black usually indicates water, but it could also signify a lava flow. Darker grays may denote materials that retain more moisture (clay soils, shale), lower areas, or forested regions. Lighter grays may indicate materials that retain little moisture (sandy soils, sandstone), higher areas, or regions of grassland. Uniform tone represents uniform soil or rock type or uniform moisture as found on lake plains or thick, flat-lying rocks. Mottled tone implies inhomogeneity of a surface, with light, drier, upland areas interspersed with dark, wetter, lowland regions. Banded tones may reflect differences in the color of flat-lying or tilted beds as well as differences in soil or rock type or moisture availability. Certain plants may grow on a particular landform and give a clue to its identity.

Vertical photographs are taken along flight strips with about 60 percent overlap at each end and about 30 percent overlap along their sides. Each photographed spot, then, appears at least twice.

Examine two consecutive vertical photographs taken from a slightly different position along a flight path, called a **stereopair**, and view them through a **stereoscope**, a device with two lenses on short legs. (One source for an inexpensive pocket stereoscope is Ward's Natural Science Establishment, Inc., 5100 West Henrietta Road, P. O. Box 92912, Rochester, NY 14692-9012.) The result will be a three-dimensional portrayal similar to that viewed through old-time stereoscopes or seen with special glasses at suspense-filled 3-D movies. Some people can see 3-D immediately, others require practice. If the stereopair is permanently mounted (Figure 1-3), 3-D viewing is easier. Adjust the space between the lenses on the stereoscope to equal that between your eyeballs—about 2.4 inches (6 cm). Look down on the stereopair through the lenses, your nose over the meeting line of the two photographs. One eye should be above the feature to be viewed in one photograph, the other over the same feature in the second photograph. The trick now is to stare *straight down*, eyes viewing in parallel paths, and attempt to focus as if looking into space. If you are successful, your eyes and brain fuse the two images into one.

With unmounted stereopairs, you must position them so the desired feature on each is separated by a space about equal to the distance between your eyes. Many people, with experience, can see features in 3-D on stereopairs without a stereoscope. Remember that with stereopairs, mounted or unmounted, vertical distances are "pulled up" or exaggerated on the order of two to five times the horizontal distances; but this allows landforms to pop out more readily. Another distortion, in this case horizontal, occurs near the edges of aerial photographs because of any photographic lens's inadequacy near its margins.

If you wonder about scale on an aerial photograph, check a topographic map of the same area. Simply compare two known points on each and work out the scale relationship between the photograph and the map.

To sharpen your landform identification eye with aerial photographs, you might page through compilations of aerial photo-

FIGURE 1-3. Vertical aerial stereopair photographs of sinkholes (see chapter 6) in cherty limestone near Oakland, southwestern Kentucky. If you lack a stereoscope, stare straight down, with each eye fixed on a common point on each photograph. Command your brain to bring the two points together as one for a 3-D effect. The darker sinkholes are wooded. The light, nonwooded sinkhole near the center of each photograph is about 500 feet (152 m) wide. Figure 6-2 is a topographic map of a similar area whose center is about 8 miles (13 km) to the right or east-northeast. (U.S. Geological Survey photographs Kentucky 2 A-B.)

graphs that explain the landforms you see in them. Mollard's *Landforms and Surface Materials of Canada*, with several hundred photographs, is comprehensive. Others include Wanless's *Aerial Stereo Photographs* and the *Atlas of Landforms* by Curran and others. The *Atlas* combines vertical and oblique aerial and ground photographs with topographic maps. Shelton's *Geology Illustrated* provides numerous high-quality oblique aerial and ground photographs of landforms.

For access to aerial photographs, you might first try county or local offices of such federal agencies as the Soil Conservation

Service, the United States Forest Service, and the Agricultural Stabilization Conservation Service. If these sources fail to produce photographs, call 800-USA-MAPS, the U.S. Geological Survey information number in Reston, Virginia, and request instructions on how to obtain aerial photographs. You will be sent an order form and a price list.

I recommend the following approach to the easy learning and appreciation of landforms. Before a trip, skim chapters 2 through 9 and look over the keys in chapter 10. If you have access to Photo-Geographic International's *Photo-Atlas of the United States* and Snead's *World Atlas of Geomorphic Features*, check them out. The *Photo-Atlas* shows complete coverage of the United States by Landsat satellite photographs. The scale is too small to see many landforms but the photographs give you an overall perspective. Snead's *World Atlas* provides locations of major landforms worldwide. If you have time, and for optimum appreciation, look over some topographic maps and aerial photographs as I have already suggested.

Suggested Reading

Bird, J. B. *The Natural Landscapes of Canada, A Study in Regional Earth Science.* Toronto: Wiley, 1980.

Blume, Helmut. *Colour Atlas of the Surface Forms of the Earth.* Cambridge, MA: Harvard University Press, 1992.

Curran, H. A., P. S. Justus, D. M. Young II, and J. B. Carver, Jr. *Atlas of Landforms.* New York: Wiley, 1984.

DeBruin, Richard, *100 Topographic Maps Illustrating Physiographic Features.* Northbrook, IL: Hubbard Press, 1970.

Mollard, J. D. *Landforms and Surface Materials of Canada: A Stereoscopic Airphoto Atlas and Glossary.* Regina, SASK: Commercial Printers, 1975.

Photo-Geographic International. *Photo-Atlas of the United States: A Complete Photographic Atlas of the U. S. A. Using Satellite Photography.* Pasadena, CA: Ward Ritchie Press, 1975.

Shelton, J. S. *Geology Illustrated.* San Francisco: Freeman, 1966.

Snead, R. E. *World Atlas of Geomorphic Features.* New York: Robert E. Krieger Publishing and Van Nostrand Reinhold, 1980.

Upton, W. B., Jr. *Landforms and Topographic Maps.* New York: Wiley, 1970.

Wanless, H. R. *Aerial Stereo Photographs; For Stereoscope Viewing in Geology, Geography, Conservation, Forestry, Surveying.* Northbrook, IL: Hubbard Press, 1978.

2

Stream-Related Landforms

The running water of streams, aided by the downslope movement of soil, sediment, and rock under gravity's pull, sculpts most of the landscape. Stream valleys, therefore, are the most frequent and widespread landforms on the continents. Streams work geologically in two dramatic ways: They cut channels and they serve as conveyor belts to remove mineral and rock debris brought to them by downslope movement, that is, by landsliding and related actions (see chapter 7). Streams incise channels with carried sand and gravel that grind against the bottom and sides of a stream channel, and by the force of the running water itself.

As downcutting steepens valley walls, valleys widen—slopes retreat away from stream channels—chiefly by downslope movement. Imagine a stream valley where only channel downcutting and rockfalls (see chapter 7) but not downslope movement operate. You would see a vertically walled gorge or canyon materialize (see the photograph that introduces the appendixes). Such valleys form where resistant rocks do not succumb to gravity with ease. **Sheet erosion**, the wearing away of the land by the flow of rainwater in broad sheets that do not follow channels, hurries the movement of rock material down valley slopes.

Streams not only erode, but also deposit sediment. A stream system of a main stream and its tributaries can be divided into three segments relative to erosion and deposition: an upstream reach where erosion prevails; a middle reach where erosion and deposition are somewhat equal; and a downstream reach where deposition prevails. Stream deposition, as well as erosion, produces landforms.

Narrow Valleys

Narrow valleys (Figure 2-1) are narrow-bottomed—streams fill their bottoms—and V-shaped in across-valley profile as viewed up- or down-valley. Not necessarily narrow as the name implies, they may be half a mile (0.8 km) or more wide at their tops. The Grand Canyons of the Colorado and Yellowstone Rivers are "nar-

FIGURE 2-1. Narrow valley, showing characteristic V-shaped cross-profile and waterfall. Grand Canyon of the Yellowstone River from Artist's Point, Yellowstone National Park, northwestern Wyoming.

row'' valleys. Narrow valleys are most often found where streams are actively downcutting, especially in their upper reaches. But they exist in other places, as where underlain by rocks resistant to stream erosion.

Waterfalls, cascades, and rapids characterize narrow valleys where the slope of the streambed or **gradient** steepens abruptly and stream velocity accelerates. At **waterfalls**, streams plunge vertically or nearly so. Niagara Falls results because the Niagara River drops from a resistant rock, called dolostone, into a plunge pool carved from weak shales and limestones that underlie the dolostone. **Cascades** consist of a series of small waterfalls or very steep **rapids**, areas of faster-than-normal flow; rapids may develop from waterfalls. Waterfalls, cascades, and rapids often migrate upstream as undercutting of weak rocks causes overlying resistant rocks to collapse.

Holes, usually deeper than wide, hollowed in streambeds of rock at waterfalls, cascades, and rapids are called **potholes**. They are ground out by the abrasive tools of sand, pebbles, cobbles, and boulders, which spin and whirl about in the swift, turbulent water.

Broad Valleys

Broad valleys are broad and flat-bottomed, much wider than they are deep. They form where side-to-side or lateral cutting prevails over downcutting, as in the lower reaches of streams. A great deal of the Mississippi River flows through a broad valley.

A broad stream valley complex, one of nature's grandest designs, is best seen from the air (Figure 2-2). The sinuous, meandering stream channel dominates the scene. Straight channels are not the norm, and in broad valleys they are rare. **Meanders**, wide loops or bends of the stream channel, develop in broad valleys because the gradient is low and the terrain erodes with ease. Higher stream velocity on the outside of a meander causes erosion there by undercutting, and the collapse of cutbanks; lower velocity on the inside causes the laying down or deposition of sediment in arclike ridges or **point bars** at the point of the meander. These ridges are often emphasized by stream-flanked vegetation. (To test the high versus low velocity on the outside and inside of meanders, paddle a canoe through a meandering stream. Better still, try snorkeling with a dependable PFD [Personal Flotational Device] and you will experience the velocity differences even more intimately!) Combined lateral cutting and deposition allow meanders to shift back and forth across a valley and even migrate, in time, down the valley because of the slope of the valley surface.

What about those stream loops isolated from the main stream channel? If the downstream limb of a meander is delayed in its migration down the valley by, say, resistant rock, the upstream limb overtakes it, and the meander is cut off from the main channel (Figure 2-3). As the ends of the abandoned meander are plugged with sediment, an **oxbow lake** is formed. If the lake dries up or fills with sediment and vegetation, it becomes a **meander scar**. (The "billabong" of the unofficial Australian national anthem, "Waltzing Matilda," is an oxbow lake.)

The flatter part of a broad valley, inundated during floods, is the **floodplain** (Figure 2-2). A floodplain is, in general, fertile for

FIGURE 2-2. Oblique aerial photograph of a broad valley with a meandering stream, point bars, meander scars, and floodplain. Laramie River, southeastern Wyoming. (Photograph 7 by J. R. Balsley, U.S. Geological Survey.)

agriculture because, with the finer sediment, increased amounts of organic matter settle on its surface as floodwaters recede. During floods, too, low ridges of silt and sand that flank a stream channel, **natural levees**, are deposited as stream velocity is checked abruptly near the channel. With each flood, the natural levees, as well as the streambed, are gradually raised above the **backswamp** or lower ground away from the river; the backswamp is surfaced with silt and clay. From the air, natural levees are evidenced by tributary streams that flow parallel to the main stream for some distance before they arrive at breaches in the levees.

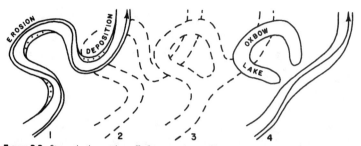

Figure 2-3. Stages in the cutting off of a meander and formation of an oxbow lake. A stream erodes on the outside of meanders and deposits sediment on the inside to form point bars (stage 1, areas stippled). The neck of a meander narrows and severs as the ends of the abandoned meander are plugged with sediment to create an oxbow lake. The sinuous line within the channel in stages 1 and 4 traces the path of highest stream velocity.

As you can see, floodplains develop as suspended sediment settles out from floodwater and accumulates. But floodplains develop also as stream meanders shift from side to side across a valley. So floodplains result from erosion and reworking of stream sediment as well as from **overbank** deposition during floods.

On some floodplains of broad valleys, a stream consists of many interconnected channels instead of a single, meandering channel. Bars and islands abound. Such a **braided stream** (Figure 2-4), which resembles the strands of a braid, occurs where the supplied sediment is more than the stream can carry.

When a meandering, broad-valley stream undergoes a period of renewed downcutting or **rejuvenation** (for any of the reasons discussed in chapter 19), stream terraces or incised meanders may result. **Stream terraces** (Figure 2-4 and Figure 9-15), remnants of floodplains that flank valley walls and are cut out by lateral erosion as well as by downcutting, may or may not be paired on either side of a valley. If not, resistant rock that underlies a terrace may preserve the terrace on one side of the valley; the lack of such rock on the other side of the valley allows the stream to remove the other member of the pair. Stream terraces, which may also be cut into resistant rock, may form at several levels, dependent on the rejuvenation behavior of a stream or region. **Incised** (or **entrenched**) **meanders** (Figure 2-5 and Figure 9-8) are those incised or cut deeply into sediment or rock and without associated terraces. Downcutting is the main erosive process in the formation of incised meanders with little or no lateral erosion.

Where a stream that carries considerable sediment enters standing water, sediment is dropped as velocity is checked and

Figure 2-4. Shaded relief topographic map showing stream features, Ennis area, southwestern Montana. The Madison River is braided in the upper left, stream terraces are visible on the left, and the Cedar Creek alluvial fan dominates the center. The numbered squares of the grid are one mile (1.6 km) on a side. (From the U.S. Geological Survey Ennis Quadrangle, 1949.)

forms a **delta**. The name implies this body of sediment is most often fan-shaped or triangular like the Greek letter delta. The Nile delta in Egypt, whose shape is partly molded by waves and currents, fits the classic delta shape. But few deltas do. The Mississippi delta, where stream processes dominate over those of shorelines, is asymmetrical with irregular margins. A delta fans or spreads out because the main stream splits into several smaller streams or **distributaries** as the velocity slackens and sediment is dropped. New distributary systems or lobes are often built dur-

Figure 2-5. Incised meander. Goosenecks of the San Juan State Park, near Mexican Hat, southeastern Utah. The San Juan River has incised its meanders 1,200 feet (366 m) into sandstone, limestone, and shale.

ing floods. A geologic challenge is to recognize an ancient delta whose form rises subtly above a former lake bottom (see Figure 3-9, bottom).

Similar to deltas are **alluvial fans** (Figures 2-4, 2-6), fan-shaped bodies at the base of steep slopes. They form where streams drop sediment as their velocities are checked by marked drops in gradients. Alluvial (**alluvium** is stream sediment) fans occur most often in arid or semiarid regions where intermittent streams, which flow through mountain canyons, spill out onto a lowland. They fan out or spread as the main stream shifts laterally and splits into smaller distributaries. Alluvial fans, made up largely of coarser sand and gravel rather than the finer sand and mud of deltas, are associated with narrow rather than broad valleys.

Landscape Change by Stream Erosion

We have looked at narrow and broad valleys as if they might be distinct and separate entities. But each stream valley is always part of a larger drainage system that molds a particular landscape (Figure 2-7). A drainage system of a main stream and its tributaries gradually extends upslope toward a drainage divide, the boundary

FIGURE 2-6. Alluvial fans at the base of a mountain front, Mojave Desert, California. Compare with the alluvial fan in Figure 2-4. (Sketched from a U.S. Geological Survey photograph by J. R. Balsley.)

between adjacent drainage systems, by **headward erosion**, a wearing away in the direction of the headwaters. Each tributary valley lengthens its upper, or headwater, reach as slower sheet erosion converts to faster stream erosion at the head of the valley.

Geologists have conceptualized stream erosion, accompanied by downslope movement of rock material and sheet erosion, as the cause of successive changes in a landscape. No one has witnessed a complete series of stream-induced landscape changes at any one place, but different stages in the series of changes can be observed in different places. **Base level**, the lowest level to which a stream can erode—such as sea level or, temporarily, a lake, reservoir, or resistant rock layer—is the controlling factor. The lower the landscape, or the closer to base level, the more change that has transpired. You should remember that interruptions in the progression of landscape changes may occur at any time.

In a humid region (Figure 2-7), the landscape passes from one of low relief to high relief and back to low relief. Highest relief develops at the stage (intermediate) with the greatest number of tributaries. Divides between streams change from broad to narrow

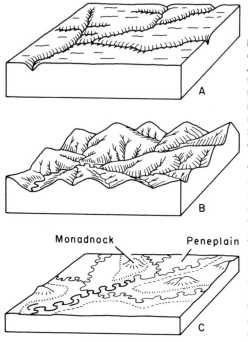

FIGURE 2-7. Landscape change in a humid region. *A.* early stage: Divides between streams are broad, tributaries are few, and relief is low; stream valleys are narrow, and streams have steep gradients with rapids and waterfalls (see Figure 2-1). *B.* intermediate stage: Divides between streams are narrow, tributaries are numerous, and relief is highest; stream valleys are broad, and meanders and floodplains develop. *C.* late stage: The region is reduced to a low-relief surface (peneplain) near sea level with scattered erosional remnants (monadnocks); stream valleys are very broad, and floodplains are wider than stream meander belts.

to much reduced. Streams initially have high gradients and flow through narrow valleys with their characteristic features. Later, gradients are reduced, and broad valleys with their characteristic features are produced. Finally, if no interruptions occur, the changing landscape becomes a late-stage, low-relief erosional surface or **peneplain** (PEEN-uh-plain) with scattered erosional remnants or **monadnocks** (muh-NADD-knocks). Floodplains become wider than the meander belts—swaths of meanders defined by down-valley imaginary lines that touch the outer edges of the meanders—of the highly meandering streams on a low-relief surface.

In an arid region with through-flowing streams, landscape changes are similar to those in a humid region. Landforms, however, are more angular, the retreat of slopes is more evident, and wind action may be important. As the region is dissected, flat-lying resistant rock layers leave wide tablelands or **plateaus**, which rise above more readily erodible areas. In time, erosion-ravaged plateaus reduce to smaller, steep-sided, flat-topped uplands or **mesas**, which diminish to isolated hills or **buttes**.

In an arid region with internal drainage (with no through-flowing streams) and accompanied by the formation of fault-block mountains (see Figure 9-15 and chapter 10) with intervening basins, the landscape alters in a different manner. The Basin and Range Province (Appendix D) of Nevada and adjacent regions is a good place to witness this kind of landscape alteration. At the start, the linear fault-block mountains project above linear fault-block basins. Relief lessens as the mountains wear down and the basins fill with sediment. Streams deposit their sediment along mountain fronts in alluvial fans. Erosional surfaces that are cut into rock along mountain fronts and veneered with sediment, **pediments** (PED-uh-muhnts) widen as the mountain ranges diminish. Shallow, intermittent **playa** (PLY-uh) **lakes** in the basins accumulate salts. Finally, the landscape reduces to a low plain with scattered erosional remnants of the once lofty mountain ranges.

Suggested Reading

Knighton, David. *Fluvial Forms and Processes*. Baltimore: Edward Arnold, 1984.

Morisawa, Marie. *Streams: Their Dynamics and Morphology*. New York: McGraw-Hill, 1968.

Richards, Keith. *Rivers: Form and Processes in Alluvial Channels*. New York: Methuen, 1982.

3

Glacier-Related Landforms

Imagine you are flying in a high-altitude jetliner over southern Alaska; you smirk slyly at the *Mad* magazine glued to your lap. The captain's voice crackles through the aircraft: "Good afternoon, ladies and gentlemen. This is Captain Barnes. We are on schedule, and presently crossing the Alaska Range. Thought you might want to look at the glaciers that are directly beneath us."

"Look, there they *are*!" exclaims an elderly gentleman as he points an excited finger toward his window.

Your magazine spills to the floor as you curiously press your nose against the window. There, like striped, snaky locks of Medusa's head, you see them; they issue in all directions from the lofty snow fields. What a fantastic sight!

Now, if I have your curiosity piqued, let's take a closer look at glaciers and the landforms they shape.

Glaciers and Glacial Ice

Glaciers are thick masses of flowing ice, although some may have ceased to flow. Icebergs don't qualify as glaciers, although they may calve from a glacier that enters the sea or a lake.

Two main kinds of glaciers exist: valley and continental. **Valley** or **alpine glaciers** (Figure 3-1), confined to mountain valleys, are literal streams of ice; they resemble streams in that tributary glaciers join a main trunk glacier. Valley glaciers, several hundred feet to many tens of miles long and a few hundred to several thousand feet thick, begin in the snow fields of high mountain ranges in many parts of the world, even in the Tropics. Valley glaciers that spill onto low-lying terrain at the feet of mountain fronts and form broad lobes are called **piedmont glaciers**.

Continental glaciers or **ice sheets**—small ones are called **ice caps**—cover large parts of continents. Antarctica and Greenland are blanketed by them; on these continents, glaciers are 10,000 feet (3,000 m) thick or more, enough to bury entire mountain ranges. Can you perceive ice *two miles* (3.2 km) or more thick?

Today, glaciers cover about 10 percent of Earth's land surface;

FIGURE 3-1. Valley glaciers, latitude 66 degrees 42 minutes north, longitude 65 degrees 47 minutes west, southeastern Baffin Island, Canada. Lateral moraines and a medial moraine are visible at the lower right of the photograph. (Aerial photograph T332R-150 © 1949 Her Majesty the Queen in Right of Canada, reproduced with permission from the National Air Photo Library, Department of Energy, Mines and Resources, Canada.)

90 percent of that ice is on Antarctica. But during the Pleistocene Epoch (see chapter 11), which began about two million years ago, glaciers were more extensive. Their margins, however, fluctuated several times, to expand and encroach at one time, to melt back at another. The last extensive encroachment took place 20,000 to 15,000 years ago when glaciers covered 30 percent of Earth's land surface. Ice covered most of northern North America—including Canada, the northern United States, and Greenland—northern Europe and northern Asia, Antarctica, and southernmost South

America. Glaciers on Antarctica and Greenland today remain as the most conspicuous remnants of the great Pleistocene ice sheets.

What is needed for glacial ice to form? Simply, a cool, humid climate and more snow to accumulate than melt each year. Glacial ice originates from considerable snow by pressure, that is, snow compaction, and recrystallization. Such ice is made, in fact, by a metamorphic process (see chapter 17). Highly porous, low-density masses of snow are pressed together. Points of snow crystals melt from the pressure, and water freezes and recrystallizes in the intervening spaces where there is less pressure. In time, the snowflakes transform into tiny grains. (Such granular snow is what you find in old snowbanks in late winter or early spring.) Further pressure and recrystallization produce dense, nonporous, glacial ice of interlocking ice crystals—in essence, a metamorphic rock. This transformation, from snow to glacial ice, may take from a year or so to tens of years, depending on the climate.

That glaciers move is obvious from the flow lines seen on the surface of valley glaciers as emphasized by rock debris (Figure 3-1)—the striped Medusa's locks mentioned at the beginning of the chapter. But how can ice, that brittle substance in your glass, "flow"? Beneath an upper zone about 100 to 200 feet (30 to 61 m) thick where **crevasses** (cruh-VASS-uhz)—cracks or fissures—form as the ice plunges over steep spots in the valley floor, the ice is a plastic, yielding substance—like a thick, heavy fluid. Folds in the ice seen near the fronts of glaciers attest to this. As a heavy mass of ice succumbs to gravity, flowage occurs by gliding along tiny planes within ice crystals as well as by ice crystals rotating and sliding past one another. Glaciers move, too, by slippage along their bottoms and sides as shown by grooved, scratched, and polished rock exposed after the ice has melted away. At glacier fronts, thinner, brittle ice moves by sliding along shear planes.

Glacial ice moves about as fast as groundwater (see chapter 6) percolates through porous rock or sediment. Most glaciers "race" along at speeds of less than an inch to several feet per day; surging glaciers may occasionally spurt along at a few to several hundred feet per day.

Work of Glaciers

Glaciers wear down rocks and sediment mostly by **glacial plucking** and **abrasion**. Meltwater seeps into cracks in rock beneath and along the sides of a glacier, freezes, and expands. Blocks of rocks are wedged loose, frozen to the base of a glacier, and *plucked* out as the glacier moves along. The plucked rocks, like the sand grains in sandpaper, *abrade*—rasp, grind, groove, scratch, and polish—the rocks on which the glacier passes as well as abrade themselves. Many gravel-sized particles have characteristic grooved and ground faces or facets, crudely similar to those on cut gemstones (Figure 3-2), and differ from particles shaped in streams, which all have rounded surfaces.

Glaciers carry rock material largely in suspension at the base, sides, and top of valley glaciers and mostly near the base of continental glaciers. Some rock material is also bulldozed in front.

When glaciers melt, rock material is deposited. Material let down directly by the melting ice is called **till** (Figure 3-3), a poorly sorted mixture of particles of many sizes that range from boulders to clay. Till lacks distinct layering or bedding and contains the sculpted tools of abrasion—faceted, scratched, and grooved gravel particles. Sediment worked and transported by meltwater is much better sorted and displays good bedding: the sand and gravel of meltwater streams (Figure 3-4) and the silt and clay of glacial lakes.

Figure 3-2. Glacially grooved and faceted dolostone cobble, from near Inkster, northeastern North Dakota. Cobble is 2.9 inches (7.4 cm) high.

FIGURE 3-3. Glacial till, exposed in a stream cutbank, showing general lack of bedding. A boulder protrudes from the till at the left. The exposure is about 35 feet (11 m) high.

Landforms of Valley Glaciers

Valley glaciers tend to deepen, widen, and straighten former stream valleys and smooth out many irregularities (Figure 3-5). The rounded topography of stream erosion (in humid regions) becomes the angular topography of glacial erosion.

The characteristic cross-valley profile of a **glacial valley** is U-shaped (Figure 3-6), unless later sediment fill has flattened the valley floor. A profile along the valley's length is apt to show steplike irregularities with scooped out **rock basins** frequently containing lakes or **tarns**. Along coasts, flooded glacial valleys form **fiords** such as in coastal Norway and British Columbia. Tributary glaciers don't scour as deeply as the main glaciers, so when ice melts, higher tributary **hanging valleys** arise from which waterfalls often plunge.

At the head or upper end of a glacial valley is a half-bowl-like depression or **cirque** (SIRK) (Figures 3-5, 3-7) where a glacier orig-

FIGURE 3-4. Glacial meltwater sand and gravel, or outwash sediment, showing distinct cross-bedding (see chapter 18). The pebble in the lower right is 1.8 inches (4.6 cm) wide.

inates. The characteristic cliffed walls form and extend up-valley (headward) by ice wedging and plucking, the washing action of meltwater, avalanches, and rockfalls. Abrasion scours the floor of a rock basin, often occupied by a tarn. Two cirques that come together by headward erosion on opposite sides of a divide produce an **arête** (uh-RATE) or sharp-crested ridge; three or more cirques create a pyramidal peak or **horn**, typified by the famous Matterhorn in the Swiss Alps.

Several landforms arise from the deposition of rock debris. Ridges along the sides of valley glaciers, or **lateral moraines** (Figures 3-1, 3-8), are created as debris accumulates by valley wall erosion, avalanches, and rockfalls. Where a tributary glacier merges with the main glacier, lateral moraines merge as well to form **medial moraines** (see Figure 3-1), several of which may ribbon a glacier's surface. Medial moraines are short-lived in glacial valleys because streams rework them during and after a glacier's melting. Between lateral moraines on the valley floor you will find an undulating surface of low hills and closed depressions, a blanketlike **ground moraine** (see Figure 3-9) of till let down by the melting ice. Lateral moraines often merge with an **end** or **terminal moraine** (Figure 3-9), an arclike ridge of till that forms at the snout or terminus of a glacier. The end moraine forms when

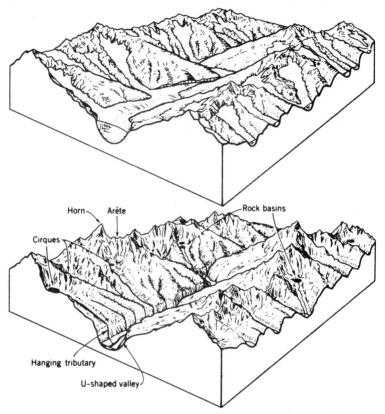

Horn
Arête
Rock basins
Cirques
Hanging tributary
U-shaped valley

FIGURE 3-5. Erosional features of valley glaciers. Glaciers tend to deepen, widen, and straighten former stream valleys they occupy (top). After glaciers melt, characteristic landforms (bottom) evidence their former existence. (From R. F. Flint and B. J. Skinner, *Physical Geology*, 1974, Figure 11.12, used with permission of John Wiley & Sons, Inc.)

an ice front stabilizes for a time: The glacier wastes away at the same rate as it is nourished. An end moraine may dam meltwater to create a lake on its up-valley side (Figure 3-7). If the ice front recedes and restabilizes, a **recessional moraine** (see Figure 3-9)—up-valley from the end moraine—is laid down. Down-valley and below the end moraine is an almost flat **outwash plain** (see Figure 3-9) of stream sediment, "washed out" from the glacier by meltwater and rainwater.

Streams that flow on the glacier or in tunnels within or beneath it lay down sand, gravel, and silt within their twisting, icy channels. When the ice melts, the channel sediment is let down

FIGURE 3-6. Glacial valley with a characteristic U-shaped cross-valley profile, Yosemite Valley, Yosemite National Park, eastern California. The bottom of the valley is somewhat flattened because of sediment fill after glaciation. El Capitan is the cliff on the left, Bridalveil Fall drops from a hanging valley on the right, and Half Dome—an exfoliation dome (see chapter 23)—is in the center far distance. (Photograph 748 by F. E. Matthes, U.S. Geological Survey, 1923.)

on the landscape to form sinuous ridges, **eskers** (see Figure 3-14), that seem to lope over the uneven glaciated terrain. Eskers pass downstream into outwash plains and deltas (see Figure 3-9), raised above the surrounding terrain after meltwater lakes disappear. If a glacial stream dumps sediment into an opening in the ice, the sediment assumes the configuration of a steep-sided hill called a **kame** (CAME), or a fairly straight ridge called a **crevasse filling**. After all the ice melts, the resulting landform takes on the shape of the opening in the ice.

The topography that results from the sculpting of a mountainous region by glacial ice is distinctive. Rugged, angular landforms predominate. Characteristic U-shaped valleys are interspersed with sharp-crested divides and jagged peaks (Figure 3-5).

FIGURE 3-7. Shaded relief topographic map of terrain sculptured by valley glaciers, showing glaciated valleys, cirques, rock basin lakes, and an end moraine fringing Turquoise Lake (lower right). Near Leadville, west-central Colorado. The numbered squares of the grid on the right side of the map are one mile (1.6 km) on a side. (From the U.S. Geological Survey Holy Cross Quadrangle, 1949.)

Landforms of Continental Glaciers

Unspectacular by most standards, the landforms of continental glaciers, in the main, are inconspicuous and often missed by the casual traveler. But they cover the acreage. Such landforms in northern North America, for instance, can be found over an area greater than the size of the Antarctic ice sheet, attesting to once extensive ice coverage. Your eye is snared, perhaps because of the monotony, by an undulating or hilly terrain with closed depressions, many filled with ponds, marshes, bogs, or lakes. Stream drainage systems on the younger surfaces, or where till is thick, are poorly developed or nonexistent. This terrain is the kind you

FIGURE 3-8. Field sketch of Athabasca Glacier, Jasper National Park, southwestern Alberta, Canada; June 15, 1959. Glacier-fringing lateral moraines are conspicuous.

can expect to see in much of Minnesota, Wisconsin, Michigan, New York, and Maine. On the surface and embedded within are numerous boulders, some house-sized; they differ in makeup from the surrounding rock. Foreign boulders of granite, gneiss, and dolostone, for example, may rest on or near indigenous exposures of sandstone or shale. Transported some distance from their source, these **erratics** (ear-AT-icks) are one of the first clues for glaciers in places where glaciers no longer exist. What besides glacial ice could naturally move huge boulders great distances?

Erosional landforms of continental glaciers are hard to spot in many places. They consist of large, almost flat lowlands of grooved and scratched rock stripped of most or all soil and sediment cover, such as found in eastern Canada and northern Europe. In places, look for asymmetrical rock knobs or **sheep rocks** (Figure 3-10)—the technical French equivalent is *roche moutonnée* (RAWSH moot-uhn-AY; literally, woolly rock)—formed by abrasion on the less steep, up-glacier side and by plucking on the steeper, down-glacier side. (Down-glacier is the side or direction toward which the glacier was moving.) Such rocks, we can see, are useful in deciphering past ice movement. More conspicuous landforms are the rock basins scooped out of valleys by separate ice lobes along the scalloped margins of ice sheets. Filling such basins are the Great Lakes and the smaller, long and narrow finger lakes, which include the north-trending Finger Lakes of west-central New York.

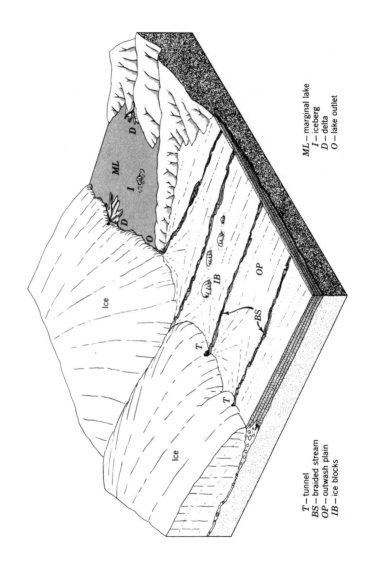

ML – marginal lake
I – iceberg
D – delta
O – lake outlet

T – tunnel
BS – braided stream
OP – outwash plain
IB – ice blocks

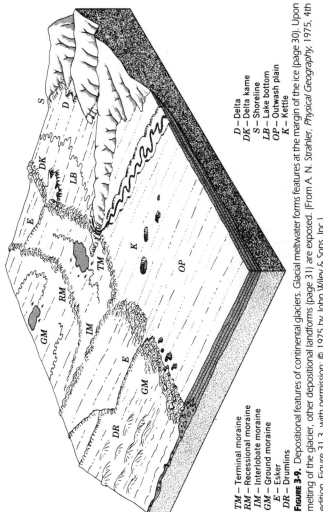

TM – Terminal moraine
RM – Recessional moraine
IM – Interlobate moraine
GM – Ground moraine
E – Esker
DR – Drumlins

D – Delta
DK – Delta kame
S – Shoreline
LB – Lake bottom
OP – Outwash plain
K – Kettle

Figure 3-9. Depositional features of continental glaciers. Glacial meltwater forms features at the margin of the ice (page 30). Upon melting of the glacier, other depositional landforms (page 31) are exposed. (From A. N. Strahler, *Physical Geography*, 1975, 4th edition, Figure 31.3, with permission; © 1975 by John Wiley & Sons, Inc.)

31

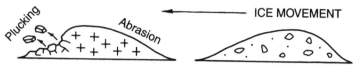

FIGURE 3-10. Generalized profiles of a sheep rock and drumlin in relation to the direction of ice movement. Sheep rocks are knobs of hard rock and drumlins consist mostly of till.

FIGURE 3-11. End moraine, with many glacial erratics on the surface.

Moraines of continental glaciers (Figure 3-9) are similar to those of valley glaciers, but lateral and medial moraines are absent. End moraines (Figure 3-11) may be multiple and complex in places as they form few- to several-miles-wide bands of concentric ridges that produce a washboard effect. Continuations of end moraines between adjacent ice lobes are **interlobate moraines**. Ground moraines (Figure 3-12) are the most extensive, with less relief than end moraines. Their subdued relief derives from the uneven laying down of till or the laying down upon uneven surfaces that underlie them. On some ground moraines you will find streamlined, asymmetrical hills or **drumlins** (Figures 3-10, 3-13) that resemble inverted teaspoons (minus the handles) in map view; some may be more elongate. Most consist of till, others contain sand and gravel, and some are rock-cored with a veneer of till. Molded by moving ice and oriented parallel to such movement, they trend at right angles to end moraines. Drumlins are usually less than half

Figure 3-12. Ground moraine with glacial erratics, showing less relief than that of end moraine (see Figure 3-11) and a water-filled depression or swale.

a mile (0.8 km) long and 150 feet (46 m) high. The gentler slope along a drumlin's length points in the direction the ice was moving. Drumlins generally occur in fields or swarms, as in southeastern Wisconsin and west-central New York north of the Finger Lakes.

Other features formed by direct contact with stagnant, nonmoving ice—eskers (Figure 3-14), kames (Figure 3-15), crevasse fillings, and outwash plains—are similar to those of valley glaciers. Eskers, however, may be longer and the outwash plains more extensive. Blocks of ice, separated from the main mass of ice, may become partly or wholly buried in outwash sediment or the till of ground moraines. Upon melting, steeper-walled depressions—**kettles** (Figures 3-9, 3-16)—form that may become lakes, swamps, or bogs.

As a glacier melts, considerable water accumulates as meltwater streams mold eskers, kames, and outwash plains. Other meltwater streams siphon off the water elsewhere and when flow

FIGURE 3-13. Surface overridden by a continental glacier, showing a drumlin field and numerous lake-filled depressions; latitude 62 degrees 45 minutes north, longitude 106 degrees zero minutes west, east of Great Slave Lake, District of Mackenzie, northwestern Canada. Several drumlins with blunt ends that point toward the horizon indicate the glacier moved from the horizon toward the bottom of the photograph (see Figure 3-10). (Aerial photograph T82R-160 © 1946 Her Majesty the Queen in Right of Canada, reproduced with permission from the National Air Photo Library, Department of Energy, Mines and Resources, Canada.)

ceases, abandoned **meltwater channels** remain behind, perhaps with **underfit streams**—those too small for the valleys they occupy. Much of the meltwater eventually accumulates in lakes.

With the advance of glacial ice, preexistent stream courses are diverted or blocked altogether to form streams or lakes at or near the margins of the ice sheets. The present courses of the Missouri and Ohio Rivers approximate the southernmost extent of continental glaciers and document such diversion. A major drainage

FIGURE 3-14. Dahlen esker, near Dahlen, northeastern North Dakota. (Photograph by J. R. Reid.)

FIGURE 3-15. Woods-covered kame.

blockage was that of the Red River of the North. This created glacial Lake Agassiz (AG-uh-see), largest of the ice-marginal lakes in North America, named after a famous nineteenth-century zoologist and glaciologist. Its extent, which varied as the ice margin fluctuated, reached an area greater than that of all the Great Lakes

FIGURE 3-16. Forest-flanked kettle.

FIGURE 3-17. Aerial view of the Glacial Lake Agassiz plain, near Grand Forks, northeastern North Dakota. (Photograph by J. R. Reid.)

FIGURE 3-18. Ground view of the fertile Glacial Lake Agassiz plain, showing a field of sunflowers. Near Fargo, southeastern North Dakota.

combined and occupied parts of Manitoba, Ontario, and Saskatchewan as well as eastern North Dakota and northwestern Minnesota. Lakes Winnipeg, Winnipegosis, and Manitoba are remnants of this once great lake. Today, the lake is evidenced by a vast, flat, highly fertile **lake plain** (Figures 3-17, 3-18) fringed by several ancient shorelines, pitted with economically important sand-gravel pits in places, which mark various positions of the lake's margin.

Suggested Reading

Bailey, R. H., and The Editors of Time-Life Books. *Planet Earth: Glacier.* Alexandria, VA: Time-Life Books, 1982.

Post, Austin, and E. R. LaChapelle. *Glacier Ice.* Seattle: University of Washington Press, 1971.

Price, R. J. *Glacial and Fluvioglacial Landforms.* New York: Hagner Publishing, 1973.

Sharp, R. P. *Living Ice: Understanding Glaciers and Glaciation.* Cambridge, NY: Cambridge University Press, 1991.

Shoreline-Related Landforms

Shorelines, where land and sea meet, are intriguing places to watch conflicting destructive and constructive geologic processes at work. Battering waves tear apart rocks, grind them down with their abrasive tools of gravel and sand, and, with longshore currents, carry the rock debris away. Earth movements may raise shorelines for renewed attack by wave erosion. Streams provide sediment that they use to build the land out into deltas or that waves and longshore currents sort and mold into such landforms as bars and barrier islands. So landforms along shorelines, as elsewhere, take shape by tearing down as well as by building up. But, as we will see at the end of the chapter, many landforms along shorelines were built by manipulators other than waves and currents.

Work of Waves and Currents

Waves, more significant in the sea than in lakes, are generated by wind. Wave motion transfers the wind energy from one place to another. Offshore in deep water, water particles move negligibly; it's the form of the waves that passes forward. As in a field of waving grain, the stalks and heads bend forward with the wind but return to their original positions—the stalks remain rooted in place—as a wave sweeps through the field.

What can you tell about waves' behavior by simply watching them from shore? A wave's energy depends on its length, the distance from one crest or high point to another, and on its height, the distance from a crest to a trough (the lowest point). Waves "feel," disturb, or erode the bottom to a depth equal to about one-half of the wavelength. Waves with greater wavelengths, therefore, can erode to greater depths. As waves approach the shore, at a depth less than one-half of their wavelength, they slow down, crowd together, heighten, steepen, curl over, and break. **Breakers**, "broken waves," tend to form at a depth of one to one and one-half times the wave height. Nearshore ocean waves, except during severe storms, are seldom more than 20 feet (6 m)

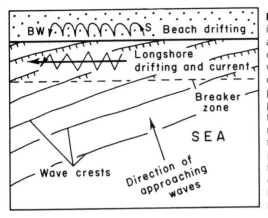

FIGURE 4-1. Beach drifting (curved pattern with arrows) and longshore drifting (zigzag pattern with arrow) of sediment caused by waves that approach the beach (stippled) at an angle. Within the breaker zone (tick marks on wave crests) is the longshore current (straight line with arrow) that drives longshore drifting. Swash (S) and backwash (BW) drive beach drifting.

high. So the **surf** or **breaker zone** of "broken water" (Figure 4-1) normally is limited to a narrow band from the shoreline to a depth of 20 feet to 30 feet (9 m).

The impact of waves as they slam a rocky shore smashes and loosens rocks, particularly those already cracked. Water driven into cracks compresses air that, in turn, widens existing cracks and wedges and pries apart rock blocks. Spray-producing **blowholes** along sea cliffs are dramatic places where wave-induced compressed air is forcibly released through openings. Storm waves move rock or concrete blocks weighing many hundreds of tons.

Abrasion, as noted for stream and glacial erosion, is the grinding of rock against rock, and an effective wave erosion process. Sand and gravel particles, the tools of abrasion, grind against rocky cliffs as well as against themselves.

In a minor way, waves also erode by dissolving rock; soluble limestone and dolostone are especially susceptible.

Waves erode jutting headlands or promontories more powerfully than they do intervening bays, because wave fronts bend as they approach a shore. As a wave front nears a headland, that part closest to the headland—where water is shallower—feels bottom first and is retarded. Those parts of the wave front on either side of the headland, however, proceed at normal speed and are bent around until they parallel the shore. Wave bending, therefore, concentrates energy and erosion on the headlands, and partially accounts for irregular shorelines becoming smoother and straighter with time.

As breaking waves splash against a low shore at a low angle (less than a right angle), the uprushing water or **swash** carries sediment up the beach slope and returns it back down to a different place by the **backwash**, pulled by gravity. In a continuous series of small, curved, swash-backwash paths, sediment moves along a beach by **beach drifting** (Figure 4-1). Coarser grains move by rolling, sliding, and jumping, and finer ones are suspended in the water.

Sediment moves, too, in the deeper, turbulent water of the breaker or surf zone. As breaking waves approach the shore at a low angle, water piles up at first and then is forced to flow parallel to shore as a **longshore current**. Longshore currents can also derive from wind-induced oceanic currents whose movements are deflected by land masses and tend to nearly parallel shorelines. Water piled up from breaking waves may break out seaward, at right angles to shore, as **rip currents** that are capable of eroding shallow channels in the seafloor. If you are caught in a rip current, attempt to swim parallel to shore to escape the narrow current. You can recognize rip currents by gaps in breakers and by streaks of darker, deeper water that move seaward, often covered with foam or with floating objects.

Although most sediment is coarse and moves within the surf zone and beach, some finer sediment moves outside of the surf zone by waves and currents. Oscillating waves move sediment particles back and forth, but the net movement is offshore because the particles are pulled down by gravity along the sloping seafloor. Each particle is sorted out from the rest by the energy required to move it. When wave action becomes too feeble, the particle comes to rest. Coarse particles form steeper slopes, finer particles more gentle slopes. If the sediment available reaches a balance with the prevalent wave and current energy, the shoreline profile, from shallow to deep water, tends to become concave upward, steeper near shore and more gently sloping in deeper water.

Other water movement is of less geologic significance than waves and longshore currents. Seismic sea waves, termed by the Japanese **tsunamis** (suh-NAHM-ee), are set off by tremors from earthquakes, volcanic eruptions, or submarine landslides. Racing at speeds of a few hundred to several hundred miles per hour, they produce a high, severely eroding surf, which, although brief, may destroy human life and property. Places like the Hawaiian Islands are particularly vulnerable to tsunamis. Tides are of geologic importance mostly because they allow wave erosion to take place at more than one level. In narrow bays and inlets, tidal currents can loosen and move sediment.

Landforms of Marine Erosion

Breakers that slam straight against a shore promote landforms of erosion. Such landforms are fabricated more readily if the shore rocks are poorly lithified (hardened) or are well fractured. **Sea cliffs** (Figure 4-2) are formed not only by wave erosion but also by landsliding as steep, undercut slopes become oversteepened. **Hanging valleys**, analogous to those developed in regions of valley glaciation, abruptly terminate at sea cliffs where some stream valleys meet the sea. Recesses in sea cliffs may hollow out to form **sea caves** (see Figure 10-2), which, if on opposite sides of a headland, may be excavated through to form **sea arches**. **Stacks**, isolated pinnacles or small islands (Figure 4-3; see also the photograph that introduces Part I and Figure 10-2), result from the collapse of sea arches or the erosion of vertically fractured headlands.

As wave impact and abrasion pound, saw, and grind the sea cliff back, a **wave-cut bench** or platform develops at the base. Exposed at low tide in some places (see the photograph that introduces Part II), the wave-cut bench widens until a critical width absorbs most of the wave energy. A beach forms along the low-energy shoreline, and the sea cliff diminishes as weathering, landsliding, and, perhaps, stream action continue their effects. In regions of coastal uplift, wave-cut benches rise above sea level to form **marine terraces**. Several of these, raised during the late Pleistocene, are well displayed in the Palos Verdes Hills south of Los Angeles, California; the highest and oldest is about 1,300 feet (396 m) above sea level.

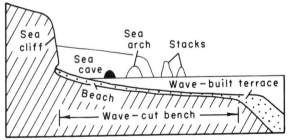

FIGURE 4-2. Profile of a shoreline of primarily erosion and associated features.

FIGURE 4-3. Shoreline of primarily erosion, showing wave-cut cliffs and many stacks, Curry County, southwestern Oregon. Heavy, mineral-rich black sand (see chapter 24) accumulates on the small beach. (Courtesy of Oregon State Highway Department, photograph 6674.)

Landforms of Marine Deposition

Sediment moved by longshore and beach drifting is laid down in places of low energy to form characteristic landforms. This sediment is brought in mostly by streams that enter the sea, but also originates by erosion of coasts. On occasion, coarser sediment may be washed shoreward by storm waves. Perhaps the most obvious and well-known landform of deposition is the **beach**, a shore of wave-washed sediment that extends from the low waterline upward to the first land vegetation or a sea cliff. (Other definitions may be less encompassing.) Beaches include the upper **backshore**, upward from the high waterline, and the intertidal, lower **foreshore**, which may contain ridgelike **bars** at its lower part. The word *beach* conjures up images of a shore of sand—an ideal white, dazzling sand as on west Florida beaches—but some beaches consist of pebbles, cobbles, and even boulders. The type of beach depends on the available sediment and the wave energy.

Beaches are in a constant state of change. They may move slowly landward as coasts undergo heavy wave attack, and migrate seaward as much sediment accumulates. And beaches tend to lose sand during storms and regain it during more halcyon times. Since storms prevail during winter and spring and are less frequent during summer and fall, some changes in a beach are seasonal. At La Jolla, California, for example, a sand beach is present in summer and fall and a gravel beach—the sand is removed by storms—prevails during the winter and spring.

Humans try to stabilize beaches from longshore movement by constructing low walls (**groins**) at right angles to shore. But these structures don't work all that well. Some sand is trapped on the up-drift side of the walls, but only temporarily. And shore erosion is the usual consequence on the down-drift side.

Along a fairly straight shoreline interrupted by bays or estuaries, longshore and beach drifting extend the beach and deposit sediment into the deeper water of these embayments to form a **spit** (Figure 4-4), a ridge of sand or gravel that projects from land into open water. Where longshore movement, which is always toward the free end of a spit, is deflected landward, a curved spit or **hook** results. Sandy Hook, New Jersey, and Cape Cod, Massachusetts, are good examples of hooks. Further extension of a spit blocks the mouth of a bay to form a **baymouth bar** or bay barrier. Active tidal currents may breach the bar in places or not allow it to form. If a spit extends outward and connects an island to the mainland or to another island, a **tombolo** (TOME-buh-low) is formed.

Elongate ridges of sand that invariably parallel low-lying coasts, but are separated from them by lagoons, are **barrier islands**. They may form as (1) tidal currents or storm waves breach spits, (2) beach ridges-with-dunes drown by sea level rises as glacial ice melts, and (3) offshore bars migrate shoreward. Padre Island, Texas, backed by its accompanying lagoon, Laguna Madre, is a well-known barrier island.

One last feature of marine deposition, but one not readily visible above sea level, is the **wave-built terrace** (Figure 4-2). Remember the wave-cut bench? The wave-built terrace is a similar embankment that consists of wave-washed sediment and is located seaward of the wave-cut bench and surf zone.

Evolution of Shorelines

Shorelines, most of which are irregular at first, tend to become smooth and straight or gently curved with time. This change occurs as shoreline erosion and deposition perform in concert. If we assume no interruption by outside forces, shoreline evolution is predictable. But the *rate* of evolution is not. Shorelines with more

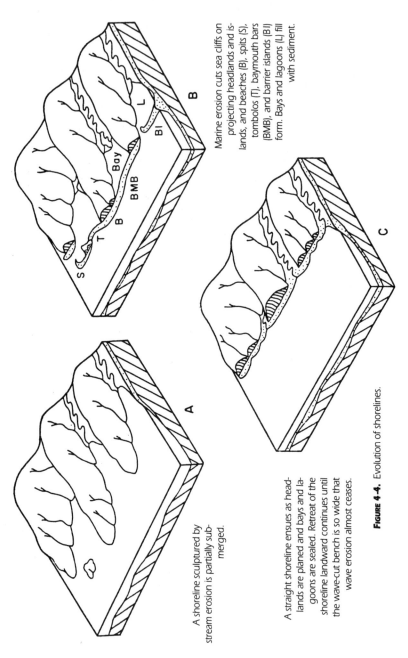

Marine erosion cuts sea cliffs on projecting headlands and islands, and beaches (B), spits (S), tombolos (T), baymouth bars (BMB), and barrier islands (BI) form. Bays and lagoons (L) fill with sediment.

A shoreline sculptured by stream erosion is partially submerged.

A straight shoreline ensues as headlands and bays and lagoons are sealed. Retreat of the shoreline landward continues until the wave-cut bench is so wide that wave erosion almost ceases.

Figure 4-4. Evolution of shorelines.

44

erodible rocks and with rocks more exposed to wave action will straighten faster. Let's imagine how a drowned shoreline, originally sculpted by stream erosion, changes with time (Figure 4-4).

Marine erosion cuts sea cliffs on projected headlands and islands, and a wave-cut bench begins to form. Beaches develop at the base of sea cliffs. With more sediment, beaches extend into spits, baymouth bars, barrier islands, and tombolos. Bays seal to become lagoons that fill with sediment, largely because of delta-building at their heads. Any existing islands are wiped out. The planed headlands and sealed off bays, then, delineate a relatively straight shoreline. The shoreline retreats farther landward until the wave-cut bench reaches such a width that wave erosion is inhibited or almost eliminated.

This pattern occurs if the shoreline remains quite stable. Should sea level rise or fall, or the coast rise or subside, the progression of events just described would be interrupted. A shoreline rarely changes in a progressive and complete manner without interruption.

Classification of Shorelines

You want to approach any shoreline classification with the thought that the configuration of many shorelines is markedly affected by a worldwide sea-level rise caused by the melting of Pleistocene glaciers. Shoreline types 1, 3, and 4 (Table 4-1) partic-

TABLE 4-1. Classification of Shorelines[1]

Characteristic Features	Land or Sea Processes Predominate[2]	Erosion or Deposition Predominates[2]	Other	Name
Drowned stream system	Land	Erosion	Valleys become bays and estuaries, divides become peninsulas	1. Shoreline of stream erosion
Deltas, drowned alluvial fans	Land	Deposition	———	2. Shoreline of stream deposition
Drowned valley glacier system	Land	Erosion	Valleys become fiords, divides become peninsulas and islands	3. Shoreline of glacial erosion

(continued)

TABLE 4-1. Continued.

Characteristic Features	Land or Sea Processes Predominate[2]	Erosion or Deposition Predominates[2]	Other	Name
No, or partial, stream system; low-lying highly irregular shoreline	Land	Deposition	Partly submerged moraines, drumlins, eskers, kames	4. Shoreline of glacial deposition
Cut lava flows, breached volcano craters	Land	Erosion	———	5. Shoreline of volcanism[3]
Faults, folds	Land	Erosion	Fault-controlled shorelines straight; fold-controlled shorelines straight or irregular, with grain to eroded, folded beds	6. Shoreline of faulting or folding[3]
Sea cliffs, arches, caves and stacks; wave-cut benches (low tide)	Sea	Erosion	Uplift of shoreline implied in places	7. Shoreline of marine erosion
Beaches, spits, bars, barrier islands	Sea	Deposition	Much sediment available	8. Shoreline of marine deposition
Coral reefs, mangrove swamps or marsh plants	Sea	Deposition	———	9. Shoreline of organisms

[1]Marine shorelines are implied in this table but all but some types of Shoreline 9 may occur in lakes as well.
[2]Either predominates now or did so in the past.
[3]May be considered part of Shoreline 7.

ularly reflect this rise. A second point to consider is that more types of shorelines result from processes on land than from those that occur in the sea. In spite of the many shoreline types—not all of which are given in Table 4-1—this chapter dwells on only two, types 7 and 8; landforms that give rise to nearly all of the other shorelines are covered in other chapters. Shorelines of predominantly marine erosion (type 7) (see Figures 4-2, 4-3) are common in Oregon and California, and those of mainly marine deposition (type 8) are frequent along the United States Atlantic and Gulf coasts. For "Shorelines of Organisms" (type 9), keep in mind that typical tropical coral reefs—also composed of lime-secreting algae and other organisms besides coral—are of three main types: (1) **fringing** (attached to a landmass); (2) **barrier** (separated from a landmass by a lagoon, like a barrier island); and (3) **atoll** (A-tawl) (generally ringlike with an enclosed central lagoon). Reefs are usually submerged at high tide.

This classification, as with most others—whether of minerals, rocks, fossils, or other natural objects or features—is not foolproof. On many shorelines shaped by marine, nonorganic processes, for example, *both* erosion and deposition occur. You must determine which of the two processes predominates to apply the classification. In other cases, you might require further information. In coastal Maine, for example, you might call a highly irregular shoreline, which lacks a stream system, one of glacial deposition. In fact, though, knowing that scoured rock basins and finger lakes are present would reveal a shoreline of (continental) glacial erosion. In spite of shortcomings, this classification should enable you to make the right choice in most cases, even with only the aid of maps and aerial photographs.

Suggested Reading

Bird, C. F., and M. L. Schwartz, eds. *The World's Coastlines*. New York: Van Nostrand Reinhold, 1985.

Davis, J. L. *Geographical Variations in Coastal Development*. New York: Longman, 1980.

Snead, R. E. *Coastal Landforms and Surface Features, A Photographic Atlas and Glossary*. Stroudsburg, PA: Hutchinson Ross Publishing, 1982.

Wind-Related Landforms

Unlike water and ice, wind lacks significant erosive power, and wind erosion produces few landforms. Most wind-related land-forms materialize in arid or semiarid regions when sand moved by wind is deposited as the speed of the wind is arrested. If you can't picture wind-related landforms readily, imagine yourself a central character in a desert movie; you rock along under a blazing sun in a camel caravan that inches through a sand sea of undulating dunes. The wind comes up and a sandstorm engulfs you. Much to your surprise, there on your camel, you don't feel the stinging sand projectiles on your face. I'll touch on the reason for this later.

Although the main wind-related landforms, dunes, occur in deserts, other places with a persistent wind and a source of sand produce dunes as well. Many shorelines, you might remember from chapter 4, are reservoirs of sand derived, in the main, from streams that enter the sea. Onshore winds shape this sand into dunes. Consider the coastal dunes in relatively wet Oregon and Michigan as examples of dunes in nondesertic regions. Stream courses, with their channels and floodplains, provide sand for re-working by wind as do areas of glacial outwash fashioned by meltwater streams. And, whether in true deserts or not, areas of loosely cemented sandstone provide another sand source.

Sediment finer than sand—dust, of silt or clay—is, of course, also carried in enormous amounts by wind. Consider, for example, the great dust storms of the Great Plains during the 1930s that caused bothersome fine sediment to infiltrate dwellings and animals alike. But dust does not accumulate in conspicuous, easily recognizable landforms.

Work of the Wind

You can think of wind as a thin, easily movable fluid; water is thicker, and, in chapter 3, we considered glacial ice as a thick, heavy fluid. Wind, consequently, can carry only small sediment particles—mostly of sand size and smaller—and is much more selective of the sediment carried. Much of what geologists know about the wind's ability to pick up and move sand grains and the mechanics of this process was worked out by R. A. Bagnold and published in his classic book, *The Physics of Blown Sand and Desert Dunes* (1941).

Sand begins to move at a wind speed of about 11 miles per hour (18 km per hour) as the grains roll and slide. As the speed picks up, grains lift and jump into the air. Those that land on a hard rock surface or gravel continue to bounce along. Some strike other sand grains and cause a splash effect as each ejected grain strikes one or more others and the grain jumping spreads. Before long, a surface of sand is set into motion. Let's magnify the sand grains to the size of Ping-Pong balls. Drop a single ball on the game table, and the sphere bounces until its energy is spent. Now place a *layer* of balls on the table. Throw a ball with force onto this layer, and watch the others jump and scatter. Most sand grains react in a similar fashion and move by jumping, more so than by rolling and sliding.

But sand grains don't jump all that high. Most skip within a few inches of the ground and rarely above six feet (2 m). Sand-blasting effects on poles, rocks, and other objects are seldom significant above a height of 1.5 feet (0.5 m). So people's heads and shoulders often project above sandstorms. (Their legs may be sandblasted, but their upper body parts are okay!) Now you know why you did not feel the sting of sand grains while perched on your imaginary camel.

The wind's selective carrying ability causes the grains of most dune sand to fall in the size range of 0.006 inch to 0.012 inch (0.15 mm to 0.30 mm), what geologists call fine sand. Other grades of sand are very fine, medium, coarse, and very coarse. So, you see, dune sand is near the fine end of the sand scale.

Dust particles do not roll, slide, or jump, but are held *suspended* in turbulent, eddying air. Less wind speed is needed to move dust than sand, but dust particles may be difficult to lift initially. Why? Because the fine dust particles present a smooth surface to the wind and are cohesive—they stick together. Some disturbance, such as that caused by off-road vehicles, animals, or jumping sand grains, is almost always needed to allow wind to grasp the dust with ease.

Landforms of Erosion

Wind erodes as it lifts and removes sediment and abrades rock. The lifting and removal of sediment may scoop out **blowouts**, hollows or depressions, many feet to several miles in diameter.

Geologists consider many depressions in the United States Great Plains to be blowouts. How do you tell? Check for any alignment or elongation with prevailing wind direction or look for flat-topped pedestals of sediment that tend to remain behind in blowouts, held back by vegetation. Look, too, for a residue lag gravel or **desert pavement**, which may line the floor of the basin, left behind as the wind removes the finer sand and dust. A resistant desert pavement and the water table (see chapter 6) limit the depth of a blowout.

Abrasion is the sandblasting effect that grooves, pits, polishes, and facets large rock surfaces or gravel particles. (We've already covered the abrasion produced by streams and glaciers.) Certain wind-sculpted gravel particles or **ventifacts**—not to be confused with human-fashioned stones or artifacts—may have two or more flat surfaces or facets, formed as prevailing wind changes direction or as a pebble, cobble, or boulder is turned over to expose a new surface to abrasive attack.

Larger features of abrasion in some deserts are linear ridges or **yardangs** (YAHR-dahngz), most easily sculpted in soft sediment or sedimentary rock. The rock material must be cohesive enough so steep slopes are retained. Yardangs, typically shaped like inverted boat hulls, orient parallel to wind direction. Spectacular examples have developed in the Lut Desert of eastern Iran and reach almost 492 feet (150 m) high, exceed 985 feet (300 m) in length, and are separated by troughs 330 feet (100 m) or more wide. Often in clusters, streamlined yardangs, shaped by flowing air, are analogous to drumlins, which are molded by moving ice.

Landforms of Deposition

Dunes, mounds or ridges of sand, are the most prevalent of wind-deposited landforms. Many develop around an obstacle, such as a rock or bush, which creates a wind shadow or pocket of quieter air in which eddies occur. The wind shadow, mostly downwind from the obstacle but to a lesser degree upwind, accumulates sand until a dune forms and creates its own wind shadow. A dune migrates as sand jumps, rolls, and slides up the gentler upwind slope, builds up at the crest, and slips or slides down the steeper downwind slope or **slip face** in thin, tonguelike masses. Sliding occurs when the downwind slope reaches about 34°, the angle of rest, the greatest slope at which dry sand is stable. Slicing through a dune with a huge, imaginary knife would reveal that most of the internal layering parallels the slip face. Dunes, on a larger scale, resemble the miniature sand ripples (see Figure 16-19) on stream-beds, lake and sea bottoms, and on the backs of dunes. Quartz, a hard, durable mineral (see chapter 14), makes up most dunes. But even a soft mineral, like gypsum, can constitute dunes, as those at White Sands National Monument, New Mexico. Other materials include volcanic ash and even such heavy minerals as magnetite.

Common types of dunes are transverse, barchan, longitudinal, U-shaped, and star (Figure 5-1). Most often in groups, dunes may merge and intergrade into complexes. Wind speed and constancy of direction, sand supply, and amount of vegetation primarily affect their formation (Figure 5-2). **Transverse dunes** (Figure 5-3), at right angles or transverse to prevailing winds, form under low to moderate, constant winds, which move a considerable supply of sand. Little or no vegetation is associated with these dunes, which prevail in deserts and along shorelines. Transverse dunes may be up to several thousand feet long and often up to 30 feet (10 m) high. An area of large transverse dunes is the Namib Desert in southwestern Africa.

Barchan (bar-KAHN) **dunes** (Figure 5-4) perhaps offer the most interest. Barchans are crescent-shaped dunes with horns or tips that point downwind and curve around the slip face. They are often well developed on desert floors where moderate, con-

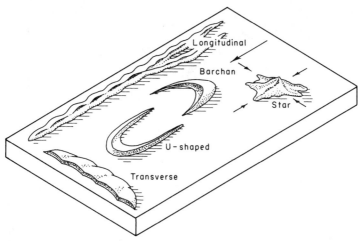

Figure 5-1. Main types of sand dunes. Arrows indicate wind direction; the long arrow relates to the longitudinal, barchan, U-shaped, and transverse dunes. Dunes are not shown to relative scale.

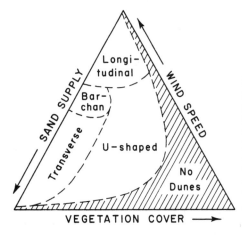

FIGURE 5-2. Conditions of formation of common types of sand dunes. Arrows point in the direction of increase of each condition of formation. A barchan, for example, forms under scanty sand supply and vegetation cover and moderate wind speed. (Modified from J. T. Hack, "Dunes of the Western Navajo Country," *Geographical Review* 31 (1941), p. 260.)

FIGURE 5-3. Transverse dunes, Saudi Arabia. Slip faces toward the upper right indicate the wind blew from the lower left. (Courtesy of Aramco.)

stant winds move and shape a scanty supply of sand. Vegetation is scarce. Barchans are somewhat small, up to about 1,300 feet (400 m) wide; their height is generally about one-tenth of their width. They often migrate about 15 feet to 100 feet (5 m to 30 m) per year, the smaller ones somewhat faster. Barchans may form at the margins of a transverse dune field where sand is limited. Vast areas of complex barchans occur in the Libyan Desert. Smaller areas of well-developed barchans include White Sands

Figure 5-4. Barchan dunes along the Columbia River near Biggs, northern Oregon. Shadowed slip faces on the right indicate the wind blew from the left. (Photograph 504 by G. K. Gilbert, U.S. Geological Survey.)

National Monument, New Mexico, and parts of southeastern Washington.

Longitudinal dunes (Figure 5-5)—also known by the Arabic **seif** (SAFE), meaning sword—are long and narrow and parallel prevailing winds. Actually, winds blow parallel at times, but at an angle at others as the dunes widen. Conditions necessary to form longitudinal dunes include high wind speed somewhat variable in direction, scanty sand supply, and meager or no vegetation. Longitudinal dunes may reach several hundred feet high, as in southern Saudi Arabia and eastern Iran, and several hundred miles in length. Extensive areas noted for longitudinal dunes are the Sahara and the large deserts of western Australia. Longitudinal dunes may be thought of as the depositional counterparts of yardangs.

Now, let's pause for a moment and attempt to visualize a relationship between the three dune types just described to help remember how they form. With your back to the wind, imagine your arms, extended sideways straight out from your body, forming a transverse dune under a low to moderate wind and a good supply of sand. As the wind speeds up and sand diminishes, your arms swing forward to form a barchan. The wind blows harder still, and the barchan "smears out" into a longitudinal dune as your arms touch, fully extended forward (Figure 5-2).

U-shaped or **parabolic dunes** somewhat resemble barchans

FIGURE 5-5. Longitudinal dunes, Saudi Arabia. (Courtesy of Aramco.)

but have the slip face on the outside of the U, which is open upwind. Constant low to moderate winds scoop blowouts in areas of considerable sand, particularly along shorelines, and U-shaped dunes, which surround the blowout, become snagged by vegetation. Elongate U-shaped dunes assume a hairpinlike shape.

Star dunes (Figure 5-6) are isolated, pyramid-shaped sand peaks, which resemble a star from above, with several sharp-crested ridges that radiate from a central point. The wind blows from several directions and piles up sand against a central mass. Up to a few hundred feet high, they may occur at junctions where linear dunes intersect. Star dunes are well displayed in southern Saudi Arabia and western Egypt.

Keep in mind that all dunes do not fit into one of the four categories just outlined. Some are simply irregular hills or "mountains" (Figure 5-7) of sand. And when old dunes are covered by vegetation they may be difficult to recognize (Figure 5-8).

FIGURE 5-6. Star dune, Rub'al Khali region, southeastern Saudi Arabia. (Courtesy of Aramco.)

FIGURE 5-7. Sand "mountains," Rub'al Khali region, southeastern Saudi Arabia. (Courtesy of Aramco.)

FIGURE 5-8. Dunes covered by vegetation.

Before we leave sand dunes, let me ask you this: Can dunes form in anything besides sand? Answer: Yes—in *snow*. Most of the dune forms we've examined also take shape in snow. If you live or travel in snowy regions that are also "blessed" with the necessary ingredient, wind, look for them. Keep in mind the conditions necessary for the formation of each. So, if you really desire to see a *snow barchan*, look where a moderate wind is blowing scanty snow around. And watch for all sizes. Some snow barchans may be only a few to several feet wide.

Suggested Reading

Brookfield, M. E., and T. S. Ahlbrandt, eds. *Eolian Sediments and Processes.* New York: Elsevier, 1983.

Greeley, Ronald, and J. D. Iversen. *Wind As a Geological Process on Earth, Mars, Venus, and Titan.* Cambridge, NY: Cambridge University Press, 1985.

Groundwater-Related Landforms

Envision yourself on a flight over central Florida. Your seatmate, next to a window, calls out, "Hey, look at all those lakes down there!" You lean toward your companion, and glimpse the terrain below. Numerous small lakes, all right, several of them almost circular. Your geological mind races for an explanation. With insufficient thought, you explain: "They've formed in jumbled sediment dumped by a glacier, some as insulated ice blocks melted out later and the basins filled with water." After speaking, though, you sense you've committed a geological blunder. Glaciers in Florida? A second glance confirms that there aren't any real hills between the lakes. This is flat country pitted with lakes. The circular ones resemble water-filled bomb craters. But no major battlefield in modern times occurred here. Hmm . . .

A day later you ask a Floridian geologist about the lakes. He tells you they are the work of groundwater. Groundwater? Since you've only heard of innocent groundwater drawn from wells, you listen, transfixed, to the narrative.

Groundwater

Groundwater is the water in the spaces of sediment and rock beneath Earth's surface; this water occupies pores between rock and mineral grains, cracks, cavities dissolved out of rock, and gas bubble cavities at the surfaces of lava flows (see chapter 15). The greater the **porosity**, the percentage of pore space, the more groundwater a sediment or rock can hold. Most groundwater originates as precipitation that infiltrates into porous soil, sediment, and rock.

Water that seeps into the ground finds its way into one of two zones. In the upper, the **zone of aeration** (Figure 6-1), most pore space is filled with air, except, of course, right after a rain or wet snowfall. You know, though, that soil, sediment, and rock just beneath the surface tend to contain some moisture. Beneath the zone of aeration is the **zone of saturation** where all pore space is saturated with water.

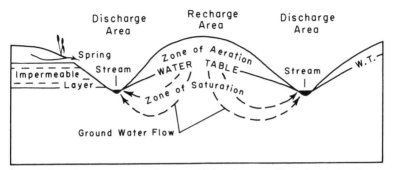

Figure 6-1. Occurrence of groundwater, mostly below the water table, and generalized flow patterns through uniformly permeable rock toward stream valleys. A spring issues above the level of the water table (left) because of an underlying impermeable rock layer, such as shale. The water table may be flatter in limestone regions.

At the boundary between the two zones, the top of the zone of saturation, is the **water table**. Most often the water table reflects the topography—higher under hills, lower under valleys, or flat where the ground surface is flat. Springs are places where the water table intersects the ground surface, frequent at the edges of perennial streams, lakes, and marshes. The water table rises and falls with wet and dry periods.

Once it reaches the zone of saturation, groundwater moves from areas of a high water table to those of a low, or from areas of high to low water pressure. Movement takes place along sweeping, curved paths that trend downward as well as laterally, in the direction the water table slopes, but not directly down that slope. This is because a water table surface resembles a movable, underground wave with water continually moving downward, by the force of gravity, from the higher parts under greater pressure. The slow movement of groundwater can be seen at the sources of springs. Rates of flow most often vary from less than about a foot a year to several hundred feet per day; only in caves and tunnels does groundwater flow equal that of slow streams. On a large scale, we can think of a groundwater system, of higher **recharge** areas where surface water enters and lower **discharge** areas where groundwater leaves after having percolated through the system.

Movement of groundwater depends largely upon **permeability** (purr-mee-uh-BILL-uht-ee), the ability of an Earth material to transmit water and other fluids. Rocks not only must have pore spaces, but these pore spaces must be connected. Sandstone and conglomerate are often highly permeable if pore spaces are not filled with mineral matter. Rocks that seem "tight," such as basalt and dense limestones (see chapters 15 and 16), may be highly permeable if fractured. Shale, although highly porous, is, in most cases, poorly permeable, because the pores are too small to allow easy movement of groundwater or the pores are not connected. You can perceive how the size of pore space affects permeability if you touch a thumb and forefinger together and place a drop of water at their point of contact. Slowly separate the two. At first, the water drop is held suspended by the attraction of thumb and forefinger upon the drop and by water particles upon each other. Upon further separation, which corresponds to an increase in the size of a pore space, the water drop slips through. You can estimate permeability, high or low, as you place a drop of water on a freshly broken rock surface and see how fast the drop penetrates.

Work of Groundwater

Groundwater accomplishes geologic work—as do surface water, glacial ice, and wind—by erosion and deposition. It erodes mainly by dissolving rocks, most often carbonate rocks, rock gypsum, and rock salt (see chapter 16). Rock gypsum and rock salt are rare at or near the surface, and dolostone is less readily dissolved than is limestone (or marble). So groundwater primarily dissolves limestone.

Rainwater and groundwater become somewhat carbonated as they combine with carbon dioxide from the air and soil. (Carbonated beverages get their "fizz" from added carbon dioxide.) The result is carbonic acid, the most important dissolving agent in groundwater.

Although difficult to dissolve in water, limestone readily dissolves in carbonic acid:

Carbonic acid + limestone (calcite) = calcium bicarbonate
(in solution) + water + carbon dioxide.

Deposition or precipitation of limy material, the converse process, also depends on carbon dioxide. As calcium bicarbonate–laden water drips or trickles in caves and caverns, carbon dioxide is released as water evaporates, or the gas is passed off as water is agitated. Increased concentration of the limy matter causes it to precipitate from solution as the mineral calcite or the rock limestone.

Landforms of Erosion

The most obvious erosional landforms are embodied within **karst topography**, a solution-controlled landscape named after the limestone Karst district in western Yugoslavia on the east side of the Adriatic Sea. Other regions of well-developed karst include southern France, southeastern Asia, the Nullarbor area of southern Australia, northern Yucatan, Jamaica, Puerto Rico, central Florida, the Appalachian belt from Pennsylvania to Alabama, central Kentucky to southern Indiana, and the Ozark area of southern Missouri.

The most widespread of karst landforms are **sinkholes** (Figures 6-2, 6-3; see also Figure 1-3), solution cavities open to the sky. They form by solution at the surface or by the collapse of **caves** and **caverns**, roofed over, underground solution cavities (caverns are larger than caves). A few feet to several hundred feet in diameter, hundreds of sinkholes may occupy a square mile in some places. Throats of sinkholes may clog with mud to produce ponds and lakes. Sinkhole ponds and lakes may form, too, where the water table is high, as in central Florida. Sinkholes may merge and coalesce to form elongate, blind-ended or closed **solution valleys**.

Surface water diverted into the subterranean solution system produces **disappearing streams** (Figure 6-4), which may descend into and follow cavities for some distance and emerge to flow on the surface once again. Stream sediment in some caverns and natural tunnels attests that underground stream erosion may play a part, but most cavities in soluble rock seem to result from solution. The collapse of tunnels creates **natural bridges**, the roof remnants of those tunnels left standing. Such a bridge is 215-foot (66-m) high Natural Bridge near Lexington in west-central Virginia, crossed by U.S. Highway 11.

What is needed for karst to form? (1) Limestone or some other soluble rock. (2) Soluble rock with many fractures and closely spaced layering surfaces along which acidic groundwater concentrates solution activity. (Disseminated water that moves through homogeneously porous and permeable rock without fractures and closely spaced layering surfaces is apt to pass through without forming solution cavities.) The rock, although fractured, must have sufficient strength so as not to collapse after it partly dissolves. (3) A humid to subhumid climate that provides at least moderate precipitation to ensure a continuous replenishment of groundwater. (4) Continually moving groundwater that maintains

FIGURE 6-2. Shaded relief topographic map of karst with numerous sinkholes and solution valleys—mostly in the lower part of the map, southwestern Kentucky. The southern boundary of Mammoth Cave National Park—diagonally ruled—is in the upper part of the map. The air distance between Rocky Hill (near center) and Liberty (upper left) is 3.8 miles (6.1 km). Rocky Hill is 8 miles (13 km) east-northeast of the 500-foot (152-m) sinkhole in Figure 1-3. (From U.S. Geological Survey Mammoth Cave Quadrangle, 1955.)

FIGURE 6-3. Sinkhole in Shelby County, central Alabama, the "December Giant": 425 feet (130 m) long, 350 feet (107 m) wide, and 150 feet (46 m) deep. Slumping (see Chapter 7) is well developed. (Photograph 140 by U.S. Geological Survey; December 2, 1972.)

the solution of rock. Stream valleys entrenched into soluble rocks encourage groundwater to percolate toward them in a watery journey from areas of a higher water table.

How does karst evolve in a temperate climate? Streams dissect a soluble rock terrain until deep valleys are cut. Groundwater dissolves the rock along fractures and layering surfaces in its travels toward the valleys. Caves and caverns riddle the rock, and sinkholes, solution valleys, and disappearing streams develop on the surface. Sinkholes and solution valleys become more numerous and larger. In time, most of the original surface is destroyed, and a stream drainage system becomes obliterated. Most of the soluble rock dissolves away. If and when insoluble rock materializes at the surface, a stream drainage system reappears.

In the Tropics with heavy rainfall, solution occurs mostly at the surface and is less significant at depth. Conelike (Figure 6-5) and towerlike hills, consequently, prevail over sinkholes and solution valleys by the time the original surface is destroyed.

FIGURE 6-4. Disappearing stream in limestone canyon. The stream, flowing from the lower right, seeps into its bed in the middle of the photograph, and the remainder of the channel (upper right) is dry.

FIGURE 6-5. Karst in limestone dominated by conical hills in a tropical climate, near Manatı, Puerto Rico. (Photograph 371 by W. H. Monroe, U.S. Geological Survey.)

Landforms of Deposition

Visualize limestone caves and caverns excavated by acidic water below the water table. If the water table is lowered, as by uplift of the region or by groundwater-draining valleys cut more deeply, air-filled caves and caverns become sites of limestone deposition. As water evaporates and releases carbon dioxide, the dripping water lays down **dripstone**, iciclelike **stalactites** (stuh-LACK-tights) that hang from the ceiling (*c* in the word can remind you of *ceiling*) and inverted iciclelike **stalagmites** (stuh-LAG-mights) (*g* in the word for *ground*) that project above the ground or floor. Stalactites and stalagmites fuse to form **columns** (Figure 6-6). Flowing or trickling water lays down **flowstone** in the form of rock tapestries, ribbons, and falls. Both dripstone and flowstone are types of travertine (see chapter 16). Among the famous caves and caverns with many and varied limestone deposits are Mammoth Cave, Kentucky, and Carlsbad Caverns, New Mexico.

In areas of present or recent igneous activity, such as Yellowstone National Park, Iceland, and New Zealand, groundwater issues to the surface as **hot springs** and **geysers**, most of which are hot springs that erupt periodically. (Some rare geysers erupt cold water by the expelling of carbon dioxide trapped underground.) At the sites of these thermal features, groundwater-

FIGURE 6-6. Stalactites (hang from the ceiling), stalagmites (project above the cavern floor), and columns (fused stalactites and stalagmites), Carlsbad Caverns National Park, southeastern New Mexico. (Photograph 150-211 by the National Park Service.)

deposited rock material builds mounds, cones (Figure 6-7), and terraces upon evaporation, cooling, loss of gas, drop in pressure, or precipitation by algae. Where the source rock is rich in silica, such as the rock rhyolite, a deposit of porous **siliceous sinter** (see chapter 16) is laid down. Hot groundwater that passes through limestone lays down porous travertine, as in the terraces at Mammoth Hot Springs (Figure 6-8) in Yellowstone National Park.

FIGURE 6-7. Siliceous sinter cone of Castle Geyser, once a quiet hot spring, Yellowstone National Park, northwestern Wyoming.

FIGURE 6-8. Terraces of limy travertine (see chapter 16), Mammoth Hot Springs, Yellowstone National Park, northwestern Wyoming.

Suggested Reading

Sweeting, M. M. *Karst Landforms.* New York: Columbia University Press, 1973.

Trudgill, S. T. *Limestone Geomorphology.* New York: Wiley, 1985.

Landslide-Related Landforms

A full moon illuminates the campground this still, mid-August night. But you can't sleep although you're snug in your sleeping bag near the bottom of an impressive canyon. Your sister sleeps undisturbed nearby and your parents have doused the lights in the house trailer. You glance at your watch about 11:35 P.M. and concentrate on sleep.

A few minutes later, ground tremors jar you alert. You sit up with a sense of imminent danger. Trees whip back and forth with a fury. Is this real or a nightmare? Above the din of the crazed trees you hear a thunderous roar. The silent night erupts into cacophony.

As your alarmed parents dash from the trailer, a powerful blast of air slams into the campground. Your father grasps a tree and is strung out flagwise before he is forced to let go. Buffeted by the air blast, your body is pummeled by trees and rocks as you are hurled along like a helpless rag doll. A sharp pain pierces your left leg. The clear night turns dark and conceals the destruction.

In the morning, only you—bruised and with a broken leg— and your mother survive in your family. Your father and sister share the same fate with twenty-four other campers in the canyon.

It sounds unreal. But it happened. On August 17, 1959, at 11:37 P.M., the Hebgen Lake earthquake, centered a few miles northwest of Yellowstone National Park, triggered the Madison landslide (Figure 7-1) 17 miles (27.4 km) west of the park on the south wall of the canyon cut by the Madison River. Nearly 40 million cubic yards (31 million cubic meters) of rock debris rushed down the south wall of the canyon and buried a mile (1.6 km) of river and highway up to a depth of 220 feet (67 m). This slide mass dammed the Madison River and created a lake that, three weeks later, extended upstream 6 miles (9.6 km) and reached a depth of 190 feet (58 m). Slide debris traveled up to a mile (1.6 km) and forced its way as high as 430 feet (131 m) above the riverbed on the north canyon wall. One block that rode the slide mass down is house-sized, almost 30 feet (9 m) on a side (Figure 7-2).

FIGURE 7-1. Rock debris of the Madison slide that dammed the Madison River and formed Earthquake lake—in the background, Madison County, southwestern Montana. The slide scar is off the view to the right. Rock debris forced its way to 430 feet (131 m) above the riverbed on the opposite (north) canyon wall (left). (Photograph 216 by J. R. Stacy, U.S. Geological Survey.)

FIGURE 7-2. Dolostone block moved to the opposite (north) canyon wall by the Madison slide. Height of the person is 5.5 feet (1.7 m).

The air blast mentioned in our story, and reported by several eyewitnesses, was most likely caused by rapidly expelled air trapped by the descending slide mass. Some believe such trapped air provides a cushion or lubricant for the slide mass to move farther than is possible without the air cushion.

What caused the Madison slide, one of the three largest rapid landslides in North America to occur within historic time? (The other two were the Gros Ventre slide near Grand Teton National Park in 1925 and the Turtle Mountain slide near Frank, Alberta, in 1903.) An earthquake was the cause, to be sure, but suitable geologic conditions allowed the landslide to happen. On the south canyon wall, weathered, sheared gneiss and schist (see chapter 17)—with stress-induced layering and shear zones inclined at a high angle toward the canyon—were waiting for dislodgment. Fractured dolostone was also inclined toward the canyon.

Now, let's step back and examine the conditions that enhance the downslope movement of rock and rock debris. Here, I'll use *debris* to mean any loose rock material, soil and sediment included, that blankets solid rock. Gravity, of course, is the driving force. Downslope movement becomes effective when the internal resistance of any Earth material to move down a slope is overcome, by say, oversteepening of a slope. Oversteepening may occur by stream and glacier downcutting, wave erosion along shorelines, or human excavation. Landslides along steep highway cuts are notorious. Sudden shocks, as from earthquakes—this was the case in the Madison slide—blasting, or sonic booms from aircraft may also overcome an Earth material's resistance to movement. Water enhances movement by adding weight and, when combined with clayey materials, creates a lubricated surface upon which overlying materials may slide. Water may partially saturate Earth materials, so they may flow as well as slide or fall. After periods of heavy rains or snow melt, steep slopes are prone to landsliding. Lack or scarcity of vegetation encourages downslope movement. And fractures and layering inclined downslope, as in the Madison slide, do so as well.

Kinds of Landslides and Related Landforms

Downslope movement of rock and rock debris can be considered fast or slow; fast movement is that which you can see, slow is that you cannot. Geologists don't always agree as to what types of downslope movement should be considered landslides. Some

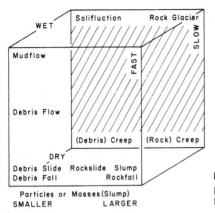

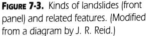

FIGURE 7-3. Kinds of landslides (front panel) and related features. (Modified from a diagram by J. R. Reid.)

say landslides are only the downward sliding or falling of dry rock or debris; others would include flows, wet or dry. Since flowage may accompany sliding, I will include all types of fast downslope movement within the category of landslides (Figure 7-3).

Rockfalls are landslides in which rock drops from cliffs or steep slopes. Rolling, bounding, and ricocheting may also be involved. **Debris falls** are the debris counterparts of rockfalls. Rockfalls and debris falls form accumulations of rock and debris at the base of slopes, **talus** (TAY-luhs) (Figure 7-4), that tend to resemble half-cones.

Rockslides, the most catastrophic of landslides, are rapid slides of rock along surfaces of weakness, such as rock layering or fractures. The Madison, Gros Ventre (Figure 7-5), and Turtle Mountain (Figure 7-6) landslides are all rockslides. In the Gros Ventre slide, the Gros Ventre River had oversteepened the lower slopes. Heavy rains and melting snow saturated sandstone and underlying shale, both inclined toward the river valley. The heavy, water-saturated sandstone simply slid down on the greasy shale.

Debris slides, debris counterparts of rockslides, may roll or slide. A snow avalanche is similar to a debris slide. Both rockslides and debris slides produce bare slide scars and uneven slide masses. In slide masses of debris slides, in particular, hills or hummocks and ridges develop and are separated by intervening depressions; these features give rise to a topography similar to that of certain glacial moraines (see chapter 3).

Figure 7-4. Talus. Note the dead tree in the foreground brought down with the rock debris.

Slumps (Figures 7-7, 7-8; see also Figure 6-3) differ from rock-slides and debris slides in that blocks or masses of rock or debris move as discrete units, usually with backward rotation on curved surfaces down and away from scarps or cliffs (see chapter 9) from which they descend. Ponds or lakes may develop in the elongate depressions in back of and between rotated blocks. Below the

FIGURE 7-5. Gros Ventre slide, near Grand Teton National Park, northwestern Wyoming. The almost bare slide scar is evident, below which is uneven terrain of vegetated rock debris. This slide dammed the Gros Ventre River and formed a lake similar to that upstream of the Madison slide (see Figure 7-1).

scarps, rather chaotic topography may occur, as for rockslides and debris slides. Near-parallel arclike ridges may alternate with similarly shaped depressions (Figure 7-9), especially where water-saturated materials may flow in the lower parts of slumps. Heavy rain may initiate slumping or contribute toward further movement once such movement has begun.

Debris flows and mudflows form where rock debris becomes water soaked. **Debris flows** may have the consistency of fresh cement or a thick fluid; many occur in the lower parts of slumps. **Mudflows** are more fluid than debris flows and contain a high percentage of mud; they follow stream valleys or channels and spill out into lobes or fans when they reach low-lying terrain. Mudflows prevail in dry regions with scarce vegetation and are generated by heavy, though infrequent, rains. Their high density allows them to carry buildings as well as boulders which weigh many tons. Mudflows also move volcanic debris along the flanks of volcanoes. Both debris flows and mudflows leave scars barren of soil and vegetation and lobelike ridges or corrugations at their fronts.

Figure 7-6. Turtle Mountain slide, Frank, southern Alberta. This slide moved along steeply inclined fractures in limestone that overlies weak shale, siltstone, and coal; the slide killed 66 people in the town of Frank. Alberta Highway 3 and the Canadian Pacific Railway cross the slide mass. (Aerial photograph T31L-214 © 1944 Her Majesty the Queen in Right of Canada, reproduced with permission from the National Air Photo Library, Department of Energy, Mines and Resources, Canada.)

As a final thought about rapid downslope movements, be aware that falls, slides, and flows may all occur underwater even though the resultant landforms are not, as a rule, visible.

Fewer slow downslope movements exist than rapid ones. **Creep** is the very slow downslope movement—a fraction of an inch to perhaps a few inches per year—of rock, soil, and sediment. Creep prevails on smooth vegetated slopes in temperate and tropical climates. In exposures, tilted layers are seen to curve downslope within the weathered zone (see Figure 17-2) and tree roots trail behind their trunks. On the surface, lower parts of tree trunks bend downslope, and posts, poles, and gravestones tilt; roads may be slung downslope. In areas of periodic freezing, frost heaving contributes in large measure to creep. Expansion upon freezing

FIGURE 7-7. Slump associated with a debris flow. Note the scarp and the backward rotation of the slump mass.

FIGURE 7-8. Slump, showing bare scarp (cliff at upper part of photograph) and vegetated slump mass slightly rotated backward.

forces rock, soil, and sediment particles upward at right angles to the slope; upon thawing, such particles are let down vertically. Repeated freezes and thaws, then, pass particles downslope in small increments in a slow but continuous manner. Organisms also contribute to creep: Burrowing animals pile dug-out material on the downslope side of their burrows; large grazers push debris downslope with their hooves as they follow traditional paths; and plants wedge loose material downslope by their roots. Creep may produce lobelike bulges on hillsides.

FIGURE 7-9. Landslide topography, mostly from slumping, of near-parallel arclike ridges and intervening depressions, caused by stream (Peace River) downcutting and slope failure. Near the town of Peace River, west-central Alberta, Canada. (Aerial photograph A21819-40 © 1970 Her Majesty the Queen in Right of Canada, reproduced with permission from the National Air Photo Library, Department of Energy, Mines and Resources, Canada.)

Considered a kind of creep to some and flowage to others, **solifluction** (SO-luh-fluck-shuhn—from the Latin *solum*, "soil," and *"fluctuare*, "to flow") is the slow downslope movement of water-saturated debris. Most pronounced in polar or high altitude areas of permanently frozen ground or permafrost, movement occurs during periods of thaw. Meltwater saturates thawed debris to a shallow depth that flows over a permanently frozen substrate, even on gentle slopes. Solifluction forms lobes or terracelike landforms on slopes.

Rock glaciers are tongues or streams of angular rock fragments at the base of cliffs or in valleys of cold, mountainous regions. Flowage is indicated by steep, lobed fronts and parallel, arclike ridges on their surfaces. Movement seems to take place by the flow of ice in the spaces between rock fragments. Rock glaciers, active in such places as Alaska, resemble ice glaciers and some may be debris-covered remnants of former ice glaciers.

Related to downslope, gravity-induced movement of rock and debris is **subsidence**, the downward rapid or slow sinking of parts of Earth's crust. Most subsidence near Earth's surface is caused by human removal of underground fluid, such as oil and groundwater, and by the collapse of natural caves and caverns. Overwithdrawal of oil and water from pore space in rock and sediment leaves these Earth materials unsupported; they compact, subside, and cause the formation of depressions and basins at the surface. In the San Joaquin Valley of California, considerable subsidence has resulted from overwithdrawal of groundwater; the same is true in Mexico City. At Long Beach, California, subsidence has resulted because of excessive pumping from a nearby oil field.

Collapse over dissolved limestone, rock salt, and rock gypsum forms sinkholes (see Figure 6-3). Similar features form where people pump water underground to mine salt or sulfur by dissolving these materials. Salt-laden water is pumped back to the surface and unsupported cavity roofs subside.

Subsidence may also result in other ways. In regions of underground mining, such as the coal-bearing Appalachian region of the eastern United States, collapse of mine roofs produces pits at the surface, most often elongated and aligned. In addition, subsidence on a smaller scale may occur as coal seams burn naturally and overlying materials collapse (see Figure 10-8). Volcanic craters and the larger calderas (see Figure 8-2) may form by subsidence as molten rock is withdrawn.

Suggested Reading

Coates, D. R. *Landslides. Reviews in Engineering Geology, v. 3*. Boulder, CO: Geological Society of America, 1977.

Hadley, J. B. "Landslides and Related Phenomena Accompanying the Hebgen Lake Earthquake of August 17, 1959," *U.S. Geological Survey Professional Paper 435-K* (1964): 107–138.

Witkind, I. J. "Events on the Night of August 17, 1959—The Human Story." *U.S. Geological Survey Professional Paper 435-A* (1964): 1–4.

8

Volcanic Landforms

Volcanoes and lava flows are familiar to most of us even though we may not have seen them. Who in North America, for example, is unaware of Mt. St. Helens in southwestern Washington, which erupted on May 18, 1980?

In this chapter we focus on how to recognize various volcanoes and lava flow-related landforms from a distance. For information on the rocks of volcanic landforms and igneous features, you might wish to check chapter 15.

Volcanoes

Volcanoes are hills or mountains built up of **lava** (hot, molten rock), fragmented rock, or both, spewed from vents or fractures. At their tops are circular or elliptical depressions—called **craters** if less than a mile (0.6 km) in diameter, or **calderas** (kal-DARE-uhz) if larger. Both craters and calderas form by explosion, collapse, or both processes.

More than 700 volcanoes have been active during recorded history, and most occur in narrow belts. The circum-Pacific belt, or Ring of Fire, extends from southern Chile northward in sporadic fashion along the western edges of the Americas; from the Aleutian Islands the belt continues to Japan, the Philippines, the East Indies, and New Zealand. Volcanoes are scattered also within the Pacific, as in the Hawaiian Islands. Another major belt trends east-west from the Mediterranean region through southern Asia and joins the East Indies. The mid-Atlantic belt is believed to contain numerous volcanoes as well, but they become visible only at such places as Iceland, the Azores, and Tristan da Cunha.

Volcano belts correspond to the major earthquake belts. Earthquakes, in fact, are often monitored to help predict volcanic eruptions. The belts of volcanoes and earthquakes in close association are believed to delineate the boundaries of major Earth plates (see chapter 12), which are in constant motion.

Volcanoes present different profiles (Figure 8-1) because of the materials of which they are constructed. **Shield volcanoes** (Fig-

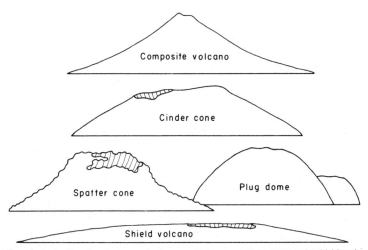

FIGURE 8-1. Profiles of major types of volcanoes. Profiles are not drawn to scale; shield and composite volcanoes are the largest, others are smaller. Diagonal ruling indicates craters or a caldera (shield type).

ure 8-2) are flat domes—slopes are generally less than 10°—that resemble a warrior's shield in profile. They are composed in most part of silica-poor basalt lava, hot (about 1,600 to 2,200°F [900 to 1,200°C]) and free-flowing, which results in gentle slopes. Although lava usually pours quietly from the crater and fractures along a volcano's flanks, gushing lava fountains occur. Hawaiian volcanoes, such as Mauna Loa, and several in Iceland are of the shield type. Mauna Loa is the world's largest known active volcano, many hundreds of square miles in area; it rises about 30,000 feet (9,140 m) above the seafloor. This may seem huge, but the largest shield volcano on Mars, Olympus Mons, is twice as large and towers above surrounding plains. Calderas are common at the summits of shield volcanoes, formed largely by collapse as lava is drained from subterranean chambers.

Gas-charged, basaltic lava fountains may build up rough, steep-sided **spatter cones** of pasty spatter or blobs of lava. Generally small, they may reach a few thousand feet high.

Silica-rich lava, similar in composition to rhyolite or andesite, is cooler and thicker and flows in a sluggish manner. Some lava barely flows at all and heaps up into steep-sided, bulbous **plug domes** over vents. Plug domes are similar in size to spatter cones. An area of plug domes is Mono Craters in eastern California.

Figure 8-2. Caldera of the shield volcano Kilauea, Hawaii, Hawaiian Islands. View is northward with Mauna Kea, another shield volcano, in the background; an extensive lava field separates the two volcanoes. Within the caldera, bordered by fault scarps, is the Halemaumau "Fire Pit" or crater near its southwest edge and lava flows on its floor, one of which has oozed out of the crater (bottom of the photograph). (U.S. Geological Survey photograph Hawaii 8A.)

The explosive accumulation of volcanic ash and coarser fragmental volcanic material, including cinders, about a vent forms **cinder cones** (Figure 8-3). Cone slopes are generally 30° to 35°, at the angle of rest of loose volcanic fragments. Cinder cones often group in clusters, and basalt flows may extend from their bases. One famous cinder cone, Paricutín (pah-ree-koo-TEEN), was born in a western Mexican cornfield in 1943 and ceased activity nine years later. At the close of eruptions, this cone rose 1,345 feet (410 m) high, large for a cinder cone.

Constructed of a combination of lava and fragmental material, **composite volcanoes** (Figure 8-4) display slopes of about 30° close to summits and 5° near their bases. Materials of these vol-

FIGURE 8-3. Cinder cone (top) and associated lava flow; SP Mountain and SP flow, 26 miles (42 km) north of Flagstaff, north-central Arizona (see Figure 10-6). The cone is 820 feet (250 m) high and 4,000 feet (1,200 m) in diameter at its base. (U.S. Geological Survey Photograph I-35 GS-VVP.)

canoes reflect alternating periods of explosive and quiet eruptions and, most often, have the composition of andesite, but range from rhyolite to basalt. Most of the world's larger volcanoes are of this type; examples include Mayon in the Philippines, Fujiyama in Japan, El Misti in Peru, Merapi in Java, and Mts. St. Helens and Shasta in the United States Cascades. Crater Lake (Figure 8-5) in the Oregon Cascades, almost 2,000 feet (610 m) deep, occupies a

FIGURE 8-4. Dormant composite volcano with lava flows at the base, Mt. Shasta, northern California. (Photograph 3668 by J. S. Shelton.)

caldera within a former composite volcano called Mt. Mazama. Back in the Pleistocene Epoch, valley glaciers streamed down the slopes of this peak. Eruptions and collapse hollowed out the famous caldera. Later, three cinder cones appeared, one of which—Wizard Island, with a lava flow issuing from its base—projects above lake level.

Lava Flows and Fields

Lava flows are outpourings of molten lava or the solidified rock equivalent of that lava. Flows issue from cracks or vents. Basaltic lavas with little gas move slowly and form flows many feet thick. The surfaces of such flows are of a rough, jumbled mass of angular, jagged blocks and clinkers. The Hawaiian term for such flows is **aa** (AH-ah) (Figure 8-6). **Pahoehoe** (Pah-HOE-ee-hoe-ee) **flows**, composed of basaltic lava with considerable gas, flow faster, are thinner, and have wrinkled or ropy surfaces (Figure 8-7). As mentioned in the discussion of plug domes, rhyolitic or an-

FIGURE 8-5. Caldera within a former composite volcano, Crater Lake, Crater Lake National Park, southwestern Oregon. Wizard Island, a cinder cone with a lava flow at its base, is in the foreground.

FIGURE 8-6. Rough, jagged *aa* lava flow with a cinder cone in the distance, Craters of the Moon National Monument, south-central Idaho.

desitic lavas are stiff and pasty, move slower than basaltic lavas, and produce flows with steeper sides.

Flows have lobed margins and develop characteristic landforms on their surfaces. **Pressure ridges**, usually at right angles to the direction of flow movement, form as the semirigid surface is squeezed and the interior remains fluid and mobile. Cracks often adorn the crests of ridges, and lava may issue secondarily from them. **Squeeze-ups** are moundlike equivalents of pressure ridges. Where basaltic lava is neither too stiff nor too fluid and flows with a moderate gradient, it may be confined in places to **lava channels**, open at the top, or roofed-over **lava tubes** or **tunnels**; both may extend for several miles. Drained, cooled tubes lure the inquisitive cave explorer. Some tubes are well insulated and retain ice the entire year. The collapse of tubes creates elongate depressions that resemble channels; short roof remnants of tubes produce natural arches or bridges.

Broad areas of lava flows, in frequent association with groups of cinder or spatter cones, are called **lava fields** (Figure 8-2 and Figure 10-6) or **plains**. Such areas display all of the flow-associated landforms mentioned here and are extensive within the Snake River region of southern Idaho.

Figure 8-7. Fractured *pahoehoe* lava flow with ropy surface, Valley of Fires State Park, near Carrizozo, south-central New Mexico. Numerous gas bubble cavities are visible on the fracture surface.

Lava fields are prevalent on the moon and Mars. The dark, lowland areas of the moon, **maria** (MAR-ee-uh), represent "seas" of basalt, extruded after the light, heavily cratered highlands or **terrae** (TEAR-ee) developed. Flow margins are not always obvious, presumably because of the extreme fluidity of the lava. Sinuous or winding rilles on the moon, and some on Mars, may be lava channels or collapsed lava tubes.

Evolution of Volcanic Terrains

After the extrusion of volcanic materials, a terrain undergoes progressive change unless renewed volcanism interrupts such change. Under light volcanism, lava flows follow stream valleys and dam streams. Diverted water runs along the sides of the more resistant lava flows and concentrates erosion there to create new valleys in those places. In time, the once low-lying areas of lava flows become elevated, elongate, twisted tablelands as the surrounding, more erodible rock wastes downward and away. These tablelands succumb further to erosion and degenerate to separated mesas and buttes. Those volcanoes, made up for the most part of fragmented volcanic material, erode to skeletal volcanic neck remnants (see Figure 10-3 and Figure 15-14) of more resistant rocks.

Under heavy volcanism, with emplacement of many lava flows, a landscape may become completely buried. Drainage, as in regions of light volcanism, is diverted, this time around the margins of extensive lava fields. Some streams with steeper gradients, however, may cut through the lava pile. With continued erosion, the more resistant, coalesced lava fields become an elevated lava plateau as surrounding softer rocks are worn down. One such plateau is the Columbia-Snake River Plateau (Figure 8-8), which occurs for the most part in Oregon, Washington, and Idaho, where the basalt flow pile exceeds 10,000 feet (3,000 m); the plateau is incised by the Columbia and Snake Rivers. Most of the flows in Oregon and Washington were emplaced during the Miocene Epoch about 15 million years ago. Those in Idaho continued into recent times; most of the flows in the Craters of the Moon National Monument (Figure 8-6) of southern Idaho are about 2,000 years old. Another extensive lava plateau is the Deccan Plateau in India. Lava plateaus are cut further into mesas and buttes, which are eventually destroyed.

In the sea, violent wave action consumes volcanic materials, the weaker fragmented materials first. Outright violent explosions, generated by entrapped steam, may blow away entire volcanoes.

FIGURE 8-8. Stacked basalt flows within the Columbia-Snake River Plateau cut by the Snake River, downstream from Palouse Falls, southeastern Washington. Right-angled bends in the stream are controlled by rock fractures. Wind-blown silt overlies the basalt in the right background. (Photograph 29 by F. O. Jones, U.S. Geological Survey.)

Suggested Reading

Bullard, F. M. *Volcanoes of the Earth.* Austin: University of Texas Press, 1984.

Foxworthy, B. L., and Mary Hill. "Volcanic Eruptions of 1980 at Mount St. Helens: The First 100 Days." *U.S. Geological Survey Professional Paper 1249* (1982): 1–25.

Green, Jack, and N. M. Short, eds. *Volcanic Landforms and Surface Features: A Photographic Atlas and Glossary.* New York: Springer-Verlag, 1971.

Lambert, M. B. *Volcanoes.* Seattle: University of Washington Press, 1980.

Wood, C. A., and Jürgen Kienle. *Volcanoes of North America: United States and Canada.* Cambridge, NY: Cambridge University Press, 1990.

9

Rock Deformation-Related Landforms

Stresses continually assault Earth's crust; earthquakes, other than those that accompany volcanic eruptions and similar localized events, evidence the crust's yielding to those stresses as rock masses jerk and grind along large-scale fractures. Old fractures signify similar crustal breakage in the past. But many rocks are also tilted and bent or folded into a variety of configurations. So rocks not only break as they yield to stress but also fold and bend. Rocks *bend*? In chapter 3, we learned that ice, commonly thought of as brittle, *flows* in glaciers at depth. And glacial ice can be considered a rock made up in most part of a single mineral. Rocks, other than glacial ice, bend when subjected to high pressures and temperatures, both of which exist at considerable depths.

Landforms related to rock deformation of layered rocks are largely linear ridges and intervening valleys, molded by **differential erosion**, or faster erosion of some rocks than others. The differential rate varies with the degree of lithification, the minerals present, and the climate. Within an arid climate, the sedimentary rocks sandstone, conglomerate, and limestone produce ridges, and shale forms valleys. In a humid climate, both limestone and shale characterize the valleys.

Dip and Strike

Picture yourself ambling along the rocky, southern shoreline of Lake Superior in northern Michigan. You notice a sandstone bed tilted toward the lake to the north-northwest. This tilt or inclination of the bed is its **dip**, estimated or measured (see chapter 20) from a horizontal surface, in this case the water level. What is the greatest dip a tilted layer can have? Answer: 90° or a vertical right angle.

The trend or **strike** of the bed is delineated by the horizontal waterline that meets the bed. Strike, always at right angles to dip, is here east-northeast. Geologists can measure and orient any inclined rock layer or fracture in space by means of strike and dip. Those values are necessary to project inclined beds and fractures beyond where they are visible.

Fold-Controlled Landforms

Monoclines (MAHN-uh-klynz) (Greek *monos*, "single," plus Latin *clinare*, "slope") are the simplest of folds, single steplike bends in flat-lying or gently dipping beds. As they erode, monoclines give rise to linear ridges and valleys.

Anticlines (ANT-uh-klynz) (Figure 9-1) are upfolds or up-arched folds. To visualize anticlines, place several sheets of paper on a table. Push opposite edges of the sheets toward each other with both hands. A buckling upward of the paper creates an anticline; each sheet corresponds to a folded rock layer. The sides or flanks of anticlines dip away from one another. **Domes** (Figure 9-2) are basically anticlines in which the beds dip outward more or less equally in all directions; many geologists, however, include rather elongate anticlines within domes. A well-known elongate dome is the Black Hills in western South Dakota and northeastern Wyoming. About 130 miles by 60 miles (209 km by 96 km), it trends north-northwest; this eroded dome is asymmetrical, for strata dip more steeply on the east side. The higher, exposed core of Precambrian age intrusive igneous and metamorphic rocks is flanked by progressively younger sedimentary layers, eroded to

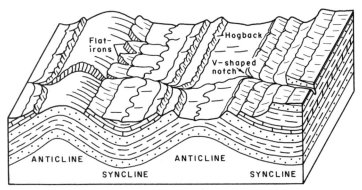

FIGURE 9-1. Eroded anticlines and synclines and resultant landforms. V-shaped notches, seen looking down on the eroded surface, point in the direction that beds dip. Rock symbols in the front and right panels are: dots = sandstone, lines = shale, and brick pattern = limestone.

FIGURE 9-2. Vertical aerial (top) and ground views (bottom) of a nearly circular dome, Green Mountain, near Sundance, northeastern Wyoming. The darker pine-covered central part consists of sandstone, dolostone, and shale. Lighter, noticeably tilted beds with flatirons that flank the uplift and with fewer trees are of limestone. The outermost, lightest beds that lack trees are of shale and rock gypsum. The dome was punched upward by a buried, intrusive laccolith (see chapter 15). (Upper photograph is 278-146 of the U.S. Department of Agriculture, ASCS.)

curved ridges and valleys, as you trace them outward from the center of the dome.

Synclines (SIN-klynz) are downfolds or downarched folds. Take the sheets of paper off the table and buckle them downward: You now have a syncline. Inclined beds, represented by the sheets, dip toward one another. Downfold counterparts of domes are **basins**. Keep in mind these are structural, not topographic, basins; that is, such basins result from the downbending of rocks, not simply from the lowering of elevation. Basins and domes vary from less than a mile to several hundred miles in extent. Both display concentric bands of strata upon erosion.

Many larger folds result from horizontal squeezing or compressive stresses at considerable depth, where high confining pressure and temperature reduce the strength of rocks. Smaller domes, however, can be produced by other means, as by igneous or salt intrusion. Intrusion of molten rock or magma can dome up overlying strata (Figure 9-2 and Figure 15-18). Intrusion of salt is more difficult to perceive, but does exist. Again, high pressure, in this case downward pressure from the weight of overlying strata, punches up pillars or columns of less dense salt in places from a thick "mother layer" at considerable depth. Rock layers that overlie the rising salt pillars are domed upward. Hundreds of these domes are known within the United States Gulf Coast area, both on land and submerged. Two that are visible at the surface but have little relief—circular and about 2 miles (3.2 km) in diameter—are the Avery and Weeks Islands salt domes in southern Louisiana.

Now, let's look more closely at what happens when erosion cuts through anticlines and synclines, which usually occur in groups. I've already mentioned the formation of parallel ridges held up by resistant rocks with intervening valleys on weaker rocks (Figure 9-1), similar as for monoclines but more complex. Ridges that are eroded from steeply dipped beds are called **hogbacks**. Where they are cut through by regularly spaced streams or gullies, triangular segments in hogbacks or **flatirons** (Figure 9-3) develop; flatirons resemble the old style of iron for pressing clothes. Ridges of lesser-dipping beds are **cuestas** (KWESS-tuhz) (Figure 9-4).

For either the cuesta or hogback, if the dip is less than 45°, the gentler slope is inclined in the same direction as the beds dip. This asymmetry of slope in cross profile helps you distinguish anticlines from synclines on aerial photographs and topographic maps or while in an aircraft. So, if asymmetrical ridges on the flanks of a fold have their gentler slopes directed away from one another, the fold is an anticline. The opposite is true for a syncline. Another approach is to look for **V**-shaped notches (Figure 9-1), as seen looking down on an eroded surface, in the hogbacks or cues-

FIGURE 9-3. Hogback—Mt. Rundle, southern Alberta, Canada—held up by resistant limestones that dip steeply to the right. In the near foreground, smaller Tunnel Mountain rises above Banff and the Bow River that cuts through the hogback. Flatirons are evident in the left distance. The view is to the southeast from Mt. Norquay. (Source of the photograph is unknown.)

FIGURE 9-4. Vegetated cuesta formed by resistant beds that dip at a low angle to the left.

tas where streams or gullies cut through them. Points of the Vs point in the direction of dip. Vs directed outward from the center of a fold, therefore, identify anticlines; those directed inward signify synclines. Long, narrow Vs indicate gentle dips; short, wide Vs denote steep dips. If no Vs exist, the beds are vertical.

Center lines or axes of folds may be higher or lower in elevation than the flanks, depending on the location of the most resistant rocks. Structurally high anticlines may have their centers at lower elevations than their flanks (Figures 9-1, 9-5), and struc-

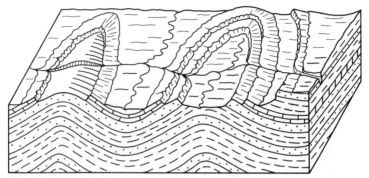

FIGURE 9-5. Eroded plunging anticlines and synclines display curved ridges and valleys that converge and diverge. Imagine the folds in Figure 9-1 tilted away from you and eroded.

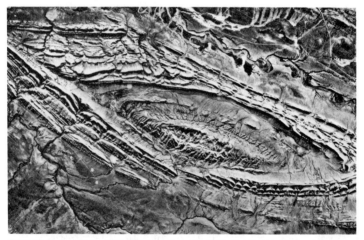

FIGURE 9-6. Eroded anticline plunges in two directions (to left and right), evidenced by elliptical hogbacks—with conspicuous V-shaped notches—and intervening valleys. Younger shale and sandstone beds occur away from the center line or axis of the anticline. Little Dome near Pavillion, Fremont County, northwest-central Wyoming. Maverick Spring Draw meanders in the upper part of the photograph. (U.S. Geological Survey photograph Wyoming 7A.)

turally low synclines may display their centers at higher elevations than their flanks.

Refer back to the sheets of paper. Off the table, create at least three folds in the paper sheets. Now, tilt the folds along their lengths, toward you or away; this angle of tilt is the **plunge** of the folds. The next step may be hard to visualize at first: What do

Figure 9-7. Folsom Point syncline—plunges toward the bottom of the photograph—evidenced by curved parallel ridges and valleys and V-shaped notches where cut by streams. Northern Alaska; the Utukok River cuts through the syncline in the foreground. Younger beds occur toward the axis, drawn on the photograph, of the syncline. (Photograph 366 by R. M. Chapman, U.S. Geological Survey.)

plunging folds look like on surfaces of erosion? In a nutshell, they produce a curved pattern of converging and diverging ridges and associated valleys (Figures 9-5 to 9-8); the pattern is zigzaglike where several anticlines and synclines occur together. If this is unclear, submerge your plunging paper folds part way in a sink or lake, whose surface simulates one of erosion. You will see a curved, zigzag line where the water's surface meets the paper. In the direction of plunge, rock ridges converge toward the closed end of a loop in anticlines and diverge away from the closed loop in synclines.

A **trellis drainage pattern** (Figure 9-9) of streams develops on associated, eroded anticlines and synclines, which may or may not plunge. Similar in configuration to a trellis for climbing vines, long, parallel tributaries in valleys of weak rocks join the fold-transecting main streams at nearly right angles. The Ridge and Valley Province (see Appendix D) of the Appalachian Mountains excellently portrays zigzag ridges and valleys of eroded plunging

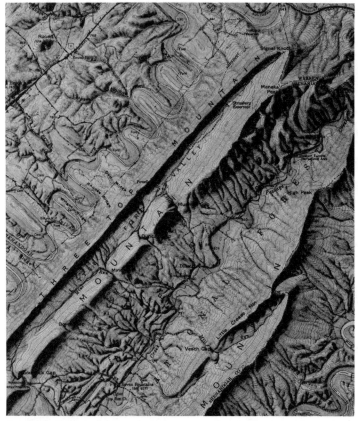

FIGURE 9-8. Shaded relief map of mountains and valleys that result from the erosion of plunging folds, near Strasburg, Virginia. V-shaped notches along Green Mountain, to the right of Three Top Mountain, and asymmetrical slopes of the long ridge on the right of the map indicate a syncline underlies the valley between; this valley is about 2 miles (3.2 km) wide in the upper right. A syncline also underlies Little Fort Valley with the crest of an anticline along Green Mountain. All folds plunge toward the lower left. Both the North and South Forks of the Shenandoah River, which flank the folds, display incised meanders. (From the U.S. Geological Survey Strasburg Quadrangle, 1947.)

folds and a concomitant trellis drainage pattern. This is in marked contrast to the common **dendritic drainage pattern**, like irregular branches of a tree, that develops on flat-lying rocks or on uniform igneous or metamorphic rocks.

Remember that as domes erode, they develop curved, alternate ridges and valleys in concentric or near-elliptical patterns, and

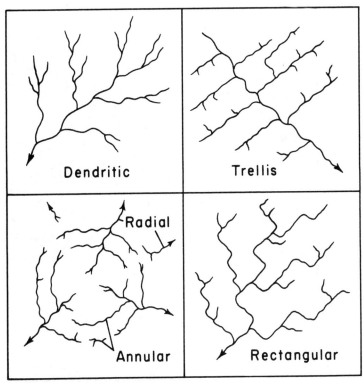

FIGURE 9-9. Main types of stream drainage patterns.

these patterns influence stream drainage. At first, a **radial drainage pattern** (Figure 9-9)—streams diverge from the center—develops on an eroded dome. (Such a drainage pattern may also develop on a mountain peak.) Later, a ringlike **annular drainage pattern** in part replaces the radial pattern. Both radial and annular drainages have developed on the Black Hills dome.

Fracture-Controlled Landforms

Joints (Figure 9-10) are fractures in rocks along which no appreciable slippage has occurred. They usually occur in sets or directions of two or more and, therefore, divide rock layers into distinctive blocks. We are concerned here with joints produced by large-scale stresses on rocks, not with those that result from cooling of magma (see chapter 15) or unloading by erosion.

Figure 9-10. Joints in the igneous rock felsite (see chapter 15).

In some places, such as Zion and Arches National Parks in southern Utah, vertical joints cut sandstone beds (Figure 9-11) cemented by calcite. Groundwater and surface water seeps into the joints and enlarges them as the calcite dissolves. Water, wind, and gravity remove the sand grains. In time, rock slabs or fins, similar in shape to the back fins of fish, are formed. Continued erosion attacks the slabs or fins from the sides and sculpts alcoves that are ultimately cut through to produce natural arches (see Figure 13-1). These arches resemble the natural bridges in sandstone and limestone that originate by groundwater action (see chapter 6). Where intersecting joints are closely spaced, weathering (see chapter 23) attacks from several sides to form rock pillars or columns. This phenomenon is well displayed at Bryce Canyon National Park, also in southern Utah.

Joints may also control stream drainage, which results in aligned, parallel valleys, or a **rectangular drainage pattern** (Figure 9-9); in this drainage pattern both main streams and tributaries make right-angled bends. Such a pattern develops in uniform rocks of any type as well as in foliated metamorphic rocks (see chapter 17).

Faults (Figure 9-12) are fractures that differ from joints in that appreciable slippage of rock masses has occurred along them. Geologists recognize two main types of faults that dip at less than a

FIGURE 9-11. Joint-controlled linear depressions and rock fins (left mid-distance) in sandstone, Arches National Park, southeastern Utah. Vegetation in the joints emphasizes them. The view is westward along the northeast flank of the Salt Valley anticline; beds in the right distance dip to the right. (Photograph 691 by S. W. Lohman, U.S. Geological Survey.)

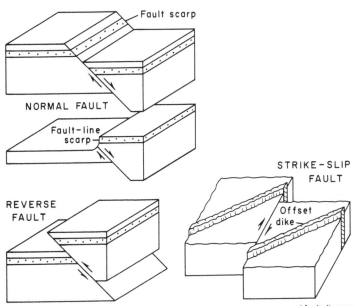

FIGURE 9-12. Main types of faults and associated features. In the lower normal fault diagram, a fault-line scarp owes its relief largely to later differential erosion; a resistant sandstone bed is dotted.

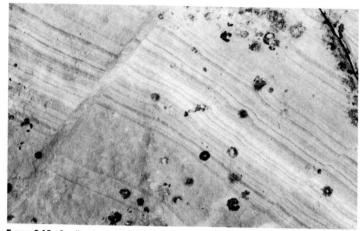

Figure 9-13. Small-scale normal faulting of thin layers or laminae in sandstone. Displacement of the laminae is 2.1 inches (5.3 cm).

vertical angle. A **normal fault** (Figure 9-13) is one in which the block above the fault has moved down relative to the block beneath it. (I say "relative to" because the upper block may have moved down, the lower block may have moved up, or both may have moved in opposite directions.) In a **reverse fault** (Figure 9-14), on the other hand, the upper block has moved up relative to the lower block. A low angle reverse fault, say with a dip of less than 45°, is the common **thrust fault**. Normal faults are caused by pulling apart or tensional stresses, reverse faults by pushing together or compressive stresses.

High angle normal and reverse faults form **scarps** (Figure 9-12 and Figure 8-2), steep slopes or cliffs parallel to the faults. **Fault scarps** are due entirely to faulting. Older **fault-line scarps** owe their relief to faulting plus later differential erosion, in particular where a more resistant bed contributes to the formation of such scarps (Figure 9-12, normal fault). Fault scarps are associated with recent geologic features, such as where they pass across alluvial fans or abut against scarp-dammed streams. They are short-lived and eroded by streams, glaciers, and landslides. The eastern fronts of the Sierra Nevada Mountains in eastern California and the Teton Mountains in northwestern Wyoming (Figure 9-15) are highly eroded fault scarps. A fresher scarp faces west on the western edge of the Wasatch Mountains in northern Utah. Many scarps, of course, are much smaller than the three mentioned.

FIGURE 9-14. Reverse faulting—the fault is dashed and arrows show the directions of relative movement—of poorly lithified, fine-grained sedimentary strata. Displacement is at least 12 feet (3.6 m).

Two normal faults that dip toward one another produce a down-dropped block or **graben** (GRAHB-uhn), which results in a straight-sided **rift valley**. Normal faults often occur in groups and form a series of grabens with intervening high, linear plateaus or mountains. The Basin and Range Province (Appendix D), which covers Nevada and environs, is such a region of generally north-

FIGURE 9-15. Glacier-sculptured, east-facing fault scarp of the Teton Range projects 7,000 feet (2,135 m) above low-lying Jackson Hole, Grand Teton National Park, northwestern Wyoming. Lacking foothills, the Tetons represent a block that moved up along a normal fault relative to the downward-moving block of Jackson Hole. Stream terraces flank the Snake River in the mid-distance.

trending grabens and small mountain ranges. In eastern Africa, the rift valleys with lakes, such as Lake Tanganyika, occupy grabens as does the Dead Sea in Jordan.

Along **strike-slip faults** (Figures 9-12, 9-16), displacement of rock masses is mostly horizontal and parallel to the strike or trend of the faults. A famous example is the San Andreas—actually a zone of faults—which extends from the Gulf of California generally north-northwestward to north of San Francisco. Movement along strike-slip faults is evidenced by offset dikes (see chapter 15), ridges, fences, streams, and orchards. Movement to the right (Figure 9-12) is the case for the San Andreas. That is, if you stand on one side of the fault and look across to the other, you see that linear features have shifted to the right. San Francisco rests on the east side of the San Andreas, Los Angeles on the west. A wag has said that in the geologic future the two cities, carried along in opposite directions on their respective blocks or Earth plates, will someday be one!

Because of little or no up or down movement, landforms of strike-slip faults are inconspicuous. Shallow, linear valleys and

FIGURE 9-16. San Andreas strike-slip fault zone, San Luis Obispo County, southern California. (Photograph 194 by R. E. Wallace, U.S. Geological Survey.)

low, linear ridges—from slivers of rock caught along a fault—are the main features. Offset ridges and stream valleys are associated landforms.

Like joints, faults can produce linear ridges and valleys, single or in parallel groups. Fault systems may also intersect so as to impart a rectangular drainage system.

Suggested Reading

Twidale, C. R. *Structural Landforms: Landforms Associated with Granitic Rocks, Faults, and Folded Strata.* Cambridge, MA: MIT Press, 1971.

10

Keys for Identification
of Landforms

This chapter constitutes a concise grouping of the main landforms, those covered in chapters 2 through 9, but also includes others, such as those produced by humans. Mainly, though, this chapter provides a means for quick identification of landforms through the use of keys similar to those used by biologists to identify plants and animals.

These keys use the setting of a landform as the primary basis for identification, followed by composition and other characteristics. Each numbered step in a key offers you two choices. If the first choice doesn't provide an answer, a second choice, by means of a number, directs you to another couplet of choices. If you seem to end up with an illogical answer, backtrack through the key to the spot where you think you selected a wrong choice.

To identify a landform produced by a geologic agent no longer present can prove difficult. Examples include shoreline landforms of a lake evidenced now only by a lake plain (its former bottom) and glacial landforms produced by a glacier which melted long ago. Before you use any of the keys, should you skip to them first, I suggest that you skim chapters 2 through 9.

Landforms in the keys are grouped as to whether they project upward (hills, ridges, and mountains); are relatively flat (plains and related features); or form depressions (valleys and basins). **Hills** are about as long as wide, **ridges** are elongate; **mountains**, elongate or not, are larger than hills and ridges and reach heights of about 1,000 feet (300 m) or more. **Plains** are relatively flat areas, horizontal or gently sloping, and often at low elevations. Hills, ridges, or depressions may be present but relative flatness predominates. **Valleys** are elongate depressions, usually open at one or both ends. **Basins** are normally about as long as wide and enclosed.

Figure 10-1. Rock pillars in a resistant Permian sandstone, Monument Valley, near Mexican Hat, southeastern Utah. A broad butte rises in the background.

Hills

1. Restricted to base of slopes
     Landslide hill (see Figure 7-8): Scarps or cliffs above; of rock or rock debris.
     Talus (see Figure 7-4): Rock accumulation, commonly in half-cones.
   Not restricted to base of slopes   2

2. Associated with stream drainages
     Plateau: Large, wide, elevated tableland.
     Mesa: Tableland smaller than plateau.
     Butte (Figure 10-1): Small, isolated, erosional remnant, smaller than a mesa.
     Pillar (pinnacle) (Figure 10-1): Erosional column of rock.
     Monadnock (see Figure 2-7): Isolated, erosional remnant on a low-relief peneplain.
   Not associated with stream drainages   3

3. Restricted to shorelines
     Stack (Figure 10-2, see also the photograph that introduces Part I and Figure 4-3): Isolated pinnacle or small island, associated with sea cliffs, arches, caves, and hanging valleys; of rock.
   Not restricted to shorelines   4

FIGURE 10-2. View of a stack from a sea cave, Devils Elbow State Park, near Florence, western Oregon. Boulders line the floor of the sea cave.

4. Involves domed rock layers

> **Dome hill** (see Figure 15-18): Resistant rock layers punched up by laccolith (see Figure 15-14), salt intrusion, or squeezing from sides.

> Does not involve domed rock layers　　　　　　　　　5

5. In areas of hot springs or geysers

> **Thermal mound** or **cone** (see Figure 6-7): Of travertine or siliceous sinter.

> Not in areas of hot springs or geysers　　　　　　　　6

6. Bordered by terraces (flat surfaces)

> **Terraced hill**: In rock or sediment from mining or in soil from farming.

> Not bordered by terraces　　　　　　　　　　　7

7. In volcanic terrain

> **Squeeze-up**: Moundlike; on lava flows; formed by squeezing up of semirigid surface lava as interior mass remains fluid; may be associated with pressure ridges.

> **Spatter cone** (see Figure 8-1): Type of volcano; of spatter or blobs of basaltic lava; steep-sided; built up by lava fountains.

> **Plug dome** (see Figure 8-1): Type of volcano; of slow-mov-

ing rhyolitic or andesitic lava; steep-sided and bulbous; also called volcanic dome.

Cinder cone (see Figures 8-1, 8-3, 8-5): Type of volcano; of volcanic ash and coarser fragmental volcanic material including cinders; basalt flow may extend from base.

Volcanic neck (Figure 10-3 and Figure 15-14): Towerlike mass of rock that filled vent of old volcano; exposed by erosion.

Not in volcanic terrain 8

8. Of rock, different from those hills above

Exfoliation dome (see Figure 3-6): Slabs or shells weather and spall off massive rock to form rounded hill.

Rock knob: Hill of resistant rock not covered previously.

Pyramids, temples: Human-made.

Not of rock 9

9. Of till (nonuniform mixture of boulders through clay) or human-made fill

Till knob: In moraines (see Figure 3-11); of till; with foreign boulders or erratics.

Mine spoil pile: Of fill; mining equipment and rubbish may be nearby.

Burial or **construction mound**: Of fill.

FIGURE 10-3. Volcanic neck, near Kayenta, northeastern Arizona. Most of the volcano has been eroded away and the more resistant rock that occupied a former vent remains.

Of sand or gravel

> **Kame** (see Figure 3-15): Steep-sided; formed in contact with glacial ice.
>
> **Dune** (see Figure 5-6 and Figure 5-8): Inland or near coasts; of sand only.

Ridges

1. Restricted to base of slopes

> **Landslide ridge** (see Figure 7-9): Scarps or cliffs above; of rock or rock debris.

Not restricted to base of slopes   2

2. Associated with streams

> **Divide between streams** (see Figure 2-7): Of rock or sediment.
>
> **Natural bridge**: Of rock; spans erosional valley; formed by surface and underground streams.
>
> **Natural arch** (see Figure 13-1): Of rock; does not span erosional valley; may associate with intermittent (usually) or permanent streams.
>
> **Natural levee**: Flanks stream; of silt and sand.
>
> **Spoil bank**: From stream dredging or stream mining; may appear segmented.

Not associated with streams   3

3. Restricted to shorelines   4

Not restricted to shorelines   5

4. Of rock

> **Sea arch** (see the photograph that introduces Part I and Figure 4-2): Associated with sea caves and cliffs and hanging valleys.

Of sand and gravel

> **Beach** (see Figure 4-4): At shoreline and parallels it.
>
> **Spit** (see Figure 4-4): Projects into open water.
>
> **Baymouth bar** (see Figure 4-4): Blocks mouth of bay.
>
> **Tombolo** (see Figure 4-4): Connects island to mainland or other island.
>
> **Barrier island** (see Figure 4-4): Separated from low coast by lagoon.

5. Restricted to mountains

> **Arête** (see Figure 3-5): Sharp-crested, between half-bowl-like depressions (cirques); result of valley glaciation.

Not restricted to mountains   6

6. On lava flows

  Pressure ridge: At right angles to flow movement; forms by squeezing up of semirigid surface lava as interior mass remains fluid; may be associated with squeeze-ups.

  Not on lava flows   7

7. Involves tilted rock layers

  Hogback (see Figure 9-3): Rock layers steeply inclined.

  Cuesta (see Figure 9-4): Rock layers gently inclined.

  Does not involve tilted rock layers   8

8. Of rock

  Sheep rock (see Figure 3-10): Streamlined; surface scratched or grooved.

  Stone wall: Human-made, as in New England area.

  Dike wall (see Figure 9-12): Of resistant rock of igneous dike (see chapter 15).

  Of sediment   9

9. Of till or human-made fill

  Drumlin (see Figures 3-9, 3-13): Streamlined; of till.

  Moraine (see Figures 3-8, 3-9): Lateral, medial, end, recessional; may be associated with glaciers; of till with foreign boulders or erratics.

  Road or **railroad embankment**: Where abandoned, look for straight sides; human rubbish or railroad ties may be nearby; of fill.

  Mine spoil pile: Especially in coal-mining areas; of fill.

  Of sand or gravel

  Esker (see Figure 3-14): Twisting; formed in contact with glacial ice.

  Crevasse filling: Relatively straight; formed in contact with glacial ice.

  Dune (see Figure 5-1): Inland or near coasts; of sand only.

Mountains

Mountains typically occur in chains or ranges but also as isolated peaks. Peaks become jagged from secondary erosion by glaciers.

1. Entirely of volcanic rocks

  Volcanic mountain (see Figure 8-4): Commonly as isolated peak.

  Not entirely of volcanic rocks   2

2. Involves domed rock layers

Dome mountain (see Figure 9-2): Resistant rock layers punched up by laccolith intrusion or squeezing from sides.

Does not involve domed rock layers   3

3. Interior of folded and and faulted rock layers
Folded mountain (see Figure 9-8): In long belt, most extensive of mountains.

Interior not of folded and faulted rock layers   4

4. Straight and linear with linear depression on one or both sides
Fault-block mountain (see Figure 9-15): Faulting along one or both sides of mountain, adjoining depression(s) from down-dropped block(s).

Not straight and linear with linear depression on one or both sides   5

5. Rock layers often flat-lying
Erosional mountain: Result primarily of differential erosion with accompanying uplift; may be plateau, mesa, or monadnock (see *Hills*)

Plains and Related Features

1. Associated directly with streams
Floodplain (see Figure 2-2): Flat part of broad valleys inundated during floods.
Stream terrace (see Figures 2-4, 9-15): Benchlike remnant of former floodplain flanking valley walls.
Delta plain (see Figure 3-9): At mouth of present or former stream, slopes toward sea or lake; surface of delta.
Alluvial plain (see Figures 2-4, 2-6): Surface of alluvial fan or grouped fans; also, any plain of alluvium or stream sediment.
Outwash plain (see Figure 3-9): Adjacent to irregular knob and basin terrain of glacial moraines; of meltwater stream sediment.

Not associated directly with streams   2

2. Allied with shorelines
Wave-cut bench (see Figure 4-2 and photograph that introduces Part II): Slopes away from sea or lake cliff; forms **marine terrace** where raised above water level; of rock.
Wave-built terrace (see Figure 4-2): Seaward or lakeward of wave-cut bench; not readily visible except if produced by former water body; of sediment.

Figure 10-4. Tidal flat at Point Wolfe River estuary, Fundy National Park near Alma, southeastern New Brunswick. Photograph was taken on June 27, 1985, two hours after low tide.

Tidal flat (Figures 10-4, 10-5): Periodically covered and uncovered by rising and falling tide.

Coastal plain (see Figure Appendix D-1): Slopes toward the sea; generally represents raised former sea bottom.

Lake plain (see Figures 3-9, 3-17, 3-18): Former lake bottom; associated with former shoreline features; fertile; mostly of silt and clay; commonly direct or indirect result of glacier formation and extension.

Not allied with shorelines   3

3. Restricted to lava flows

   Lava field or **plain** (Figure 10-6 and Figure 8-2): Broad expanse underlain by lava flows; may be associated with volcanic cones.

   Not restricted to lava flows   4

4. Of till

   Till plain: Of low hills and shallow, closed depressions; corresponds to ground moraine (see Figures 3-9, 3-12).

   Not of till

   Pediment: Planed rock surface sloping away from mountain front or cliff; may be veneered with stream sediment; in dry regions.

Figure 10-5. Same place as that shown in Figure 10-4 on June 28, 1985, 20 minutes before high tide. The waters of the estuary merge imperceptibly with those of the Bay of Fundy. The average tidal range in this region is 20 feet to 40 feet (6 m to 12 m).

Figure 10-6. Lava field as viewed from the north rim of SP Mountain, a cinder cone; near Flagstaff, north-central Arizona (see Figure 8-3). The lava field, which extends north from the northwest base of the cinder cone, formed about 70,000 years ago.

Peneplain (see Figure 2-7): Planed rock surface unrelated to mountain front or cliff, often with scattered erosional remnants (monadnocks).

Valleys

1. Restricted to soluble rocks
     Solution valley (see Figure 6-2): Ends closed; most common in limestone regions; sinkholes and caves nearby.
   Not restricted to soluble rocks   2

2. Restricted to lava flows
     Lava channel: For confined conveyance of lava; originally open at top.
     Lava tube collapse channel or **pit**: For confined conveyance of lava; secondary collapse of roof exposes it to sky.
   Not restricted to lava flows   3

3. Straight-sided and usually flat-bottomed
     Rift valley: Bounded by steep cliffs or linear mountains; result of faulting; valley occupies top of down-dropped block.
   Not straight-sided and usually flat-bottomed   4

4. Tributary valleys present
     Stream valley (see Figures 2-1, 2-7): Tributary valleys meet main valley at its level; narrow valley with V-shaped cross-valley profile; may be straight where it follows fracture or tilted rock layers (Figures 9-8, 9-9, 9-16); may lack stream or one that is underfit as in abandoned meltwater valley.
     Meander scar (see Figure 2-2): Part of curved abandoned stream bend in broad valley; **oxbow lake** if filled with water.
     Glacial valley (see Figures 3-5, 3-6): Tributary valleys meet main valley above its level; cross-valley profile U-shaped, bottom may be flattened from sediment fill; may be secondarily occupied by stream; **fiord** is drowned glacial valley.
   Tributary valleys generally absent
     Ditch, **canal**, **channel**: Sides even; may be lined with rock, concrete, or other material; for irrigation, drainage, diversion.

Basins

Most basins are wholly or partly filled with water to form lakes or ponds.

1. Restricted to stream valleys   2

   Not restricted to stream valleys   3

2. In rock

   Pothole: Usually deeper than wide, in stream channel at sites of present or former waterfalls and rapids; worn by sand and gravel in whirling water.

   In sediment

   Backswamp: Shallow depression on floodplain away from stream in broad valley.

3. Restricted to folded or faulted rock layers

   Tectonic basin: From downfolding or downfaulting.

   Not restricted to folded or faulted rock layers   4

4. Restricted to volcanoes

   Volcanic crater (see Figures 8-2, 8-3): At top of volcano.

   Caldera (see Figures 8-2, 8-5): Similar to volcanic crater but larger.

   Not restricted to volcanoes   5

5. Overlies soluble rocks

   Sinkhole (see Figure 6-3): Solution cavity at surface; most often in or above limestone; solution valleys and caves nearby.

   Does not necessarily overlie soluble rocks   6

6. Restricted to glacial valleys (see *Valleys*)

   Cirque (see Figures 3-5, 3-7): Half-bowl-like depression at head of glacial valley, commonly with distinct basin at base.

   Not restricted to glacial valleys   7

7. Usually bordered by raised rim

   Meteor crater (Figure 10-7): Meteor fragments in vicinity and rock in crater may show effects of shock metamorphism (see chapter 17); rare on Earth, common on other planets and moon.

   Maar (MAHR): Low-relief explosion crater; in volcanic terrains; crater walls with little or no lava or fragmental volcanic material; often occupied by circular lake.

Figure 10-7. Meteor Crater, near Winslow, northeastern Arizona. This crater, 4,000 feet (1,200 m) across and 600 feet (183 m) deep, was formed by meteorite impact about 50,000 years ago. Meteor Crater is the first recognized and one of the best-preserved impact craters on Earth. Although first thought to be a crater of an extinct volcano, numerous meteorite fragments have been found on the surrounding plain, and drilling produced many within the crater itself. Up-arched sedimentary layers, a raised crater rim, and ejected rock blocks—some as large as small houses—further evidence the impact. From the air, Meteor Crater is more squarish than circular, its shape controlled by the trends of regional joints.

    Bomb crater: In areas of human conflict; associated with human rubbish and relics of war.
Not usually bordered by raised rim   8

8. Restricted to desert floor
    Playa: Contains lake after rains, accumulates salts.
Not restricted to desert floor   9

9. Characteristic of areas of mining
    Quarry, open-pit mine, **sand-gravel pit**: Site of extraction of valuable rocks or minerals; associated with spoil piles; open-pit mine may be terraced.
    Collapse (subsidence) pit or basin (see chapter 7): May be associated with spoil piles; collapse pits related to underground mines elongate or aligned; may also form by overwithdrawal of groundwater or oil and burning of coal

Figure 10-8. Small subsidence basin caused by the burning of lignite and subsequent collapse, Theodore Roosevelt National Park (South Unit), near Medora, southwestern North Dakota.

        (Figure 10-8); sinking may cause settling of buildings and local flooding.

Not characteristic of areas of mining   10

10. In rock

    Rock basin (see Figure 3-5): Grooves and scratches indicate formation by ice scour; scattered along glacial valleys and in other glaciated areas where rock is exposed.

In sediment

    Blowout: In hilly area of sand; sides often steep, cut layering of adjacent dunes.

    Kettle (see Figures 3-9, 3-16): In hilly area of till and relatively flat area of sand and gravel (outwash plain); steep-sided, at least in part; result of melting of partly or wholly buried block of ice.

    Swale (see Figure 3-12): Similar to kettle in setting but not steep-sided; result of uneven laying down of glacial sediment.

    Watering pond basin: Human-made; with bordering spoil banks; livestock may be nearby.

11

Time and Geology

Time, the elusive, abstract dimension. We "make time," "mark time," "kill time." But what really *is* time? I like this Webster's definition: "Every moment there has ever been or ever will be." No stipulation as to a beginning or an end for time. And time, at least as we know it on Earth, is continuous; there are no gaps. Most of us view time as irretrievable and irreversible, although physicists delve into the possible reversibility of time.

Time, by itself, is virtually meaningless to humans; it gains significance only when related to a happening or event. In this sense, time is a period or interval when something exists or happens, or the period or interval between a thing's nonexistence and existence or between a nonhappening or happening. We've come to accept that time and events are inseparable.

We can conceive time in a relative or a specific sense. We speak of a happening in the past, present, or future, one that occurs before, at the same time, or after another happening. One happening is relative to another; for example, World War I happened before World War II. Specific time for an event is reckoned in years, months, days, hours, minutes, seconds; when geologists date geological events in terms of years, they call this **absolute time**.

Historic time, the period of written history, goes back about 5,000 years. Time prior to historic time is **prehistoric time**. In the seventeenth century, Biblical scholars stipulated that prehistoric time extended back to about 6,000 years; this figure prevailed until the nineteenth century when several dating attempts, based

OVERLEAF. A good place to contemplate past happenings, Sunset Bay State Park near Coos Bay, southwestern Oregon. The tilted layers of sandstone and mudstone were originally flat-lying beds of sand and mud that later lithified. Earth movements tilted the rocks whose upturned edges were worn by erosion and covered by flat-lying sandstone (top of photo). The buried surface of erosion at the level where the flat-lying sandstone overlies the upturned edges of tilted rocks is an angular unconformity (see chapter 11). The flat surface of worn tilted layers in the foreground could represent an angular unconformity in the making if sea level were to rise or the coastline were to sink. This surface is the top of a wave-cut bench (see chapter 4), which is covered by the sea during high tide.

on scientific principles, pushed the beginning of prehistoric time back millions of years. Geologists have since demonstrated that *billions*, not thousands or millions, of years encompass prehistory. Prehistoric time since Earth's origin is often referred to as **geologic time**. Geologic time goes back to when Earth attained most of its mass, and perhaps a solid crust, possibly by condensation of a whirling, eddying cloud of dust and gas, the process that may also have formed other members of the solar system. The universe, of which the solar system is but an infinitesimal part, may have originated billions of years earlier. Time since the formation of the all-encompassing universe may be called **cosmic** or **universe time**.

We witness the passage of time with the continuance of day and night, the change of the seasons, birth and death. For the course of geologic time, geologists rely on the **principle of uniformitarianism** (you-nuh-four-muh-TARE-ee-uh-nihz-uhm), which says natural laws have remained unchanged through time, and, therefore, processes that shape and affect Earth today are continuations of those from the past. (More is said about uniformitarianism in chapter 19). The principle of uniformitarianism provided geologists with the perspective of an Earth much older than 6,000 years. Based on this premise, considerable time is required for major events to occur: canyons to be cut; glaciers to mold the surface as they advance and retreat; shorelines to be shaped by waves and currents; sea level to rise and inundate the land, then drain once again; and mountain ranges to be created.

Measurement of Time

To measure and record time, we are not restricted to human clocks and calendars; in fact, we cannot be for the measurement of prehistoric time. Well-known, natural time recorders that reflect seasonal changes are tree rings and "growth rings," perhaps better termed "rest rings," on clam shells. Some bristlecone pines of the American Southwest and eastern California are the most ancient trees. Counts of rings of dead and live trees have extended a record of time well beyond the 6,000 years first believed as the age of Earth. **Varves**, or annual sediment layers, also reflect seasonal changes and, therefore, record time. The best-known varves are those laid down in lakes formed by the damming of glacial meltwater. Each varve consists of a lighter, thicker, coarser summer layer and a darker, thinner, finer layer deposited during ice-covered periods. You simply count the couplets of beds for the span of a lake's existence. Varve counts of glacial lake sediments that relate to the latest glaciations give values of about 15,000 years; those of certain older, nonglacial lakes give their duration as a few million years.

All the methods we've looked at so far are restricted in the magnitude of time they measure or how they might be applied. **Radioactive** or **radiometric dating**, however, with several methods that use radioactive elements, allows us to measure any interval of time that involves Earth materials and events.

At about the turn of the twentieth century, certain varieties of elements—or **isotopes** that differ from their relatives by different atomic weights—were found to be unstable or *radioactive*. That is, the nuclei of their atoms decay, as charged particles are emitted, and the isotopes transform into different elements. The decay rate seems to be constant with time and unaffected by changes in temperature, pressure, or chemical changes. A decay rate for a radioactive element is expressed as its **half-life**, the time in years for half of the original number of atoms to decay. Uranium 235 (the number refers to the atomic weight), one of the isotopes of uranium, has a half-life of 713 million years. After this time, half of the atoms of this isotope in a sample are gone; in two half-lives or 1,426 million years, three-fourths are gone and only half of a half or only a quarter remain. Because isotopes are used to date rocks, they can be considered radioactive clocks.

To date a mineral or rock with a radioactive element, we must know the relative amount of the derived or daughter isotope in relation to the amount of the original or parent isotope. Sophisticated equipment can make these measurements. Uranium 235 decays to lead 207. If a mineral like zircon in an igneous rock contains 50 percent derived lead and 50 percent original uranium, one half-life has gone by, and the dated sample is 713 million years old. Seventy-five percent derived lead and 25 percent uranium indicate two half-lives have elapsed for a date of 1,426 million years; and 87.5 percent lead and 12.5 percent uranium tells us that three half-lives have elapsed or the sample has an age of 2,139 million years.

The chief radioactive alterations used to date minerals and rocks are: uranium to lead, potassium to argon, rubidium to strontium, thorium to lead, and carbon to nitrogen. All methods except carbon to nitrogen can date the oldest rocks because of long half-lives; the longest involves rubidium 87 with a half-life of about 50,000 million years.

The carbon to nitrogen or carbon 14 method operates in a different manner than the other methods and can date only organic materials—those that contain carbon, such as wood, bone, and shell. Carbon 14, formed as nitrogen is bombarded by cosmic rays in the upper atmosphere, is absorbed by every living organism after combining with oxygen to form carbon dioxide. When an organism dies, carbon 14 is no longer replenished and begins to diminish at its decay rate, in accordance with a half-life of 5,730 years. A date is based on the ratio of carbon 14 to ordinary carbon in a sample; the less carbon 14 found, the older the sample. Because of the short half-life involved, the carbon 14 method can only date organic materials that are younger than about 70,000 years.

Radiometric dating is a useful technique, but I would be remiss if I didn't point out some inherent fallibilities. That doesn't mean we shouldn't believe the derived dates, but we must apply them with caution. A major source of possible error involves the assumption that an analyzed sample has persisted within a closed system: that neither original nor derived materials were removed or added except by radioactive decay. An implication, too, is that no derived material was originally present. The possible error from the assumption is corrected for by the use of different dating methods, so as to check one against another. An error can also ensue from the laboratory analysis. Every date is reported with a plus or minus figure, such as 430 million years ± 10 million years; in this case the calculated date could range between 420 and 440 million years. Plus or minus 10 million years may be strictly from an error in measurement or reflect variations in several samples analyzed. A date given this way means another analyzed sample would probably fall within 10 million years on either side of 430 million, but says nothing about how good the radiometric age is in relation to the true age. The true age is approached, again, by additional analyses by different dating methods; another check is to compare a radiometric age against a relative age gained by the principle of superposition (see the next section) or by the use of fossils. At first, ± 10 million years may seem a large laboratory error. In actuality, the error is less than 3 percent of 430 million years.

Geologic Time Scale

The geologic time scale (see Figure 11-1 and Table 11-1) was developed during the eighteenth and nineteeth centuries, mostly in Europe where the science of geology was born. Development was rather haphazard, with no preconceived plan. Names of the time

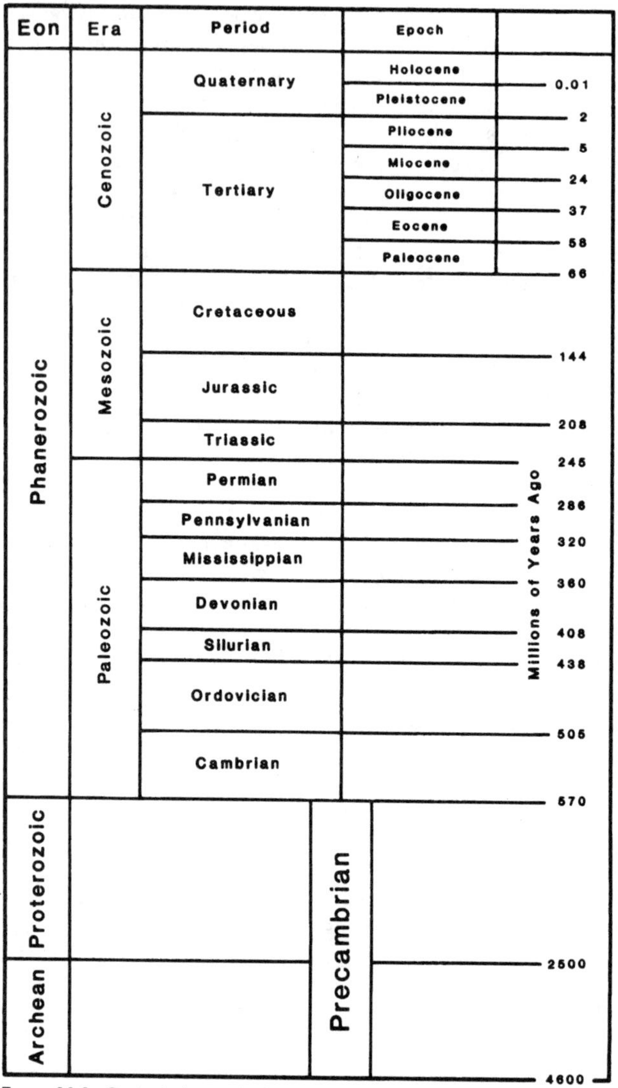

Eon	Era	Period	Epoch	
Phanerozoic	Cenozoic	Quaternary	Holocene	— 0.01
			Pleistocene	— 2
		Tertiary	Pliocene	— 5
			Miocene	— 24
			Oligocene	— 37
			Eocene	— 58
			Paleocene	— 66
	Mesozoic	Cretaceous		— 144
		Jurassic		— 208
		Triassic		— 245
	Paleozoic	Permian		— 286
		Pennsylvanian		— 320
		Mississippian		— 360
		Devonian		— 408
		Silurian		— 438
		Ordovician		— 505
		Cambrian		— 570
Proterozoic		Precambrian		— 2500
Archean				— 4600

Millions of Years Ago

Figure 11-1. Geologic time scale. Subdivisions of the Cenozoic and Precambrian are not drawn to scale. (Adapted from Allison R. Palmer, compiler, "The Decade of North American Geology Time Scale," *Geology* 11 (1983): 504.)

TABLE 11-1. Selected Biological Events During the Mesozoic and Cenozoic Eras

Period	Epoch	Selected Biological Events
Quaternary	Holocene	
	Pleistocene	First Modern Man
Tertiary	Pliocene	First Man
	Miocene	First Abundant Grasses
	Oligocene	First Monkeys, Largest Land Mammals
	Eocene	First Rhinoceroses and Mammoths
	Paleocene	First Horses
Cretaceous		Last Dinosaurs
Jurassic		First Birds
Triassic		First Dinosaurs and Mammals
Permian		Extinction of Trilobites
Pennsylvanian		First Coniferous Plants
Mississippian		First Reptiles
Devonian		First Amphibians
Silurian		First Confirmed Land Plants
Ordovician		First Land Animals (Millipedes?)
Cambrian		First Fishes

subdivisions were derived after places, a mountain range, ancient tribes, or rocks. At the outset, vertical sequences of sedimentary strata revealed their relative age by the **principle of superposition**: In an undisturbed sequence of strata, the oldest rocks are at the bottom and the youngest are at the top. But how to piece together many rock sequences to arrive at a relatively complete, unified whole?

Before we go further, realize that although rock sequences record time, they don't preserve a complete record of time. Although time is continuous, the rock record has not been; gaps or discontinuities in the rock record—**unconformities** (uhn-kuhn-FOUR-muh-teez)—are, in a practical sense, buried surfaces of erosion or no deposition. The type of unconformity easiest to visu-

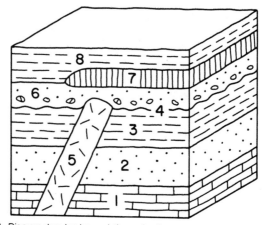

FIGURE 11-2. Diagram showing how relative and radiometric dating of rocks and events are used to formulate a time scale. Numbers indicate the correct order of events. The dike (5) (see chapter 15) is dated at 120 ± 5 million years, the lava flow (7) at 15 ± 1 million years. Layers 1 to 3 were laid down and intruded by the dike. Erosion, indicated by the wavy, erosional surface or unconformity (4), occurred after 120 million years after which layer 6 was deposited, followed by emplacement of the lava flow. Layer 6 is older than 15 million years and layer 8, deposited after the lava flow, is younger.

alize is the **angular unconformity** (see the photograph that introduces Part II); in this type, the rocks beneath the unconformity are tilted at an angle. In a **nonconformity**, eroded igneous or metamorphic rocks are buried by sedimentary rocks. The most difficult type to recognize is the **disconformity** (Figure 11-2, item 4), which separates parallel strata; this type is often identified by differences in fossils in the layers above and below the unconformity.

Even if unconformities did not exist, piecing together of rock sequences would have been necessary to construct some semblance of a whole rock record. This is so because any place on Earth preserves only the vestige of a complete rock record of geologic time. The basis for the process of piecing together is the **principle of faunal succession**, which says that fossil assemblages occur in a definite order or succession in a vertical sequence of rocks. Use of the principle allowed the matching up or demonstration of equivalence, **correlation**, of rock layers in widely separated places.

Realize, at this point, that after stacked rock layers were correlated from place to place, subdivisions of the rock record became subdivisions of the time record. After most of the relative time scale was formulated in Europe, it was extrapolated to other parts of the world by the similarity of fossils, because given rock layers tend to change age from place to place. Fossils can be considered organic or paleontological clocks.

Although usable, the geologic time scale needed calibration. This was accomplished by the radiometric dating of primarily igneous intrusive and volcanic rocks interlayered with sedimentary rocks. From the **principle of crosscutting relationships**—a rock or fault is younger than the rock it cuts across—we can see in Figure 11-2 that the dike (5) is younger than layers 1, 2, and 3. If the age of the dike rock is 120 million years ±5 million years, layers 1, 2, and 3 are older than this value. The wavy line (4) represents a disconformity. Upon erosion, boulders of resistant dike rock incorporated within layer 6 demonstrates the **principle of inclusion**: Fragments of older rocks are enclosed within younger rocks (see also Figure 15-14). A lava flow (7) encroached upon the region, later to be buried by layer 8. If the lava flow rock is dated at 15 million years ±1 million years, layer 6 has an age somewhere between 120 and 15 million years. By a combination of relative dating principles and numerous radiometric dates, ages within the rock record are continually scrutinized and the time scale becomes calibrated in more detail. The process continues.

Now, let's take a close look at the time scale. All of geologic time is first subdivided into three **eons**, the Archean (are-KEE-uhn) and Proterozoic (prohte-uh-ruh-ZOE-ick)—together called the Precambrian (pree-CAM-bree-uhn) or sometimes the Cryptozoic (krihp-tuh-ZOE-ick)—and the Phanerozoic (fan-uh-ruh-ZOE-ick). A most lopsided split, to be sure, for the Precambrian constitutes more than 85 percent of geologic time. Eons are subdivided into **eras**—Paleozoic (pay-lee-uh-ZOE-ick), Mesozoic (mehz-uh-ZOE-ick), and Cenozoic (sehn-uh-ZOE-ick); eras into **periods** (such as Cambrian); and periods into **epochs** (such as Paleocene). Only epochs for the Cenozoic are given here because of disagreement over many of the others. Some disagreement also exists over the location of the boundaries of the subdivisions. Boundaries are tied to appearances or extinctions of organisms and such physical events as mountain building. Don't expect the numbers you see here to necessarily agree with the values you might find in other publications. But the disagreements involve only a few million years, which is no big discrepancy when dealing with many millions or billions of years. Disagreements point out that geology is a healthy, growing, steadily improving science.

Should you wish to learn the time scale, I might suggest an aid to remember the periods of the Paleozoic: *Come Over Some-Day Maybe Play Poker.* Each italicized letter represents the name of a period. (I learned this from my first geology professor.) If this mnemonic seems useful, create others of your own for the rest of the time scale.

You might wonder why the time scale begins 4.6 billion years ago, the approximate age of Earth. The oldest known rocks on Earth, those from the Northwest Territories and perhaps some from western Australia, are about four billion years old. The oldest moon rocks, however, have been dated at about 4.6 billion years, as well as meteorites, believed by many to be remnants of a disrupted planet or fragments that never coalesced to form one. Since the moon and meteorites are part of the same solar system as Earth, their unity implies a common origin in process and presumably in time. So, the age of the moon and meteorites is the same as the age of Earth.

Comprehending Geologic Time

To comprehend the magnitude of geologic time is, without question, difficult. We simply lack a suitable frame of reference with which to relate. Although the perception of time on Earth is perplexing, we might try. After all, it's been said that the concept of the immensity of geologic time has been geology's greatest contribution to general thought.

Many persons reach an age of 100, so let's consider that a convenient even number with which to compare. If you were to live ten times as long, you would be 1,000 years old. And, if ten times more, to a ripe old age of 10,000. Now, that's *really* old. But if you increased your imaginary age by increments of ten times *two or five more* times, your age would be one million or one billion years. Even at one billion, Earth is still four and one-half times older.

Another way to comprehend time is to equate the age of Earth to one calendar year and consider when certain biological events (see Table 11-1) occurred as the clock ticks away. The oldest fossils are known from a time, about 3.5 billion years ago, that corresponds to more than nine months ago, and life most likely originated before then. But abundant life, or life capable of leaving a good fossil record, didn't exist until 45 days ago (beginning of the

Cambrian) in our imaginary calendar year. The first fish (Cambrian), amphibians (Devonian), reptiles (Mississippian), mammals (Triassic), and birds (Jurassic) appeared between 41 and 9 days ago. Dinosaurs lived and died out completely about 17 to 5 days ago, and recognizable humans appeared on Earth only within the last eight hours. Columbus barely discovered America (if he indeed did!) during this fictitious year about three seconds ago.

Suggested Reading

Albritton, C. C., Jr. *The Abyss of Time: Changing Conceptions of the Earth's Antiquity After the Sixteenth Century*. San Francisco: Freeman, 1980.

Berry, W. B. N. *Growth of a Prehistoric Time Scale*. San Francisco: Freeman, 1987.

Dalrymple, G. B. *The Age of the Earth*. Stanford, CA: Stanford University Press, 1991.

Eicher, D. L. *Geologic Time*. Englewood Cliffs, NJ: Prentice-Hall, 1976.

12

Reconstructing Past Events

All rocks reveal stories, but the readers must be alert and attentive in their attempt to decipher them. Geologists spend much time unraveling Earth's history from the stories they read, or believe they have read, in rocks. Read incorrectly, a story may be largely fictitious, like a tested theory proven false. In time, though, a story's veracity and completeness may be confirmed by several readers, each of whom accepts the same tale and, perhaps, assimilates more details than another reader.

Most geologists, in order to reconstruct past events, accept the premise of uniformitarianism (see chapters 11 and 19). Guided by this premise, geologists assume that events which occur today must have occurred in the past. To perceive the formation of a coral-bearing limestone now high in the Rockies, for example, geologists would first envision the precipitation of limy mud in a shallow tropical sea. But certain events of the past do not take place in the present. The approach is useful and necessary, but must be applied with some care.

This chapter demonstrates the way geologists decipher events from Earth's varied history and provides raw material for your own contemplation of the past. Approaches to decode mountain building, former continental seas, and past climates from the rocks are illustrated.

Mountain Building

Major mountains today form linear belts and are made up in large part of folded and thrust-faulted sedimentary rocks deformed by side-to-side squeezing. Such mountain belts do not distribute in haphazard fashion but occur most often at or near the margins of continents (Figure 12-1). The Rockies and other mountain belts in western North America and the Andes in western South America are examples. A few, such as the Urals of Russia and the Himalayas of southern Asia, are found toward continental interiors.

Mountain belts are not all of the same age; the mountains of the western Americas and the Himalayas formed during the Mes-

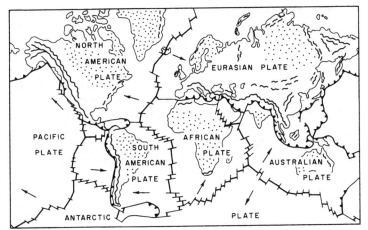

FIGURE 12-1. Tectonic map of the world showing lithospheric plates (seven major ones are named), shields (stippled), mountain belts (heavy, wiggly lines on continents: short lines indicate Paleozoic belts, longer lines indicate younger belts), and stable platforms (blank areas on continents). The plates are bounded by the midoceanic ridge (straight, heavy line offset along fine lines that depict transform faults) and oceanic trenches or earlier subduction zones (heavy barbed lines). Arrows point in the direction of plate movement.

ozoic and Cenozoic Eras, but the Appalachians and Urals are late Paleozoic mountains. Parts of the Rockies and the Himalayas still grow today. Mountain building, therefore, is a recurring event.

Let's now look at the places where other large-scale, deformational—or **tectonic**—features occur, and take note of their relationship to mountain belts. The central parts of continents consist of **shields**, low-lying, low-relief regions of mostly Precambrian metamorphic and granitic (granitelike) rocks, jointed and faulted. In North America, the Canadian Shield is exposed over most of eastern Canada. Where not exposed, shields are covered by thin sequences of sedimentary rocks and are called **stable platforms**. Within the platforms, rocks are flat-lying or warped into broad basins and domes on a regional scale.

If you could visualize the ocean basins drained, the feature that might first catch your eye is the so-called oceanic ridge, the longest mountain range on Earth: 40,000 miles (64,000 km) long and up to 9,800 feet (3,000 m) high. Unlike the makeup of continental mountain belts, the ridge consists of basalt. A prominent rift valley occupies the crest of the ridge along most of its length. The ridge is cut by numerous **transform faults** that resemble large-scale strike-slip faults. Drained ocean basins, near their margins in places, would reveal trenches that reach depths of nearly 7 miles (11 km). The most conspicuous trenches are those in the western Pacific from New Zealand to north of Japan.

Besides major features on the ocean floor, we must also glimpse Earth's interior to better understand mountain building. We cannot gain this glimpse directly, of course, in spite of Jules Verne's *Journey to the Center of the Earth*! Our knowledge of Earth's interior derives from observations of the speed and behavior of **seismic waves**, vibrations within Earth induced by earthquakes or human-made explosions. The gist of the approach is this: Seismic waves move faster through denser materials, and certain seismic waves do not pass through liquids.

From seismic waves, we know Earth is layered internally. I like the analogy of the hard-boiled egg to represent Earth. Whack the egg open for a look inside. The eggshell corresponds to Earth's thin **crust**: 3 miles to 44 miles (5 km to 70 km) thick, and thicker under continents than under ocean basins; the crust is also thicker under mountain ranges than under lowlands. Continental crust is less dense and conceived of as mostly granitic whereas the denser oceanic crust is mostly basaltic. Beneath the crust, down to a depth of 1,800 miles (2,900 km), is the generally denser **mantle**, which corresponds to the egg white; the mantle may be richer in iron and magnesium minerals than the crust, perhaps similar to the rock peridotite (see chapter 15). Below the mantle is the spherical, yolklike **core**, with a diameter of about 4,300 miles (7,000 km); its high density suggests a composition of iron with perhaps some nickel. The outer six-tenths of the core is considered to be liquid because certain seismic waves don't pass through; the inner core seems to be solid.

After reliable maps appeared, scientists noticed that certain continents would fit together jigsaw-puzzlelike, if they could be moved; in particular, South America's eastern bulge could conform to the reentrant in western Africa. This fit of now-separated continents and their shared geologic evidence, such as similar fossils, gave birth in the early 1900s to the theory of **continental drift**: Lighter continents drifted through heavier (denser) ocean basin rock, possibly driven by forces that result from Earth's rotation.

In the 1960s, after the topography of the seafloor became known, continental drift was replaced by the theory of **plate tectonics**. This theory posits that Earth's outer rind is divided into seven major, and many smaller, rigid plates (Figure 12-1). As the plates jostle about, different parts of the plates move at different speeds. Each plate might, at first, be thought of as a fragment of an eggshell as it slips on a hardened egg white sphere. But plates, about 60 miles (100 km) thick, are made up of the crust *and* uppermost mantle, or the **lithosphere** (Figure 12-2). Lithospheric plates usually include both continental and oceanic crust, such as for the North American plate, but may consist only of oceanic crust (for example, the Pacific plate). They slide along on a weaker,

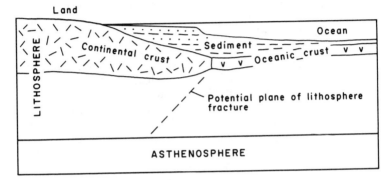

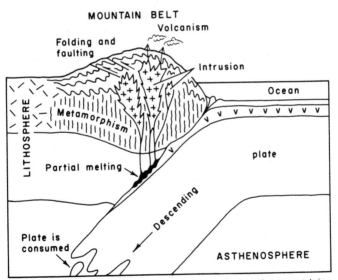

Figure 12-2. Mountain building by collision of lithospheric plates that separately include continental and oceanic crust. As the heavier oceanic plate descends, sediment (upper diagram) and crustal rocks are squeezed into an elevated mountain belt that is folded and faulted, metamorphosed, intruded, and often subjected to volcanism.

mobile, perhaps partly molten **asthenosphere** (ass-THEHN-uh-sfear) (Greek *astheneia*, "weakness") within the upper mantle that extends to a depth of 125 miles (200 km), again as based upon evidence from seismic waves. You can compare these plates to ice slabs that slide, crunch, slam, and slip under other slabs during ice breakup on a stream in spring. The stream corresponds to a mushy asthenosphere.

How does plate tectonics differ from continental drift? In plate tectonics, continents do not plow through ocean basins but thicker, rigid, lithospheric plates move over a soft asthenosphere.

What drives lithospheric plates? Most geologists seem to favor drag of the plates by convection currents brought about by heating within the asthenosphere or the entire mantle, a matter of small convection cells or large ones. Heat for entire-mantle convection would radiate from the hot, outer, liquid core. Convection currents are believed to rise in the vicinity of the oceanic ridge, drag the plates as they course laterally, and descend in the vicinity of oceanic trenches. Visualize convection currents as those cells that circulate vertically in a pot of simmering soup or in cumulus clouds as the sun's rays heat a land surface.

Considerable evidence shores up the plate tectonics theory, but we can only examine a bit here. One line of reasoning involves seafloor spreading. Along the oceanic ridge, the linear region of basalt effusion with a crested rift valley, the seafloor is known to spread to either side. Deep-sea drilling and seismic exploration show sediments are thicker along the ridge's flanks and thinner toward the crest. In addition, sediments that directly overlie the basalt become older away from the ridge on either side. Both thickness and age trends support spreading of the seafloor away from the ridge. Iceland straddles the ridge, and the rate of spreading there is measured directly across the exposed rift valley. Measurements in Iceland and indirect measurements elsewhere show seafloor spreading or plate movement as less than an inch to several inches per year.

Another line of evidence for plate tectonics comes from earthquake distribution. Most earthquakes occur in narrow zones along the oceanic ridge, oceanic trenches, and young mountain belts. Temblors along the oceanic ridge and associated transform faults have shallow origins, less than about 44 miles (70 km) below Earth's surface; those along trenches and mountain belts extend much deeper and follow a zone inclined toward a continent or an arc of volcanic islands. Earthquake zones are assumed to delineate plate boundaries that also correspond to belts of major volcanism.

You might expect all this activity where plates continually bump into or grind past one another.

New oceanic lithosphere is created at the oceanic ridge where plates separate and spread apart; basaltic magma spills out from the rift. Plates spread parallel to the transform faults that offset the ridge in many places, and, therefore, these faults indicate the direction of plate movement. At trenches and other places where plates converge, oceanic plates may descend into the mantle; in these **subduction zones**, oceanic lithosphere—at depth—is melted or assimilated, and destroyed. Some believe subduction occurs because of the weight of the sinking plate, not because the plate is dragged down by the descending part of a convection cell. Along transform faults where plates shift past one another, lithosphere is neither created nor destroyed.

You may be wondering: When are we going to get on with mountain building? The time is now. But you may have caught a hint or two about the mountain building process before this point.

Remember that squeezed mountain belts, especially the younger ones, concentrate at or near the margins of continents; and earthquakes, especially those with deep origins, tend to concentrate along young mountain belts with volcanism. From these associations you might expect plate tectonics theory postulates that mountain building occurs where converging plates slam into one another. Let's examine a case where one plate with continental crust and another with oceanic crust converge (Figure 12-2).

A thick sequence, thousands of feet, of sediments accumulates along the seaward margin of the continental plate: shallow-water sediments on the continental shelf and slope and deep-water sediments on the continental rise, as well as thinner sediments on the deep ocean floor. As the two plates come together, the heavier oceanic plate descends or subducts. The sedimentary layers of both plates are squeezed—the crust is shortened—and raised into a huge linear welt, thrust faulted at or near the surface where rocks are brittle, folded at depth under conditions of high temperature and pressure. Part of the oceanic crust, made up of deep-sea sediment, basalt, gabbro (see chapter 15), and peridotite, is scraped off the descending plate and plastered against the compressed welt. This slice of oceanic crust is the rock record of a subduction zone. Beneath the folded rocks of the welt, where pressure and temperature are high, rocks are metamorphosed; pressure-induced secondary layering of these rocks is largely vertical or nearly so, mostly at right angles to the horizontal squeezing. As the descending plate reaches depths of very high temperatures, part of it melts to generate a silica-rich magma that rises because of its natural buoyancy—it is lighter than the surrounding rock. The magma intrudes the metamorphic gneisses and schists (see chapter 17) and deformed sedimentary rocks to form granitic batholiths (see chapter 15) or extrudes at the surface to create andesitic volcanoes.

From this portrayal, we see mountain building is responsible for the emplacement of batholiths, andesitic volcanism, large-scale metamorphism, folding, and thrust faulting. Examples of continental-oceanic plate mountain belts are the late Mesozoic and early Cenozoic Rockies, the Cenozoic Andes, and the late Paleozoic Appalachians.

Mountains may also form from the convergence of two continental or two oceanic plates. When two continental plates converge, little or no subduction occurs because of the buoyancy of lower-density continental lithosphere. The late Paleozoic Ural Mountains and the Mesozoic and Cenozoic Himalayas and Alps exemplify continental plate collision. Convergence of two oceanic plates creates a well-developed subduction zone with or without metamorphism and granitic intrusion. This condition is prevalent in the western Pacific with its island arcs. The Tonga Islands (without large-scale metamorphism or granitic intrusion) and Japanese Islands (with large-scale metamorphism and granitic intrusion) are notable examples.

When convergence of the plates ceases, the mountain belt is temporarily in **isostatic** or flotational **balance**, or is in equilibrium: It floats on denser materials of the lithosphere, and downward depression and thickening of the lower root zone supports the weight of the uplifted mountain range. But uplift of the mountain range causes its immediate erosion, with sediments shed both landward and seaward. And with erosion, the isostatic balance is upset. The root zone rebounds or rises to maintain a balance as unloading by erosion occurs at the top of the mountain range. As erosion and isostatic adjustment proceed, the mountain belt becomes thinner, and its upper surface gradually approaches sea level. In time, erosion removes the thrust-faulted and folded sedimentary strata, and only metamorphic and granitic rocks are visible. These rocks that remain are the roots of a once majestic mountain range.

Remember the shields on all continents, central masses of mostly metamorphic and granitic rocks? Shields, then, represent roots of former mountain ranges. Shield rocks tend to occur in differently trending structural belts, with the older rocks toward the centers of shields. These observations lead to a far-reaching conclusion: Continents "grow" by the plastering on of successive mountain belts by plate collision.

Former Continental Seas

Today, a time of high-standing continents, it is difficult to comprehend that seas could cover the continents. But they did, many times. Present-day, restricted examples of inland seas are Hudson Bay in North America and the Black and Caspian Seas in southern Europe, all unlike the extensive continental seas of the past. From sedimentary rocks and fossils that reflect the physical, chemical, and biological environments of former sea bottoms, geologists interpret seas of the past. Let's use the Late Cambrian rock and fossil record in North America for a glimpse at how the process works.

A sedimentary facies map (Figure 12-3) shows the distribution of major rock masses. Each **facies** (FAY-sheez), a distinctive body of rock and associated fossils that reflects a particular sedimentary environment, grades laterally and vertically into another facies. The map represents a painstaking compilation of vertical rock sequences from exposures and boreholes made by many geologists over many years, and the correlation of these compilations to produce a unified portrayal. Keep in mind that any spot on the map signifies the predominance of a particular facies, not that exclusive facies.

The sandstone facies, with siltstone, contains common trilobites and brachiopods (see chapter 18) that attest to a marine origin. Well-sorted and well-rounded sand grains, together with ripple marks and cross-bedding (see chapter 16), indicate deposition of the sandstone in shallow water and the continual reworking of sand by waves and currents.

In eastern North America, the sandstone passes directly into a carbonate rock facies that contains trilobites, brachiopods, and the algae-related stromatolites (see chapter 18). Common clastic carbonates with oolites (see chapter 16), ripple marks, cross-bedding, and carbonate conglomerate signify considerable shallow-water agitation of limy sediment by waves, currents, and storms. In the west, a shallow-water marine shale intervenes between the sandstone and carbonate rock facies, and implies considerable deposition of mud.

Along the margins of the continent, rock sequences thicken (Figure 12-4) because of more downsinking or subsidence in those

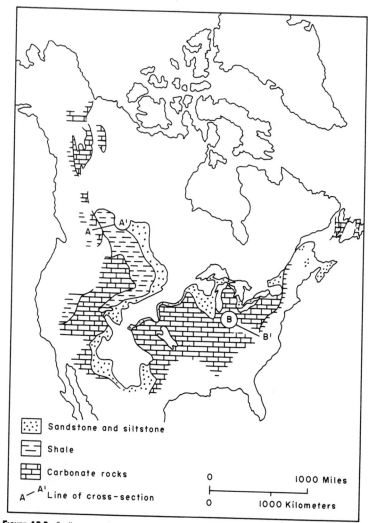

Figure 12-3. Sedimentary facies map of Late Cambrian rocks in North America. (Modified considerably from T. D. Cook and A. W. Bally, editors, *Stratigraphic Atlas of North and Central America*, Princeton University Press, 1975, p. 15.) Cross sections that relate to this map are shown in Figure 12-4.

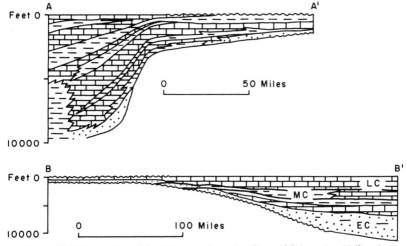

FIGURE 12-4. Cross sections of Cambrian strata (located on Figure 12-3) in western (A-A') and eastern (B-B') North America. Source of the cross sections and rock symbols are the same as for Figure 12-3. EC = Early Cambrian, MC = Middle Cambrian, LC = Late Cambrian.

places as the sediments were deposited. The carbonate rock facies gives way outward to a largely deep-water facies, which also contains rock fragment sandstone and volcanic rocks besides shale, with few marine fossils. This facies is poorly known because of later metamorphism and intrusion associated with mountain building.

Cross section B-B' (Figure 12-4) shows that Middle Cambrian rocks extend farther toward the center of the continent than do Early Cambrian rocks, and Late Cambrian rocks extend even farther. This establishes a major marine **transgression**, expansion of the sea that results in submergence of the land, during the Cambrian. Transgression is further reflected in the cross section by offshore rocks, carbonates, overlying nearshore ones, sandstone. The causes of a transgression or **regression**, contraction of the sea that results in emergence of the land, are unclear. Plate tectonics theory suggests that the arching of the oceanic ridge by strong convection could displace seawater from ocean basins onto continents. Diminishing convection could allow the oceanic ridge to subside, causing regression. Of course, sea level can rise or fall during the melting or formation of glacial ice. But glacial deposits of the appropriate age must corroborate this idea.

From the facies map we can reconstruct the **paleogeography**, ancient geography, during the Late Cambrian (Figure 12-5) in North America. Since much of the northeastern part of the continent lacks a Cambrian record—where much of the Canadian Shield is now exposed—this region is interpreted as having been a low-lying landmass. Alternative interpretations are that islands may have existed here, or the entire continent may have been inundated, but the record in the northeast was stripped away by erosion. In any case, the occurrence of the sandstone facies implies shield rocks as its source and the emergence of those rocks above sea level at least part of the time.

Past Climates

What can we say about the climate (Figure 12-5) during the Late Cambrian in North America? Extensive limestone forms today in low latitudes where warmer temperatures result in the extensive release of carbon dioxide and the prolific precipitation of calcium carbonate, as in the Bahamas or the Persian Gulf. Reef-building stromatolites during the Late Cambrian may have had similar requirements as for reef building corals, which today occur mostly within 30° of the equator. Our reasoning so far suggests a tropical or subtropical climate during the Late Cambrian in North America.

Now, let's take a different tack. When lava congeals or sediments are deposited, certain iron minerals in the form of crystals or particles—in particular, the mineral magnetite—align themselves parallel to Earth's magnetic field. This happened in the past, and mineral crystals or particles have acted as tiny, locked-in compass needles to record past pole positions; their magnetism, of course, must be be measured and interpreted correctly. Inference of pole position by this approach is approximate and is always checked against climatically sensitive rocks. Such paleomagnetic evidence passes the Cambrian paleoequator lengthwise through North America. (Consider that the equator's position has remained fixed through time, and continents, within moving plates, have shifted to give the impression of a changing equator.) When latitudes 30° north and south of the paleoequator are drawn, all of the continent is within a tropical or subtropical climate, in agreement with reasoning from extensive carbonate rocks and stromatolites.

Applying wind patterns of present-day climates places the Cambrian continent within the easterly trade wind belt, with winds

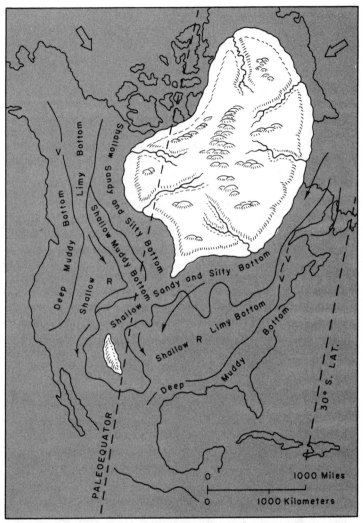

FIGURE 12-5. Reconstruction of the geography and climate during the Late Cambrian. Areas of sea-bottom sediment were derived largely from Figure 12-3. Most of the continent is inferred to have been covered by the sea except, perhaps, the northeastern part. R = stromatolite reefs, V = volcanic rocks, narrow arrows = surface oceanic currents, and broad arrows = inferred prevailing winds.

blowing obliquely toward the paleoequator. Such winds would drive the main continental sea currents, which would probably parallel sea bottom contours and be deflected in places by the irregular shoreline. A generally southerly or southwesterly flow of currents is supported by the orientations of cross-beds (see chapter 16) in the sandstones.

Although not applicable to our Late Cambrian example, other rock types are useful to infer past climates. Thick, extensive evaporites (see chapter 16), such as rock gypsum, rock anhydrite, and rock salt, indicate arid climates that cause the high evaporation necessary to allow the salts to precipitate from brines. Extensive dune sandstone, recognized by thick, wedge-shaped intervals of cross-beds (see the photograph that introduces Part IV), also requires an arid climate for its formation, and the direction of inclined cross-beds gives the prevailing wind direction. Thick, extensive coal deposits reflect moist conditions—where rainfall exceeds evaporation—but temperatures may be cool to tropical. Growth rings in petrified wood suggest a temperate climate with seasonal changes; they are absent if trees grew within a tropical climate. And, finally, **tillite**, lithified till, is a good indicator of a cool, moist climate compatible with the formation of glaciers. But other poorly sorted rocks may be confused with tillite. Questionable tillites are best verified if they rest on grooved rock surfaces.

Suggested Reading

Bally, A. W., and A. R. Palmer, eds. *The Geology of North America; An Overview, Volume A.* Boulder, CO: Geological Society of America, 1989.

Bambach, R. K., C. R. Scotese, and A. M. Ziegler. "Before Pangea: The Geographies of the Paleozoic World," *American Scientist,* 68 (1980): 26–38.

Condie, K. C. *Plate Tectonics and Crustal Evolution.* New York: Pergamon Press, 1982.

Cox, Allan, and R. B. Hart. *Plate Tectonics: How It Works.* Cambridge, MA: Blackwell Scientific Publications, 1986.

Frakes, L. A. *Climates Throughout Geologic Time.* New York: Elsevier Scientific, 1979.

Laporte, L. F. *Ancient Environments.* Englewood Cliffs, NJ: Prentice-Hall, 1979.

Stanley, S. M. *Earth and Life Through Time.* New York: Freeman, 1989.

Wright, J. B. *Outcrop Quiz.* New York: Routledge, Chapman & Hall, 1986.

Parks for Geologic Observation and Contemplation

Why do people visit parks? They come to swim, fish, boat, picnic, camp, and just plain relax. But this answer may be too simplistic. To flee their everyday routine and satisfy a need for mental re-creation compel many. Others just want to tell their friends that they have been somewhere other than their too-familiar homes. Athletic individuals see parks as places to hike, backpack, or climb. Others arrive to pursue less physically strenuous hobbies such as photography or bird-watching. Scientists use parks at times to research geologic features or organisms. A rare visitor might drop in by accident, perhaps disoriented or tugged by a gentle inquisitive urge. And other visitors, possibly only a small percentage, come to learn about nature, followed by a smaller number still who search for a natural world, intangible experience, or feeling. I may have left out someone. But these are the most obvious visitors and motives.

One definition of a park is "an area of land, usually in a natural state, for the enjoyment of the public." In this broad sense, a list of public areas at the national, state, or lesser levels is long and varied. National designated areas include parks, monuments, forests, grasslands, recreation areas, wilderness areas, seashores, lakeshores, rivers, wild and scenic rivers, refuges, preserves, scenic trails, and others. State areas encompass parks, monuments, forests, preserves, natural areas, and others. Many state features or areas derive further sanction as national Registered Natural Landmarks. One compilation of numerous natural regions, some privately owned but open to the public, is Hilowitz and Green's *Natural Wonders of America*. County and city parks expand our list even further. Implied so far are natural regions, but many parks are human creations or have been set aside for their historical significance.

What about cemeteries—are they parks? They're usually open to the public. Although preserves for the dead, cemeteries can be sources of enjoyment for the living. Cemeteries are often quiet places to pursue relaxation or contemplation. Wooded cemeteries provide habitat for many birds, and some people like to bird-watch in these quiet surroundings. Others may even observe and investigate the effects of rock weathering (see chapter 23). History buffs re-create past events from clues etched in the tombstones.

Although parks of all sizes and types exist at any level, the national parks, in particular, tend to snatch our attention because of their large size and variety. They are also treasures of our national heritage. How did the national park system come about?

On a cool, starry night in mid-September 1870, four men relaxed before a flickering campfire along the Firehole River in what is now northwestern Wyoming. The campers included a surveyor-general for Montana Territory, a second lieutenant in the United States Army, a vigilante law enforcement officer, and a judge for Montana Territory. All were part of a 15-member exploring party that had spent almost five awesome weeks in witness of such marvels as hot springs, geysers, and glass cliffs.

What should be done with such a marvelous place? they wondered out loud. Maybe each should stake his claim to the wonders before word got out. But the judge countered this idea. This area, with its unique beauty and fascinating natural features, must not be fragmented for personal gain. The region must be preserved intact for all people of the nation to enjoy—as a national park. They all agreed and vowed to promote the idea at the completion of the expedition.

Diligent promotional work paid off. Two years later, 18 years before Wyoming become a state, Yellowstone became the first national park in the United States—and the world. (Yellowstone's first park superintendent was the vigilante law enforcement officer of the 1870 expedition.) Yellowstone was the largest United States national park—2.2 million acres (0.9 million hectares)—until Wrangell-St. Elias in southern Alaska, which first became a national monument in 1978, took the honors as a national park in 1980 with 12.3 million acres (5 million hectares).

How do parks and monuments, the most common federal parks, differ? In a nutshell, parks can be established only by an act of Congress, but monuments need merely a presidential proclamation. And this may be a comforting thought: A park or monument can be abolished only by an act of Congress. A region may be protected sooner if first designated as a monument, and later elevated to a park, as was the case for Wrangell-St. Elias. Parks are usually larger than monuments and encompass a wider array of natural features. Monuments concentrate on specific natural features or preserve archaeological or historic sites. Mesa Verde, in southwestern Colorado, stands out as an exception: It is a national park established for an archaeological site.

Parks as Geologic Refuges

Most national parks, and many other national areas as well, have been established for their outstanding geologic features: Alaska's Wrangell-St. Elias for glaciers; Kentucky's Mammoth Cave for an extensive solution cave system; Wyoming's Yellowstone for unique, hydrothermal features; Utah's Arches for exquisitely sculptured natural arches (Figure 13-1); and Arizona's Petrified Forest National Park for petrified logs (Figure 13-2), to name a few. At the state level, the same is true. A sampling of state parks that exist primarily for their geological features includes: Connecticut's Dinosaur (dinosaur tracks), Hawaii's Waimea Canyon ("Grand Canyon of the Pacific"), Montana's Lewis and Clark Caverns, South Dakota's Bear Butte (laccolith), and Washington's Ginkgo Petrified Forest. Many other types of natural areas at the state and lower levels also preserve geological features.

Many parks, therefore, can be labeled geologic refuges; they maintain geological features intact, but, of course, they offer no protection from the destructive effects of natural erosion. Parks are places where interested persons can observe natural beauty created or enhanced by the geology, unadulterated by humans. Visitors can also come to learn geology if that is their desire.

Geologists like to study and research geological phenomena in parks, unhampered by the possibility of refused access and altered landscape elsewhere. More geologists and other scientists conduct their research in national parks today because these places are havens from human alteration. Parks as geologic refuges increase in aesthetic and scientific value as developers, extractors of mineral wealth, and others strive to meet the demands of a progressive, competitive society.

Geological refuges, of course, are biological and archaeological refuges as well, because geology, biology, and archaeology are often complexly intertwined. We must not attempt to fragment the natural world even though, at times, a specific emphasis is convenient or desirable.

The integrity of a park as a geologic refuge is maintained by

FIGURE 13-1. Delicate Arch of Jurassic sandstone, Arches National Park, southeastern Utah. Height of the person is 5.5 feet (1.7 m).

FIGURE 13-2. Triassic petrified (silicified) log in badlands terrain, Petrified Forest National Park near Holbrook, northeastern Arizona. Most of the logs in the park are of conifer trees.

the rules that prohibit collecting or defacing. Scientists may be allowed to collect mineral, rock, or fossil samples. But this is done only on a restricted basis, avoided when possible in highly frequented areas, and must be justified by an obvious increase in scientific knowledge.

Using Your Parks Geologically

For those who crave knowledge of the natural world, parks are outdoor museums or, to scientists, outdoor laboratories. The national park system, including parks, monuments, seashores, and other refuges, can be likened further to a great university, with campuses scattered over the country. Parks and other natural areas can be grouped according to geologic processes, landforms, rock type, fossils, and geologic history. Imagine, if you will, that you visit a substantial number of parks for their varied geology (Table 13-1) and devote a reasonable amount of time to each. Over a period of a few to several years, you may have "earned" the near equivalent of a degree in geology. And you would have gained your knowledge informally, with little effort and hassle, out of the classroom. Granted, you might lack certain higher mathematics, chemistry, and physics requirements, and certain skills in the

TABLE 13-1. United States National Parks, National Monuments, and National Seashores and Lakeshores of Geological Interest

Park (P), Monument (M), Seashore (S), Lakeshore (L)	Conspicuous Landforms[1]	Of Special Interest
ALASKA		
Admiralty Island (M)	3a	Largest population of bald eagles in U.S.
Aniakchak (M)	8	Caldera 6 miles (9.6 km) wide
Cape Krusenstern (M)	4	114 beach ridges
Denali (P)	3a	Highest mountain—McKinley—in North America
Gates of the Arctic (P)	3a	Highest peak in Brooks Range
Glacier Bay (P)	3a	Fluctuating tidewater glaciers
Katmai (P)	8	Valley of Ten Thousand Smokes
Kenai Fjords (P)	3a	Earthquakes frequent
Kobuk Valley (P)	2,5	Dune fields within Arctic Circle
Lake Clark (P)	3a,8	North end of active volcanic Aleutian chain
Misty Fiords (M)	3a	Behm Canal leads into interior
Wrangell-St. Elias (P)	3a	Largest assemblage of glaciers in North America
AMERICAN SAMOA		
American Samoa (P)	4,8	Healthy coral reef
ARIZONA		
Canyon de Chelly (M)	2	1,000-foot (305-m) sandstone cliffs
Chiricahua (M)	2	Sculptured volcanic rocks
Grand Canyon (P)	2	Mile (1.6-km) deep canyon cut in past 9 million years
Petrified Forest (P)	2	Silica-filled logs erode from multicolored badlands
Sunset Crater (M)	8	Crater is cinder cone formed 900 years ago
ARKANSAS		
Hot Springs (P)	9	Most hot water about 4,400 years old

[1]Landform numbers are those of chapters as follows:

2 = stream-related	6 = groundwater-related
3a = valley glacier-related	7 = landslide-related
3b = continental glacier-related	8 = volcanic
4 = shoreline-related	9 = rock deformation-related
5 = wind-related	23 = weathering-related

(continued)

TABLE 13-1. Continued.

Park (P), Monument (M), Seashore (S), Lakeshore (L)	Conspicuous Landforms[1]	Of Special Interest
CALIFORNIA		
Channel Islands (P)	4,5	Natural oil and gas seeps; marine terraces
Death Valley (M)	2	Lowest elevation: − 282 feet (− 86 m)
Devils Postpile (M)	3a,8	60-foot (18-m) high columns from lava upon cooling
Kings Canyon (P)	3a	Exfoliation domes in granite
Lassen Volcanic (P)	8	Volcanism in early 1900s
Lava Beds (M)	8	Cinder cones and lava-tube caves
Pinnacles (M)	2	Sculptured volcanic rocks
Point Reyes (S)	4	San Andreas fault zone between Seashore and mainland
Redwood (P)	4,7	Tsunami damage at north end
Sequoia (P)	3a	Exfoliation domes in granite
Yosemite (P)	3a	Exfoliation domes in granitic rocks
COLORADO		
Black Canyon of the Gunnison (M)	2	2,000-foot (610-m) deep canyon cut in past 2 million years
Colorado (M)	2	Mesozoic rocks directly overlie Precambrian
Dinosaur (M)	2,9	Dinosaur quarry in Jurassic sandstone
Florissant Fossil Beds (M)	2	35-million-year-old insects, leaves, and tree stumps
Great Sand Dunes (M)	5	700-foot (213-m) high transverse and barchan dunes
Mesa Verde (P)	2	Mesa Verde is cuesta
Rocky Mountain (P)	3a	Longs Peak higher than 14,000 feet (4,267 m)
FLORIDA		
Biscayne (P)	4	Most northerly coral reefs in U.S.
Canaveral (S)	4,5	White sand beaches
Everglades (P)	2,4	Coastal swamps protect shorelines against hurricanes
Gulf Islands (S)	4,5	Barrier islands Florida to Mississippi
GEORGIA		
Cumberland Island (S)	4,5	Barrier island

(continued)

TABLE 13-1. Continued.

Park (P), Monument (M), Seashore (S), Lakeshore (L)	Conspicuous Landforms[1]	Of Special Interest
HAWAII		
Haleakala (P)	8	Latest eruption about 1790
Hawaii Volcanoes (P)	8	Mauna Loa volcano rises 6 miles (9.7 km) above sea floor
IDAHO		
Craters of the Moon (M)	8	Lava from 40-mile (64-km) long Great Rift
Hagerman Fossil Beds (M)	2	Many Pliocene horse fossils
INDIANA		
Indiana Dunes (L)	4,5	Dunes tower 100 feet (30 m) above Lake Michigan
KENTUCKY		
Mammoth Cave (P)	6	Longest cave system in world
MAINE		
Acadia (P)	3b,4	Only true fiord on U.S. Atlantic Coast
MARYLAND		
Assateague Island (S)	4,5	Assateague is barrier island
MICHIGAN		
Isle Royale (P)	3b,9	Topographic "grain" parallels length of island
Pictured Rocks (L)	4,5	Multicolored cliffs on Lake Superior
Sleeping Bear Dunes (L)	4,5	Includes two Manitou Islands in Lake Michigan
MINNESOTA		
Pipestone (M)	2	Indian ceremonial pipes from Precambrian shale
Voyageurs (P)	3b	Rocks are roots of Precambrian mountains
MISSISSIPPI		
Gulf Islands (see Florida)	—	—
MONTANA		
Glacier (P)	3a	Precambrian rocks thrust over Cretaceous
NEBRASKA		
Agate Fossil Beds (M)	2	Miocene mammals
NEVADA		
Great Basin (P)	3a,6	Rock glacier, ice glacier, Lehman Caves, and natural arch

(continued)

TABLE 13-1. Continued.

Park (P), Monument (M), Seashore (S), Lakeshore (L)	Conspicuous Landforms[1]	Of Special Interest
NEW MEXICO		
Capulin Volcano (M)	8	Capulin is cinder cone
Carlsbad Caverns (P)	6	Caverns mostly in limestone of Permian barrier reef
El Malpais (M)	8	Spatter cones, lava tubes, and ice caves
White Sands (M)	5	Dunes of gypsum to 50 feet (15 m) high
NEW YORK		
Fire Island (S)	4,5	Barrier island
NORTH CAROLINA		
Cape Hatteras (S)	4,5	Seashore is barrier island
Cape Lookout (S)	4,5	Three barrier islands
Great Smoky Mountains (P)	2	In highest part of eastern U.S.
NORTH DAKOTA		
Theodore Roosevelt (P)	2	Badlands cut into lignite-bearing Paleocene rocks
OREGON		
Crater Lake (P)	8	Deepest lake in U.S. occupies caldera
John Day Fossil Beds (M)	2	Cenozoic fossils
Oregon Caves (M)	6	Caves in marble
SOUTH DAKOTA		
Badlands (P)	2	Badlands cut into Oligocene and Miocene rocks
Jewel Cave (M)	6	Named after jewel-like calcite crystals
Wind Cave (P)	6	Air currents blow through cave
TENNESSEE		
Great Smoky Mountains (see North Carolina)		
TEXAS		
Big Bend (P)	2,9	South-bounded by Big Bend of Rio Grand River
Guadalupe Mountains (P)	2	Most of mountains capped by Permian barrier reef
Padre Island (S)	4,5	Barrier island backed by Laguna Madre

(continued)

TABLE 13-1. Continued.

Park (P), Monument (M), Seashore (S), Lakeshore (L)	Conspicuous Landforms[1]	Of Special Interest
UTAH		
Arches (P)	2,23	Most natural arches in U.S.; joint controlled
Bryce Canyon (P)	2,23	Joints control location of pillars and arches
Canyonlands (P)	2,23	Joints control location of fins, pillars, and arches
Capitol Reef (P)	2,23	"Capitol" for erosional domes, "Reef" for escarpment
Cedar Breaks (M)	2,23	"Cedar" for juniper, "Breaks" for cliffs
Dinosaur (see Colorado)	——	——
Natural Bridges (M)	2,23	Three natural bridges in marine sandstone
Rainbow Bridge (M)	2	World's largest natural bridge—290 feet (88 m) high
Timpanogos Cave (M)	6	Three caverns along fault zones
Zion (P)	2,23	1,500-foot (457-m) sandstone cliffs
VIRGINIA		
Assateague Island (see Maryland)		
Shenandoah (P)	2	In Blue Ridge Mountains
VIRGIN ISLANDS		
Virgin Islands (P)	2,4	Luxurious living coral reefs
Buck Island Reef (M)	4	Luxurious living coral reef
WASHINGTON		
Mount Ranier (P)	3a,8	Dormant composite volcano in Cascades
Mount St. Helens (M)	2,8	Volcano erupted in May, 1980
North Cascades (P)	3a	More than 300 active glaciers
Olympic (P)	3a,4	60 active glaciers; hot springs along faults
WISCONSIN		
Apostle Islands (L)	3b,4	21 forest-covered islands in Lake Superior
WYOMING		
Devils Tower (M)	2,8	865-foot (264-m) tower is igneous intrusive with columnar structure
Fossil Butte (M)	2	Eocene fishes
Grand Teton (P)	3a,9	Teton Range is upfaulted block
Yellowstone (P)	2,8	Numerous hydrothermal features

use of laboratory equipment. But you would have gained more than ample background in biology and perhaps adequate knowledge in the arts, social sciences, and humanities, especially if you included a few archaeological and historic parks along the way. (I assume you would have polished your communication skills on your own.) You would have grown tall in the appreciation of natural beauty, and would have achieved spiritual enrichment as you acquired a reverence for nature's creations.

To whatever extent you wish to learn geology through parks, be prepared to expend some time. You may be familiar with a conversation that goes something like this: "Have you visited Yellowstone?" "Yes, this morning." Everyone has a personal choice to visit a park as he or she wishes, but the longer the stay, the more fulfilling the experience. Visit park museums—many parks have them—and acquire some park literature. Attend interpretive programs. Ask questions of park naturalists. If able, hike some of the trails, at least the guided nature trails. How your knowledge and appreciation of a park grow as you leave the roads, even a mile or less! And, if at all possible, stay overnight in a park. So much more is gained as you assimilate the changes in light, sounds, smells, and more geology. At day's end, review what you've learned, preferably before a campfire (Figure 13-3) where you can discuss, project, question. And contemplate the past.

Figure 13-3. Discussing and contemplating geology at day's end by the campfire.

When should you use your parks geologically? Clearly, when you are so inclined, weather is favorable, and other commitments don't interfere. These days, though, parks are not a very well kept secret. Some say people are loving their parks to death. To learn geology while you rub elbows constantly with other visitors is tough. So take advantage of less crowded times if you can accommodate them. My preferences, for temperate latitudes, are mid-May through June, and September through October. These times tend to relate to ebbs in people—and obnoxious insects. Park elevation, however, also must be considered when you decide to make a visit because of possible inclement weather conditions.

Suggested Reading

Chronic, Halka. *Pages of Stone: Geology of Western National Parks and Monuments, v. 1, Rocky Mountains and Western Great Plains*. Seattle: The Mountaineers, 1984.

———. *Pages of Stone: Geology of Western National Parks and Monuments, v. 2, Sierra Nevada, Cascades, and Pacific Coast*. Seattle: The Mountaineers, 1986.

———. *Pages of Stone: Geology of Western National Parks and Monuments, v. 3, Desert Southwest*. Seattle: The Mountaineers, 1986.

———. *Pages of Stone: Geology of Western National Parks and Monuments, v. 4, Grand Canyon and the Plateau Country*. Seattle: The Mountaineers, 1988.

Harris, A. G., and Esther Tuttle. *Geology of National Parks*. Dubuque, IA: Kendall/Hunt Publishing, 1990.

Harris, D. V., and E. P. Kiver. *The Geologic Story of the National Parks and Monuments*. New York: Wiley, 1985.

Hilowitz, Beverly, and S. E. Green, eds. *Natural Wonders of America*. New York: American Publishing, 1980.

National Geographic Society. *National Geographic's Guide to the National Parks of the United States*. Washington, DC: National Geographic Society, 1989.

PART III

Minerals, Rocks, and Fossils: The Stuff of Geology

14

Minerals

Minerals, basic components of Earth's crust, are natural, inorganic solid substances with definite chemical compositions and characteristic internal structures and physical properties. The study of minerals is **mineralogy** (min-uh-RAHL-uh-gee). Our mineral definition is quite a mouthful. Let's dissect this definition to see what each part means.

Natural, of course, means that a substance is a product of nature, not human-made. Some minerals, however, such as ruby and quartz, have been synthesized in the laboratory; such substances may closely resemble their true mineral counterparts, but they are synthetic, not natural minerals.

Inorganic solid substance signifies one that lacks an organic makeup—is formed by inorganic processes—and occurs in the solid state. (Organic refers to living, or once-living things, made of mainly carbon, hydrogen, and oxygen.) A solid state is one other than liquid or gas.

Definite chemical composition implies a stricter condition than is commonly true. Minerals are, in fact, chemicals, either elements or compounds. **Elements** consist of a single type of **atom**, a minute particle that is the basic building block of all matter. **Compounds** are made up of more than one kind of atom; most minerals are compounds. The composition of a few minerals is somewhat "definite": Quartz, for example, consists of one atom of silicon (Si) and two of oxygen (O), expressed in chemical shorthand as SiO_2. But for most minerals, atom types other than the primary ones may be present, and one atom type may substitute for another. So the "definite" chemical composition usually varies, but within certain limits; and, generally, the simpler the composition, the less the variation.

Internal structure refers to the characteristic that the atoms which make up a mineral are arranged in a specific geometric pat-

---

OVERLEAF. Wave-sculptured pebbles and cobbles on a Lake Superior gravel beach, near Grand Marais, northeastern Minnesota.

152

tern. This internal crystalline structure is responsible for a mineral's physical properties.

Physical properties are those nonchemical traits, usable in the field, that typify all minerals. These traits can often be used to identify the most common minerals, and we will consider them below.

As you can see, geologists use the word *mineral* in a different, more specific sense than do most people. Some may consider all substances as either "animal, plant, or mineral," or say food is rich in "vitamins and minerals."

Minerals are usually grouped by their chemical composition (Table 14-1). Graphite, like gold, for example, occurs in the uncombined state and is considered a native element. Pyrite, on the other hand, a sulfide, consists of the metallic element iron combined with sulfur; and orthoclase, a silicate, consists of potassium and aluminum combined with silicon and oxygen.

More than 4,000 minerals are known, and more continue to be discovered. Of this number, however, only about 20 to 30 are common, and about 10 or so—all silicates—constitute more than 90 percent of Earth's crust.

Minerals are of major importance to humans, and have been since prehistoric time. Several contain valuable metals, such as copper, lead, and iron, and are classed as metallic minerals; common examples are chalcopyrite, galena, and hematite (Table 14-2). Others, nonmetallic minerals, are utilized in the raw state or processed, but a metal is not extracted from them. Examples of this group are fluorite, graphite, and talc.

We might ask: What is the relationship between minerals and rocks? Minerals make up rocks, or, **rocks** are aggregates of minerals. This definition, however, doesn't always hold true. In some cases, a rock may consist of only one mineral rather than several, such as calcite that makes up the rock limestone. Earlier, we defined minerals as inorganic substances, so the rocks of which they are composed should be inorganic as well. But coal consists largely of organic, decomposed plant matter, although inorganic minerals may be admixed. Coal, however, qualifies as a rock because it occurs in a natural state and often contains inorganic minerals.

While we're on the subject of exceptions, what about water (or ice) and oil? Water has a rather definite chemical composition—two parts hydrogen and one part oxygen—although impurities are frequent, and, therefore, can be considered a mineral.

TABLE 14-1. Common Mineral Groups with Mineral Examples from Those in Table 14-2

Mineral Group	General Composition	Mineral Examples
Native element	Single element	Graphite
Sulfides	Element (s) + sulfur	Chalcopyrite Galena Pyrite Sphalerite
Oxides	Element (s) + oxygen	Corundum Hematite Limonite Magnetite
Halides	Element (s) + chlorine or fluorine	Fluorite Halite
Carbonates	Element (s) + carbon and oxygen	Calcite Dolomite
Sulfates	Element (s) + sulfur and oxygen	Anhydrite Gypsum
Phosphates	Element (s) + phosphorus and oxygen	Apatite
Silicates	Element (s) + silicon and oxygen	Amphibole Biotite Chlorite Garnet Muscovite Olivine Orthoclase Plagioclase Pyroxene Quartz Serpentine Staurolite Talc

Purists, however, would say only a solid, such as water in the form of ice, can be a mineral. Oil, or petroleum, has the dual problem of having an organic composition, as does coal, and a liquid form. Its highly variable composition, however, might support the contention that this hydrocarbon is a rock. A way out of this dilemma is to term oil a mineral fuel.

TABLE 14-2. Composition and Selected Use of Common Minerals

Mineral	Composition	Selected Use(s)
Amphibole	Hydrous calcium, magnesium, iron, aluminum silicate	Rock former
Anhydrite	Calcium sulfate	Soil conditioner
Apatite	Calcium, fluorine phosphate	Source of fertilizer
Biotite	Potassium, magnesium, iron, aluminum silicate	Rock former
Calcite	Calcium carbonate	Making of cement and lime (from limestone)
Chalcopyrite	Copper iron sulfide	Important ore of copper
Chlorite	Hydrous magnesium, iron aluminum silicate	Rock former
Corundum	Aluminum oxide	Abrasive and gemstone
Dolomite	Calcium magnesium carbonate	Making of cement and building stone (from dolostone)
Fluorite	Calcium fluoride (halide)	Flux in steel-making; making of hydrofluoric acid
Galena	Lead sulfide	Chief ore of lead
Garnet	Calcium, iron, magnesium, aluminum silicate	Gemstone and abrasive
Graphite	Carbon	Lubricant; making of "lead" pencils
Gypsum	Hydrous calcium sulfate	Making of plaster of Paris
Halite	Sodium chloride (halide)	Source of salt, sodium, and chlorine
Hematite	Iron oxide	Chief ore of iron
Limonite	Hydrous iron oxide	Ore of iron
Magnetite	Iron oxide	Important ore of iron
Muscovite	Potassium aluminum silicate	Electrical insulation
Olivine	Magnesium iron silicate	Refractory material for casting; minor gemstone
Orthoclase	Potassium aluminum silicate	Making of ceramics

(continued)

Table 14-2. Continued.

Mineral	Composition	Selected Use(s)
Plagioclase	Sodium calcium aluminum silicate	Making of ceramics
Pyrite	Iron sulfide	Source of sulfur for sulfuric acid
Pyroxene	Calcium, magnesium, iron, aluminum silicate	Rock former
Quartz	Silicon dioxide (silicate)	Making of glass; gemstone
Serpentine	Hydrous magnesium silicate	Chief source of asbestos (chrysotile)
Sphalerite	Zinc sulfide	Chief ore of zinc
Staurolite	Iron aluminum silicate	Minor gemstone
Talc	Hydrous magnesium silicate	Making of talcum powder

Properties for Identifying Minerals

Sophisticated laboratory methods are required for positive identification of most minerals. Included are the use of X rays, chemical analysis, and analysis of optical properties. In the last approach, a mineral is cut and ground to paper thinness and observed through a microscope to see how the mineral appears as ordinary and polarized light pass through. For the most common minerals, however, the physical properties can often serve to identify them. Properties most used in this chapter are luster, color and streak, hardness, cleavage and fracture, crystal form, and heft or specific gravity.

Luster

The appearance of a mineral in reflected light is called **luster**; there are two types: metallic and nonmetallic. Metallic luster is that which resembles a shiny metal (for example, Figure 14-3); minerals with this luster are opaque and do not transmit light. Nonmetallic luster, present in minerals that transmit light, at least through thin edges, is varied; included are glassy, resinous (as in resin), pearly, greasy (as of oily glass), silky (as of a fibrous mineral), brilliant (as in diamond), and dull (no luster).

Color and Streak

Color is the most obvious physical property of a mineral. In some minerals, as in the metallic ones, color is constant and useful for identification. In others, as in quartz, color varies. Always discern color on fresh surfaces, since minerals are often stained or tarnished. "Light-colored" (Table 14-5) means colorless, white, yellow, orange, light red, light brown, light gray, light green, and light blue. Other colors can be considered "dark" (Table 14-6). **Streak**, the color of the powdered mineral, is more diagnostic than a mineral's color in reflected light. For example, hematite may be reddish brown to black but always produces a brownish-red streak. Streak is most useful for the dark, especially metallic, minerals. Obtain streak in three ways: Rub a mineral against unglazed porcelain (easiest), rub two pieces of the same mineral together, or attempt to cut a groove in a mineral with a knife blade. If you lack access to unglazed porcelain, acquire a piece of ceramic bathroom tile (back side), which works as well. For the last two methods, try to collect the powdered mineral on paper or a light surface to ascertain streak.

Hardness

Hardness is a mineral's resistance to scratching. Certain common minerals are used in a scale of hardness (Table 14-3). Minerals with large index numbers in the scale can scratch those with

TABLE 14-3. Standard Scale of Mineral Hardness and Hardness of Common Materials

Index	Minerals	Common Materials
1	Talc (softest)	——
2	Gypsum	——
2.5	——	Fingernail
3	Calcite	Copper penny
4	Fluorite	——
5	Apatite	——
5.5	——	Knife blade, window glass
6	Orthoclase	——
6.5	——	Steel file
7	Quartz	——
8	Topaz	——
9	Corundum	——
10	Diamond (hardest)	——

smaller index numbers. Diamond is the hardest natural substance known. The hardness of a mineral is controlled by the internal arrangement of atoms. Harder minerals have a stronger bonding of atoms or **ions**—electrically charged atoms—smaller atoms (which thus have a tighter fit), or more closely packed atoms.

If you don't have access to a mineral hardness set, other common materials—a fingernail, copper penny, knife blade, window glass, or steel file (Table 14-3)—will work. Before you attempt a hardness test, make sure the mineral surface you select is fresh and unweathered. Start with a knife blade. (A good idea is to carry a small folding pocketknife with two or three blades. Reserve one blade for hardness tests only, so that all blades don't dull from scratch tests.) Hold the mineral with a firm grasp and attempt to scratch a groove in the mineral with the knife blade. Use considerable pressure for a meaningful test. Blow away any ground mineral or powder and feel for a groove with your fingernail or examine the mineral with a hand lens. If a definite groove exists, the mineral is softer than your knife blade. You may then attempt to refine the hardness value by testing the mineral with a copper penny or your fingernail. If the mineral is harder than the knife blade, a faint metallic streak from the knife blade may be left on the mineral.

Cleavage and Fracture

Cleavage is the ability of a mineral to break along smooth, flat planes. A mineral may break along one to six directions. Biotite, for example, has cleavage in one direction and breaks into thin sheets (see Figure 14-19). Galena, on the other hand, has three directions of cleavage at right angles to each other and, therefore, breaks readily into cubes (Figure 14-2). Cleavage, like hardness, is controlled by the internal arrangement of atoms and occurs along a direction of weakness; that is, a direction across which the bonding of atoms is relatively weak. When a mineral is rotated in reflected light, a "flash" of light suggests a cleavage surface. Small steps on a mineral's surface or parallel cracks, seen in transparent minerals, also indicate cleavage (Figures 14-7, 14-9).

Fracture is the tendency of a mineral to break along surfaces other than smooth, flat planes; preferred directions of weakness, as in cleavage, are not evident. Common types of fracture are shell-like or **conchoidal** (cahn-KOYD-uhl), a smooth, curved fracture that resembles the inside of a clamshell; uneven or irregular; and splintery or fibrous.

Crystal Form

A **crystal** (for example, Figure 14-30) is a symmetrical, geometric form bounded by smooth, flat surfaces—crystal faces—that reflect the ordered internal arrangement of atoms. Nearly all minerals are crystalline—have an ordered internal arrangement of atoms—but they often lack an external crystal form. Crystals form from solutions, melts (melted substances), and vapors. You can acquire a good idea of how crystals form and grow if you have access to a microscope. Place a drop of a concentrated solution of table salt and water on a glass slide. As the water evaporates, ions of sodium (Na^+) and chlorine (Cl^-) combine to form eight-faced crystals, first along the margin of the drop. Snowflakes, six-sided crystals, are well-known examples of crystallization from a (water) vapor.

The study of crystals is rather complex. We will consider only a few common crystal forms (Tables 14-4 to 14-6) to help identify the common minerals.

Be careful not to confuse a crystal face with a cleavage plane. A crystal face has only one other face parallel to it and may display growth lines. A cleavage plane has an unlimited number of potential parallel planes. Crystal faces may (Figure 14-13) or may not (Figures 14-8, 14-10) parallel cleavage planes.

Heft or Specific Gravity

Heft simply means how heavy a mineral feels when lifted in the hand. Technically, heft is **specific gravity**, or the ratio of the weight of a mineral to the weight of an equal volume of water. Quartz, with a specific gravity of 2.6, weighs 2.6 times the same volume of water. Minerals that weigh less than quartz can be considered "light," those that weigh more are "heavy." Galena and pyrite are heavy minerals. Light and heavy minerals can be sensed with a little "hefting" practice.

Other Properties

Other physical properties may be useful at times for mineral identification. These include the feel (for example, greasy, as in graphite), attraction to a magnet (present in magnetite), taste (salty in halite), bubbling when hydrochloric acid is added (calcite), and being flexible in thin layers (chlorite) or both flexible and elastic (biotite). If you intend to carry an eyedropper bottle with dilute acid, mix one part hydrochloric acid with five parts water. CAUTION: Always add acid to water, *never* water to acid.

TABLE 14-4. Mineral Identification: Metallic Luster

Softer Than Knife

Cleavage Good

Graphite (GRAPH-ite)	Color and streak black; softer than fingernail; smudges fingers; cleavage in one direction; six-sided, tabular crystals, but usually in foliated or scaly masses; greasy feel (Figure 14-1).
Galena (guh-LEE-nuh)	Color and streak lead-gray; about as hard as fingernail; cubic cleavage and crystals; heavy (Figure 14-2).

Cleavage Poor or Absent

Chalcopyrite (kal-kuh-PIE-right)	Brass-yellow, often tarnished to bronze or iridescent; streak greenish black; harder than penny; fracture uneven; usually in masses; brittle; also called "fool's gold," as is pyrite (Figure 14-3).

Harder Than Knife

Cleavage Poor or Absent

Pyrite (PIE-right)	Pale brass-yellow, darker if tarnished; streak greenish or brownish black; about as hard as steel file; fracture shell-like; cubic crystals most common, also in masses and grains; heavy; also called "fool's gold," as is chalcopyrite (Figure 14-4).
Hematite (HE-muh-tight) (crystalline variety)	Dark brown to black; streak brownish red; fracture shell-like; crystals equidimensional to tabular, also in rounded and scaly masses; heavy (Figure 14-5).
Magnetite (MAG-nuh-tight)	Color and streak black; about as hard as steel file; fracture uneven; crystals often eight-faced, also commonly in grains or masses; heavy; attracted to magnet, may also act as magnet (lodestone) (Figure 14-6).

How to Identify Minerals

To identify a mineral, evaluate the physical properties just mentioned and use the mineral identification tables (Tables 14-4 to 14-6) and illustrations. We'll consider a common mineral to see how the identification process works.

Our pale blue mineral has glassy luster, so we go to Table 14-5. The knife scratches the mineral rather easily and leaves a white powder. Checking the hardness further, we find it to be about that of a penny. Good cleavage is present, as evidenced by several

TABLE 14-5. Mineral Identification: Nonmetallic Luster, Light-Colored

Softer Than Knife

Cleavage Good

Halite (HAL-ite)	Luster glassy; colorless or white, other colors if impure; about as hard as fingernail; cleavage cubic; crystals cubic, also in masses and grains; light; salty taste (Figure 14-7).
Fluorite (FLOOR-ite)	Luster glassy; color variable, most often yellow, green, or purple; harder than penny; cleavage in four directions, parallel to faces of octahedron; crystals usually cubic, often intergrown, also in masses (Figure 14-8).
Calcite (KAL-site)	Luster glassy to dull; colorless or white, other colors if impure; hard as penny; cleavage in three directions, at oblique angles; crystal form highly varied, rhombohedrons (each face a rhombus) and scalenohedrons (each face a scalene trangle, "dog-tooth" type) most common, also in masses and grains; bubbles rapidly in dilute hydrochloric acid (Figures 14-9, 14-10).
Dolomite (DOH-luh-mite)	Luster glassy to pearly; color variable, often pink or flesh-colored; harder than penny; cleavage as in calcite; crystals commonly curved rhombohedrons (see for calcite), also in masses and grains; bubbles slowly in dilute hydrochloric acid, rapidly when mineral is powdered; less common than calcite (Figure 14-11).
Anhydrite (an-HIGH-drite)	Luster glassy to pearly; colorless, white, gray, or variously tinted; about as hard as penny; cleavage in three directions, yields cubic or rectangular fragments; crystals rare, usually in masses; often alters to gypsum by addition of water (Figure 14-12).
Gypsum (GYP-suhm)	Luster glassy, pearly, or silky; colorless, white, gray, or variously tinted; softer than fingernail; good cleavage in one direction; crystals mostly tabular, commonly intergrown ("fishtail"), also in masses or fibrous; varieties include *selenite* (colorless, crystalline), *satin spar* (fibrous), and *alabaster* (massive) (Figure 14-13).
Talc (TALCK)	Luster pearly to greasy; commonly green, white, or gray; much softer than fingernail; cleavage in one direction, thin layers flexible but not elastic; crystals rare, usually sheetlike or in compact masses (soapstone); greasy or soapy feel (Figure 14-14).
Muscovite (MUHS-kuh-vite)	Luster glassy to pearly; colorless (in thin sheets) to yellow brown, green, and red; about as hard as fingernail; cleavage in one direction, thin layers flexible and elastic; crystals tabular, often six-sided, also in sheetlike and scaly masses; one of the micas (Figure 14-15).

(continued)

TABLE 14-5. Continued.

Harder Than Knife

Cleavage Good

Orthoclase (OR-thuh-klace)	Luster glassy to pearly; usually white, gray or flesh-colored; about as hard as steel file; cleavage in two directions, at right angles; crystals usually short prisms, often intergrown, also in cleavable or granular masses; one of the feldspars (Figure 14-16).
Plagioclase (PLAY-gee-uh-klace)	Similar to orthoclase but usually white or gray and has fine parallel lines on good cleavage surfaces; one of the feldspars.

Cleavage Poor or Absent

Quartz (KWORTS)	Luster glassy; usually colorless or white, but may be any color; about as hard as steel file or harder; fracture shell-like; crystals usually six-sided prisms that appear to be capped by pyramids, also in masses; many varieties, including *rock crystal* (colorless) (Figure 14-17), *milky quartz* (white), *rose quartz* (pink) (Figure 14-18), *amethyst* (purple), *smoky quartz* (smoky yellow to black), and *agate* (banded or mossy).

---

steps on the mineral's surface, presumably in three directions at oblique angles. This cleavage pattern results in rhombohedron cleavage forms, shaped somewhat like a weakened, skewed wooden box after someone sat on one corner. The combination of hardness and cleavage characters steers us to either calcite or dolomite. If we have dilute hydrochloric acid with us, a rapid bubbling would finalize the identification to calcite.

By the way, if no acid is available, you might try lemon juice. Lemon juice contains very weak acid, so any bubbling must be viewed with a hand lens. Vinegar also contains a weak acid and may be used as a substitute for lemon juice.

If you are somewhat familiar with minerals, you might wonder: Have you been deceived by a trial example of *blue* calcite? Perhaps so. But I wished to make a point: Don't place too much emphasis on color. Rely more on other properties.

You now have the basic identification process. If you are unable to identify a mineral with one table, try another in case you made a wrong decision somewhere. If you still cannot identify the mineral, try one of the identification manuals listed at the end of this chapter. Remember, though, only relatively few minerals can be identified by their physical properties. If you become really serious about minerals, you may have to resort to chemical tests or consult a mineralogist at a university or museum.

TABLE 14-6. Mineral Identification: Monmetallic Luster, Dark-Colored

Softer Than Knife

Cleavage Good

Biotite (BY-uh-tight)	Luster glassy to pearly; usually dark green, brown, or black; hard as fingernail or penny; cleavage in one direction, thin layers flexible and elastic; crystals tabular, often six-sided, usually in sheetlike or scaly masses; one of the micas (Figure 14-19).
Chlorite (KLOR-ite)	Luster glassy to pearly; usually green to blackish green; hard as fingernail or somewhat softer; cleavage in one direction, thin layers flexible but not elastic; crystals tabular, often six-sided, usually in sheetlike scaly masses (Figure 14-20).
Sphalerite (SFAL-uh-right)	Luster resinous; usually yellow, brown, or black; harder than penny; cleavage in six directions; crystals in tetrahedrons common, usually in cleavable masses (Figure 14-21).

Cleavage Poor or Absent

Serpentine (SIR-puhn-teen)	Luster waxy, greasy, or silky; usually green, but variable; usually harder than penny; fracture shell-like or splintery; no crystals, usually in masses (Figure 14-22) or fibers (Figure 14-23) (fibrous variety is *chrysotile* asbestos); smooth or greasy feel.
Apatite (AP-uh-tight)	Luster glassy to resinous; usually green or brown; harder than penny; fracture shell-like; crystals of six-sided prisms, also in masses or grains (Figure 14-24).
Limonite (LIE-muh-night)	Luster dull to glassy; yellow, yellow-brown to black; streak yellow-brown; softer than fingernail to about that of knife; fracture shell-like to uneven; no crystals, in earthy or compact, rounded masses (Figure 14-25).
Hematite (earthy variety)	Luster dull; red and reddish brown; streak brownish red; softer than fingernail to about that of knife; fracture uneven; no crystals, in earthy masses; heavy (no photo available).

(continued)

TABLE 14-6. Continued.

Harder Than Knife

Cleavage Good

Pyroxene (pie-ROCK-seen)

Luster glassy to pearly; usually gray, green, or black; cleavage in two directions, at about right angles, forms square or rectangular cleavage fragments; crystals commonly stubby, eight-sided prisms, also in compact masses and grains; a group of minerals, most common is *augite* (AW-jite) (Figure 14-26).

Amphibole (AM-fuh-bowl)

Luster glassy to silky; usually gray, green, or black; cleavage in two directions, not at right angles, forms double wedge-shaped cleavage fragments; crystals commonly long, six-sided prisms, also in fibrous or irregular masses; a group of minerals, most common is *hornblende* (HORN-blend) (Figure 14-27).

Staurolite (STORE-uh-light)

Luster glassy to dull; brown to black; harder than steel file; fair cleavage in one direction; usually in crystals— stubby prisms—often intergrown as crosses (staurolite from Greek *stauros*, "cross") (see Figure 17-4).

Cleavage Poor or Absent

Corundum (kuh-RUN-duhm)

Luster glassy to diamondlike; color variable, usually brown, gray, red, or blue; harder than steel file; fracture uneven to shell-like; crystals six-sided, commonly barrel-shaped or tabular, also in grains; gem varieties include *ruby* (red) and *sapphire* (blue) (Figure 14-28).

Olivine (AHL-uh-veen)

Luster glassy; "olivine is olive green" (usually); hard as steel file or harder; fracture shell-like; usually in grainy masses (Figure 14-29).

Garnet (GAHR-nut)

Luster glassy to resinous; usually red, brown, or green; hard as steel file or harder; fracture shell-like or uneven; crystals equidimensional, often with 12 or 24 faces, also in grainy masses; several varieties (Figure 14-30).

Figure 14-1. Graphite, from Columbo, Ceylon, showing metallic luster and easily scratchable surfaces. Width of specimen is 4.2 inches (10.7 cm).

Figure 14-2. Galena, showing metallic luster and cubic cleavage. Smallest cleavage fragment is reflected in cleavage surface of intermediate-sized fragment. Height of largest specimen is 2.2 inches (5.6 cm).

Figure 14-3. Chalcopyrite, showing high metallic luster. Height of specimen is 2.0 inches (5.1 cm).

Figure 14-4. Cubic crystal of pyrite, showing metallic luster and shell-like fracture on front crystal face. Height of specimen is 2.2 inches (5.6 cm).

Figure 14-5. Hard, massive variety of hematite, from Minnesota, showing metallic luster and rounded surfaces. Width of specimen is 3.5 inches (8.9 cm).

Figure 14-6. Massive magnetite, from Baltimore, Maryland. Bar magnet attracted to magnetite is 0.9 inches (2.3 cm) high.

Figure 14-7. Halite, from Windsor, Ontario, showing glassy luster and cubic cleavage. Height of specimen is 3.6 inches (9.1 cm).

Figure 14-8. Intergrown cubic crystals of fluorite, showing glassy luster. Straight cracks in some crystals reflect cleavage surfaces that are oblique to crystal faces. Width of specimen is 2.6 inches (6.6 cm).

FIGURE 14-9. Cleavage fragment of calcite, from Riverside, California, showing glassy luster and three directions of cleavage. Width of left front part of specimen is 3.7 inches (9.4 cm).

FIGURE 14-10. "Dog tooth" crystals of calcite, from Ohio. Uppermost crystal displays a crack that represents a cleavage surface oblique to crystal faces. Width of crystal group is 4.6 inches (11.7 cm).

FIGURE 14-11. Curved crystals of dolomite—with smaller, darker crystals of chalcopyrite—from Joplin, Missouri, showing pearly luster. Height of specimen is 2.6 inches (6.6 cm).

Figure 14-12. Massive anhydrite, showing glassy to pearly luster. Width of specimen is 3.1 inches (7.9 cm).

Figure 14-13. Intergrown crystals of gypsum, from southwestern North Dakota, showing glassy luster. Straight crack in lower left of specimen represents a cleavage surface that parallels a crystal face. Width of specimen is 4.3 inches (10.9 cm).

Figure 14-14. Cleavable mass of talc, showing pearly to greasy luster. Width of specimen is 5.1 inches (12.9 cm).

FIGURE 14-15. Muscovite mica, from Keystone, South Dakota, showing the mineral's capability of cleaving into thin sheets. Height of specimen is 6.1 inches (15.5 cm).

FIGURE 14-16. Orthoclase feldspar, from Delaware County, Pennsylvania, showing two directions of cleavage at right angles, revealed by front and top surfaces, and pearly luster. Height of specimen is 3.1 inches (7.9 cm).

FIGURE 14-17. Transparent, six-sided crystal prisms of quartz capped by pyramids, showing glassy luster. Height of largest crystal is 1.8 inches (4.6 cm).

Figure 14-18. Massive, noncrystalline rose quartz from Hot Springs, Arkansas. Height of specimen is 4.2 inches (10.7 cm).

Figure 14-19. Biotite mica, from Renfrew County, Ontario, showing a tabular, six-sided crystal and the mineral's capability of cleaving into thin sheets. Height of specimen is 3.1 inches (7.9 cm).

FIGURE 14-20. Scaly mass of chlorite, from Chester, Vermont. Width of specimen is 2.5 inches (6.3 cm).

FIGURE 14-21. Crystals of sphalerite, from Missouri, showing resinous luster. Width of specimen is 5.7 inches (14.5 cm).

FIGURE 14-22. Massive serpentine, from Chester County, Pennsylvania, showing waxy luster and lack of cleavage. Width of specimen is 2.8 inches (7.1 cm).

Figure 14-23. Fibrous serpentine, from Waldheim, East Germany, showing delicate fibers. Height of specimen is 2.3 inches (5.8 cm).

Figure 14-24. Six-sided crystal of apatite, showing glassy to resinous luster. Height of specimen is 1.7 inches (4.3 cm).

FIGURE 14-25. Massive limonite, showing rounded surfaces. Width of specimen is 3.7 inches (9.4 cm).

FIGURE 14-26. Cleavage fragment of pyroxene. from Sydenham, Ontario, showing two directions of cleavage at about right angles as indicated by the top and right surfaces. Height of specimen is 1.1 inches (2.8 cm).

FIGURE 14-27. Cleavage fragment of amphibole, showing two directions of cleavage not at right angles. Width of specimen is 3.9 inches (9.9 cm).

FIGURE 14-28. Six-sided crystal prisms of corundum, from Mineral County, Nevada. Height of specimen on the left is 1.5 inches (3.8 cm).

FIGURE 14-29. Granular mass of olivine, from Jackson County, North Carolina, showing glassy luster. Height of specimen is 2.9 inches (7.4 cm).

Figure 14-30. Twelve-faced crystal of garnet. Height of crystal is 2.2 inches (5.6 cm).

Formation of Minerals

Minerals form in a variety of ways. Many originate from masses of molten rock at depth or from masses extruded on the surface as lava. Some heavy, metallic minerals crystallize early from molten rock at depth and sink, segregate, and concentrate near the base of the molten mass; an example is magnetite. Other, lighter minerals, such as feldspars, crystallize later from a molten mass at depth and settle at shallower depths. In the latest stages, hot, residual fluids force their way into fractures of the surrounding rock to precipitate such minerals as galena and sphalerite in veins.

Where a molten rock mass at depth comes in contact with and replaces part of the surrounding rock, minerals form by metamorphic processes (see chapter 17). Staurolite and garnet are examples of minerals formed by this means.

Many minerals form at low temperatures near Earth's surface. Precipitation from seawater has produced such minerals as hematite (some), halite, and gypsum; the last two result from the evaporation of briny water. Some minerals, such as calcite, may precipitate from groundwater. And weathering processes may produce such minerals as limonite.

Suggested Reading

Arem, Joel. *Rocks and Minerals*. Phoenix, AZ: Geoscience Press, 1991.

Chesterman, C. W. *The Audubon Society Field Guide to North American Rocks and Minerals*. New York: Alfred A. Knopf, 1978.

Hamilton, W. R., A. R. Woolley, and A. C. Bishop. *The Henry Holt Guide to Minerals, Rocks, and Fossils*. New York: Henry Holt, 1989.

Holden, Martin, and E. A. Mathez, eds. *The Encyclopedia of Gemstones and Minerals*. New York: Facts on File, 1991.

Mottana, Annibale, Rodolfo Crespi, and Guiseppe Liborio. *Simon and Schuster's Guide to Rocks and Minerals*. New York: Simon & Schuster, 1978.

Pellant, Chris. *Rocks, Minerals, & Fossils of the World*. Boston: Little, Brown, 1990.

Pough, F. H. *Peterson First Guide to Rocks and Minerals*. Boston: Houghton Mifflin, 1991.

Sorrell, C. A. *A Field Guide and Introduction to the Geology and Chemistry of Rocks and Minerals*. New York: Golden Press, 1973.

Zim, H. S., and P. R. Shaffer. *Rocks and Minerals: A Guide to Familiar Minerals, Gems, Ores and Rocks*. New York: Golden Press, 1957.

15

Igneous Rocks

In chapter 14, I mentioned that rocks are made up of minerals or are aggregates of minerals. (A few to several minerals constitute most rocks but, in some cases, only one is present.) The study of rocks is **petrology** (puh-TRAHL-uh-gee).

The three groups of rocks are igneous, sedimentary, and metamorphic. **Igneous rocks** (from the Latin *ignis*, "fire") are literally "fire-formed" rocks: They result from congealing of hot, melted rock deep within Earth, **magma**, or from that extruded at the surface as lava. Visualize magma as a molten slush—maybe on the order of thick oatmeal—made up of liquids, gases (mostly water vapor and carbon dioxide), and suspended, early-formed crystals. Basaltic magmas are generated by the partial melting of the upper mantle along spreading centers where tectonic plates move apart. Silica-rich granitic magmas are formed along subduction zones by the partial melting of descending oceanic crust and metamorphic rocks (see below) in continental crust. Formed from cooling magma, igneous rocks display mineral grains that are interlocked. These rocks are the subject of this chapter.

Sedimentary rocks (from the Latin *sedere*, "to settle") form from the accumulation of sediment—mineral crystals or particles of minerals and rocks or masses of organic matter—that solidifies into layered rock.

Metamorphic rocks (from the Greek *meta*, "change," and *morphe*, "form") result from the alteration of other rocks at depth by heat, pressure, and chemically active fluids and gases. Sedimentary and metamorphic rocks are covered in chapters 16 and 17.

Main Igneous Rock-Forming Minerals

Mineral identification in rocks is more difficult because the mineral grains are small—a hand lens is usually required—and crystal form is less often developed. The basic principles, however, still apply.

Only a few minerals—all silicates (see Table 14-1)—make up the bulk of igneous rocks. They can be grouped into *light-colored* and *dark-colored* minerals.

Light-Colored Minerals

The major light-colored minerals are the feldspars—the most abundant mineral group—quartz, and muscovite mica. Feldspar grains are recognized by their good cleavage in two directions at about right angles, common rectangular shape, and a hardness greater than that of a knife. If the grains are pink, red, or flesh-colored, they can be considered orthoclase. If white, gray, or yellow, and possibly with fine grooves, they can be called plagioclase. Quartz, commonly clear or white although almost any color, is glassy, lacks cleavage, and rarely displays crystal form. This mineral appears to fill the spaces between other mineral grains because it is one of the last to crystallize. Muscovite, usually colorless, white, or yellow, breaks into thin, elastic flakes when probed with a knife blade.

Dark-Colored Minerals

The dark-colored minerals—usually dark green to black—include biotite mica, olivine, pyroxene, and amphibole. Not only dark, these minerals are heavier, that is, have a higher specific gravity, than the light-colored minerals because they contain iron and magnesium. They, consequently, are also called **ferromagnesian** (*ferro* means "iron") **minerals**. Biotite resembles muscovite but is darker. Olivine appears as green, glassy grains. Pyroxene, which actually is a group of minerals, as is amphibole, occurs as grains or short crystals with two directions of cleavage at right angles. Amphibole tends to occur in grains or elongate crystals that cleave in two directions not at right angles.

Classifying and Identifying Igneous Rocks

Igneous rocks are classified on the basis of texture and mineral composition (Table 15-1). **Texture**, in a strict sense the size, shape, and arrangement of the mineral constituents of a rock, refers primarily to the *size* of mineral grains. Texture relates to the cooling history of the molten rock material from which an igneous rock originates. The main texture types are coarse-grained, fine-grained, glassy, porphyritic (not in Table 15-1), and fragmental.

Mineral crystals of coarse-grained rocks are large enough to see without a microscope—a hand lens may be needed—and most are of about the same size. If magma cools in a slow and uniform fashion at considerable depth beneath Earth's surface, ions have ample time to combine and form large, equal-sized crystals.

TABLE 15-1. Classification of Igneous Rocks

TEXTURE	MINERAL COMPOSITION			
	Light-Colored Minerals Mostly		Dark Minerals Mostly	Dark Minerals Entirely
	Feldspar exceeds B', A, P; quartz	Feldspar exceeds A, B, P; no quartz	P, O, A exceed feldspar; no quartz	O, P, A; no feldspar or quartz
Coarse-Grained	Granite and Related Rocks	Diorite	Gabbro	Peridotite Pyroxenite Hornblendite
Fine-Grained	Felsite (e.g., Rhyolite, Andesite)		Basalt	—
Glassy	Obsidian Pumice		Basalt Glass (rare) Scoria	—
Fragmental (= Pyroclastic)	Tuff Volcanic Breccia Agglomerate		—	—

[1]B = biotite, A = amphibole, P = pyroxene, O = olivine; minerals listed in order of relative abundance (most abundant first) in the sections above.

Fine-grained rocks possess crystals discernible only with a microscope. Such small crystals imply a much more rapid cooling of magma, which occurs near the surface or in the interior of lava flows, than for coarse-grained rocks.

Glassy rocks lack distinct crystals even when viewed with a microscope. They form under conditions of rapid cooling so that ions are unable to combine into a crystalline structure. Such rocks may form, for example, on the surfaces of lava flows or where lava enters water.

Rocks of the coarse- and fine-grained types may be "two-textured" or **porphyritic** (pore-fuh-RIT-ick). Two sizes of crystals are evident, which imply two stages and rates of cooling: larger crystals from slower cooling, smaller crystals from faster cooling, with both types in the same rock. If the larger crystals are particularly abundant, the rock is called a **porphyry** (PORE-fuh-ree).

Fragmental or **pyroclastic** ("fire-fragmental") **rocks** differ a great deal from the others. They consist chiefly of broken rock fragments, with glass, blown out during volcanic eruptions.

With an eye on texture and Table 15-1, let's examine the major igneous rocks.

Granite and Related Rocks

Granite (Figures 15-1 to 15-3) is a coarse-grained igneous rock composed mostly of orthoclase feldspar with quartz, and minor dark minerals, usually biotite or amphibole (Table 15-1). Muscovite may also occur.

Other granitic rocks are not easy to distinguish in the field. **Syenite** (SIGH-uhn-ite) resembles granite but lacks quartz; **quartz monzonite** contains about as much plagioclase as ortho-

Figure 15-1. Granite from St. Cloud, Minnesota. Most of lightest grains are of orthoclase feldspar; light gray grains, as in center of specimen, are of quartz; and dark grains are of amphibole and biotite. Width of specimen is 3.9 inches (9.9 cm).

FIGURE 15-2. Granite porphyry, implying two stages of molten-rock cooling. Long, light crystals are of orthoclase feldspar. Large crystal in the lower left is 0.9 inch (2.3 cm) long.

FIGURE 15-3. Exposure of weathered, jointed granite porphyry, showing characteristic rounded forms.

clase; and in **granodiorite** (gran-oh-DIE-uh-right), plagioclase exceeds orthoclase. Granitic rocks vary from white to dark gray to pink and red. **Pegmatite** (PEG-muh-tight) is a very coarse-grained rock with crystals about an inch (a few centimeters) to many feet long. Most often of granitic composition (Figure 15-4), pegmatite may contain somewhat exotic minerals, such as topaz, tourmaline, and spodumene. Pegmatite forms in a late stage of crystalli-

Figure 15-4. Granite pegmatite, of mostly feldspar (white), quartz (light gray), and muscovite (dark gray to nearly black). Height of the muscovite cluster in the upper right is 2.9 inches (7.4 cm).

Figure 15-5. Diorite, from Los Angeles County, California. Light grains are largely of plagioclase feldspar; the dark grains are of amphibole and biotite. Width of specimen is 4.1 inches (10.4 cm).

zation during which a gas-enriched, very fluid magma allows ions to move freely and form unusually large crystals.

Granite and related rocks make up most of the continental crust of Earth.

Diorite

Generally darker than the granitic rocks—light gray to green— because of more dark minerals, **diorite** (Figure 15-5) consists chiefly of plagioclase, with amphibole and biotite, and often small amounts of pyroxene and orthoclase. Quartz is absent or insignificant. Diorite, intermediate in composition between the granitic rocks and gabbro, grades into granite through the intermediate granodiorite.

Gabbro

Darker still than diorite—dark gray, green, or black—**gabbro** (Figure 15-6) tends to contain more dark minerals than plagioclase feldspar. The main dark mineral is pyroxene with minor olivine and amphibole. Quartz is absent. Gabbro is an uncommon rock at Earth's surface but is considered to be an important constituent of the lower part of the oceanic crust.

Peridotite, Pyroxenite, and Hornblendite

These three rocks, green to black, are composed almost entirely of dark minerals. **Peridotite** (puh-RID-duh-tight) (Figure 15-7) is mostly of olivine and pyroxene; in **pyroxenite** (pie-ROCK-suh-night), pyroxene predominates; and **hornblendite**, named after hornblende, the most common variety of amphibole, contains mostly amphibole. (The nonspecific term "amphibolite" would seem logical for a rock in which the variety of amphibole is uncertain. But amphibolite is reserved for a metamorphic rock.) Quartz is absent, and feldspar is almost always lacking. You might recall from chapter 12 the belief that peridotite makes up the bulk of the mantle.

Felsite

A fine-grained, light-colored igneous rock, **felsite** (Figures 15-8, 15-9) is a general term for the fine-grained equivalents of granitic

FIGURE 15-6. Gabbro, from Salem, Massachusetts. Dark minerals exceed plagioclase feldspar. Width of specimen is 4.5 inches (11.4 cm).

FIGURE 15-7. Peridotite, from Hualalai Volcano, Hawaii, Hawaii. Consists entirely of dark minerals, chiefly olivine and pyroxene. Height of specimen is 3.5 inches (8.9 cm).

FIGURE 15-8. Felsite (rhyolite), from Castle Rock, Colorado, showing shell-like fracture. Width of specimen is 4.2 inches (10.7 cm).

FIGURE 15-9. Felsite (andesite) porphyry, from the Spanish Peaks region, Colorado, showing conspicuous dark amphibole crystals in a fine-grained matrix, implying two stages of molten-rock cooling. Height of specimen is 4.5 inches (11.4 cm).

185

Figure 15-10. Basalt, from near Naalehu, Hawaii, Hawaii, with numerous gas bubble cavities (vesicular structure). Width of specimen is 4.5 inches (11.4 cm).

rocks and diorite. Thin edges of flakes or chips of felsites tend to be translucent. If the texture is porphyritic and larger crystals are identifiable, you might attempt a more specific rock name. So, if considerable orthoclase and quartz are present, with perhaps biotite or amphibole, as in granite, the rock is **rhyolite**. Likewise, a light-colored rock with identifiable crystals of plagioclase, along with amphibole and biotite and other minerals found in diorite, is **andesite** (AN-duh-zight)—or porphyritic andesite or andesite porphyry (Figure 15-9) if larger crystals are abundant.

Basalt

The dark-colored, fine-grained equivalent of gabbro is **basalt** (buh-SALT) (Figure 15-10), the most common fine-grained igneous rock that makes up most of the oceanic crust. Basalt appears dull, almost velvety. Thin edges of flakes or chips of this rock are not translucent as in felsite. Numerous, smooth cavities or **vesicles**, which represent entrapped gas bubbles released from lava as it cooled, are common in the upper part of basalt lava flows. Vesicles result in **vesicular structure** (Figure 15-10), found in other fine-grained and glassy rocks as well. The vesicles may later fill with mineral matter.

Glassy Rocks

Obsidian (Figure 15-11) is a natural glass with shell-like fracture. Most often black, obsidian is also gray, brown, or red. The edges of thin flakes are transparent or translucent. Native Americans fashioned knives, projectile points, and other implements and

FIGURE 15-11. Obsidian, showing excellent shell-like fracture. Width of specimen is 6.7 inches (17.0 cm).

FIGURE 15-12. Pumice, from Pumice Desert, Crater Lake, Oregon, showing glass fibers and gas bubble cavities. Width of specimen is 4.9 inches (12.4 cm).

weapons from obsidian. Most obsidians have a composition similar to that of granitic rocks. **Pitchstone**, a variety of obsidian, owes its resinous or pitchlike luster to a relatively high water content. **Pumice** (PUHM-uhs) (Figure 15-12) is a glass froth of glass fibers separated by numerous vesicles. Because it is so porous and the gas bubbles are sealed, pumice floats on water. Pumice is white, gray, yellow, or brown. As for obsidian, pumice has a composition like that of granitic rocks.

Scoria is a cindery, slaglike rock with more vesicles than vesicular basalt—there may be as much empty space as rock—and with larger vesicles than pumice. Reddish brown to gray and black, scoria often has a basaltic composition. Brown to black **basalt glass** is rare. This is because basaltic lavas are "thinner" or less viscous than felsitic lavas, and ions can combine more readily to form crystalline rather than noncrystalline rocks.

FIGURE 15-13. Volcanic breccia, from Owens River, Nevada. Rock contains coarse, angular, volcanic rock fragments within a finer tuff matrix. Width of specimen is 5.8 inches (14.7 cm).

Fragmental Rocks

As gases under pressure are released from magma rising toward Earth's surface, fragments of new and old lava are blown out from volcanic vents. Fragments smaller than 0.08 inch (2 mm) constitute **volcanic ash** and **dust**; those larger than about 2.5 inches (64 mm) are called **bombs**—rounded, ejected while molten—and **blocks**—angular, ejected after solidification. Fragments intermediate in size between ash and dust and bombs and blocks may be called **cinders**.

Tuff (TOUGH) is a fine-grained, fragmental rock made up largely of volcanic ash and dust. This rock has a rough feel from the sharp ash and dust particles. Tuff is lightweight and most often light-colored: white, gray, yellow, light brown, or pink.

Volcanic breccia (BRETCH-ee-uh) (Figure 15-13), of large, angular fragments, and **agglomerate**, of large, rounded fragments, are fragmental rocks of volcanic blocks or bombs mixed with ash and dust. They tend to be gray, yellow, brown, and red.

Occurrence of Igneous Rocks

Of the rocks exposed on the land surface, an average of 34 percent are crystalline—igneous and metamorphic—and an average of 66 percent are sedimentary. Crystalline rocks, however, underlie all sedimentary rocks. By volume, crystalline rocks constitute about 95 percent of Earth's crust to a depth of about 9 miles (15 km). One-half of the crystalline rocks exposed are igneous.

Igneous rocks occur in two types of rock bodies: extrusive and intrusive. **Extrusive** bodies result from magma *extruded* on the surface, whereas **intrusive** bodies form as magma *intrudes* into fractures of surrounding rocks at depth or melts and assimilates

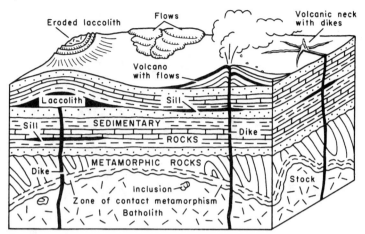

Figure 15-14. Block diagram showing occurrences of extrusive and intrusive igneous rock bodies.

them (Figure 15-14). Percentages of extrusive and intrusive rocks exposed on the land surface are similar.

Extrusive Rock Bodies

Extrusive rock bodies are of two main types: lava flows and volcanoes. These are covered in chapter 8. Flows are made up of basalt and felsite, in addition to porphyries of these rock types. Volcanic glass often develops on the surfaces of flows. Rocks associated with volcanoes are those of lava flows as well as those of the fragmental type.

Columnar structure (Figure 15-15) most often occurs in basalt of flows and other bodies, but is found in other igneous rocks as well. A mass of closely fitted columns less than 3 feet (1 m) to more than 300 feet (100 m) long, columnar structure results from a system of shrinkage cracks or joints that form as lava or magma loses heat. If the lava or magma is homogeneous and cools slowly and regularly, centers of shrinkage are equally spaced. Tension occurs between the centers, and cracks form at right angles to the direction of tension. In the ideal case, double cracking across three main tensional axes produces hexagons that form columns as the cracks penetrate downward. If the centers of shrinkage are unequally spaced, variably sided columns (other than six-sided) occur. Columnar structure is well displayed in the extensive and many "stacked" basaltic flows (see Figure 8-8) of the Columbia-Snake River Plateau of Washington, Oregon, and Idaho.

Figure 15-15. Columnar structure in an intrusive of felsite porphyry, Devils Tower, Devils Tower National Monument, northeastern Wyoming. The tapered columns are up to 10 feet (3 m) in diameter. Most geologists consider the tower the neck of an ancient volcano that formed 40 million years ago; others favor an erosional remnant of a sill or laccolith.

Intrusive Rock Bodies

Volcanic necks (Figure 15-14 and Figure 10-3) are towerlike masses of rock that seal the vents and conduits of former and recently dormant volcanoes, and become visible upon removal of the more easily erodible surrounding rocks. They are common in

Figure 15-16. Pegmatitic granite dike (light) intruded into quartz biotite schist. Width of the dike is 2.5 feet (0.8 m).

northwestern New Mexico and adjacent Arizona. Rocks frequent in volcanic necks are coarse- and fine-grained porphyries and glassy and fragmental rocks.

Dikes (Figures 15-16, 15-17) are tabular intrusive bodies—their length and breadth is great in relation to their thickness—that form as magma squeezes into vertical or near-vertical frac-

FIGURE 15-17. Light felsite dikes intruded into slate and schist and connected to light sills in the highest hill to the left; Homestake Mining Company open cut, Lead, Black Hills, southwestern South Dakota. Height of the tallest trees is about 40 feet (12 m).

tures. They can be less than a few tenths of an inch to hundreds of feet thick and may extend for many miles. Dikes tend to occur in groups—they follow fracture systems—and often radiate from volcanic necks (Figure 15-14). Columnar structure develops in some dikes, at right angles to the cool fracture walls, and the columns resemble stacked cordwood. Dikes resistant to erosion produce rock walls that traverse the countryside. One region of abundant dikes is the Spanish Peaks area of southern Colorado. All fine-grained rocks and their porphyries occur in dikes, as well as coarse-grained porphyries, gabbro, peridotite, and pegmatite.

Sills (Figure 15-17) are also tabular intrusives but differ from dikes in that magma has been forced *between* layers of older rock. They often occur where magma has been injected into weak, easily penetrated, stratified rock. Sills are of similar dimensions to dikes and may be offshoots of them. They may also display columnar structure; a famous example is the basaltic, 1,000-foot (300-m) thick Palisades sill exposed along the Hudson River in New Jersey west of New York City. Sills differ from buried lava flows in that baked or altered rocks occur above and below them, fragments of the surrounding rock may occur in them, and they lack vesicular structure and weathered and eroded tops. Rocks in

Figure 15-18. Eroded laccolith of felsite porphyry flanked by upturned edges of sedimentary strata, Bear Butte, near Sturgis, southwestern South Dakota.

sills are similar to those found in dikes except for pegmatite. Those of basaltic composition prevail.

Laccoliths are mushroom-shaped intrusives formed as thick or viscous magma, fed from below or a side, forces between rock layers and domes up the overlying strata. They, therefore, have an arched top and a rather flat base. Laccoliths are roughly circular or elliptical in plain view and up to thousands of feet thick and many miles in diameter. Well-known laccoliths occur in the Henry Mountains of southeastern Utah. Resistant laccoliths stand as prominent hills or mountains, often surrounded by concentric ridges of eroded, domed rock layers (Figure 15-18). Sills and dikes may associate with laccoliths. Most types of igneous rocks are found in laccoliths. Coarse-grained porphyritic rocks are common.

Batholiths are the largest of intrusives and the largest rock bodies of Earth's crust. They may cover thousands of square miles and assume elongate, elliptical, or circular shapes. Batholiths tend to first increase in size with depth but may decrease in size at greater depth. Emplaced at depths of thousands of feet beneath the surface, these intrusives are exposed only where extensive erosion has occurred. Fragments of older surrounding rock, **inclusions** (Figure 15-14), are often preserved within an emplaced batholith. Batholiths tend to occur along the axes of mountain belts and reflect formation along subduction zones. Well-known examples in western North America are the Coast Range batholith of western British Columbia and the Idaho batholith of central Idaho and western Montana.

Granitic rocks are typically found in batholiths, but gabbro and diorite may also occur. Coarse-grained porphyries, too, can be expected in places.

Stocks are, in essence, small batholiths, less than about 40 square miles (100 square km) in exposed area. Certain stocks are simply offshoots of batholiths. Both stocks and batholiths erode to high areas, and may display well-developed jointing.

The rocks found in stocks, generally granitic, are similar to those of batholiths, but diorite, gabbro, and peridotite are also common.

Suggested Reading

Arem, Joel. *Rocks and Minerals*. Phoenix, AZ: Geoscience Press, 1991.

Chesterman, C. W. *The Audubon Society Field Guide to North American Rocks and Minerals*. New York: Alfred A. Knopf, 1978.

Hamilton, W. R., A. R. Woolley, and A. C. Bishop. *The Henry Holt Guide to Minerals, Rocks, and Minerals*. New York: Henry Holt, 1989.

Mottana, Annibale, Rodolfo Crespi, and Guiseppe Liborio. *Simon and Schuster's Guide to Rocks and Minerals*. New York: Simon & Schuster, 1978.

Pellant, Chris. *Rocks, Minerals & Fossils of the World*. Boston: Little, Brown, 1990.

Pough, F. H. *Peterson First Guide to Rocks and Minerals*. Boston: Houghton Mifflin, 1991.

Sorrell, C. A. *A Field Guide and Introduction to the Geology and Chemistry of Rocks and Minerals*. New York: Golden Press, 1973.

Zim, H. S., and P. R. Shaffer. *Rocks and Minerals: A Guide to Familiar Minerals, Gems, Ores and Rocks*. New York: Golden Press, 1957.

16

Sedimentary Rocks

Sedimentary rocks consist of solidified or lithified **sediment**—particles of minerals or rock fragments, mineral crystals, or organic matter. Sediments such as gravel, sand, and lime mud, for example, lithify to conglomerate, sandstone, and limestone. Sedimentary rocks that consist of particles or fragments are called **clastic** (from the Greek *klastos*, "broken into pieces"), those of mineral crystals or organic matter are **nonclastic**.

Exposed on 66 percent of the land surface, on the average, sedimentary rocks are more apt to be seen on the landscape than igneous and metamorphic rocks. On the bottoms of oceans, too, sediments prevail over other Earth materials.

Main Sedimentary Rock-Forming Minerals

Clastic rocks consist chiefly of quartz, feldspars, rock fragments, micas, clay minerals, iron oxides, and calcite (Table 16-1). The clay minerals are hydrated (water is bound with them chemically) aluminum silicates; for example, kaolinite (KAY-uh-luh-night). Individual clay minerals can be identified only with sophisticated laboratory equipment. The most common iron oxides are hematite and limonite, which serve to color and cement clastic sediments. Quartz and calcite constitute particles and also cement sediments.

Nonclastic, chemically precipitated rocks are made up mostly of calcite, dolomite, gypsum, anhydrite, halite, quartz and related minerals, hematite, limonite, and apatite (Table 16-2). The carbon-bearing rocks consist of plant material.

Classification, Identification, and Origin of Sedimentary Rock

Clastic rocks are classified, first, on the basis of the size and, second, on the composition of sedimentary particles. Composition of constituents is the sole basis for the general classification of nonclastic rocks.

TABLE 16-1. Classification of Clastic Sedimentary Rocks

Particle Size	Main Constituents (s)	Sediment	Rock
Coarse (>0.08 inch or 2 mm)	Rock fragments, quartz	Gravel	Conglomerate (rounded particles), Breccia (angular particles)
Medium (0.002-0.08 inch or 0.06-2 mm)	Quartz Feldspar Rock fragments	Sand	Sandstone Quartz Sandstone Feldspar Sandstone (Arkose) Rock Fragment Sandstone
Fine (<0.002 inch or 0.06 mm)	Clay minerals, quartz	Silt (coarser) + Clay (finer) = Mud	Mudstone (blocky) Siltstone Claystone Shale (fissile)
Coarse to Fine	Calcite	Limy gravel, sand, or mud	Clastic Limestone

TABLE 16-2. Classification of Nonclastic Sedimentary Rocks

Main Constituent(s)	Rock Group	Rock
Calcite Dolomite	Carbonate	Limestone Dolostone
Gypsum Anhydrite Halite	Evaporite	Rock Gypsum Rock Anhydrite Rock Salt
Quartz and related minerals (chalcedony, opal)	Siliceous	Chert (light) Flint (dark) Diatomite
Hematite, limonite, siderite	Iron-rich	Ironstone (massive)
Magnetite, hematite, pyrite		Iron Formation (banded)
Plant material	Carbonaceous	Peat Lignite Coal Bituminous Coal Anthracite Coal
Apatite	Phosphate	Phosphate Rock (Phosphorite)

Clastic Rocks

Coarse-grained clastic rocks (Table 16-1) consist of lithified **gravel**, made up of an appreciable amount of particles greater than 0.08 inch (2 mm) in diameter. Ideally, "appreciable" means 50 percent or more, but geologists may call a sediment "gravel" with only 10 percent gravel-sized particles. Gravel includes **boulders** (greater than 10.1 inches or 256 mm in diameter), **cobbles** (2.5 inches to 10.1 inches or 64 mm to 256 mm), and **pebbles** (0.08 inches to 2.5 inches or 2mm to 64 mm).

Lithified gravel is **conglomerate** (Figure 16-1) if the particle edges are rounded, **breccia** (Figure 16-2) if the particle edges are sharp or angular. (Loose sediment of coarse angular particles may be called **rubble**.) Besides the coarse-grained constituents of rock fragments (most common) or minerals, these rocks commonly have a **matrix** of finer sediment, a mineral **cement** that binds the particles, or both. A more detailed name, then, is based on the composition of the framework particles, the matrix, and the composition of the cement. How detailed the name depends on your choice. A coarse-grained clastic rock of largely quartz pebbles in a sandstone matrix and cemented by calcite may be called by a variety of names: pebble conglomerate; quartz pebble conglomerate; sandy conglomerate; sandy, quartz-pebble conglomerate; or limy (or **calcareous**), sandy, quartz-pebble conglomerate.

Conglomerates accumulate in such **sedimentary environ-**

Figure 16-1. Conglomerate, of rounded pebbles of chert and other rock fragments. Cavities represent places once occupied by pebbles. Height of specimen is 4.5 inches (11.4 cm).

FIGURE 16-2. Breccia, of angular, pebble-sized chert fragments. Height of specimen is 3.3 inches (8.4 cm).

ments—places with certain physical, chemical, and biological conditions in which sediments are deposited—as alluvial fans, stream channels, and beaches. Breccias may form at the base of cliffs or steep slopes by rockfalls or rockslides.

Coarse-grained clastic sedimentary rocks grade into volcanic agglomerate and volcanic breccia as the amount of igneous fragmental rock (see chapter 15) material increases.

Medium-grained clastic rocks consist of lithified **sand**, of which 50 percent or more of the particles are 0.002 inch to 0.08 inch (0.06 mm to 2 mm) in diameter. Sand feels gritty when rubbed between your fingers. **Sandstone** (Figure 16-3) with conspicuous coarser or finer particles than sand is a conglomeratic or muddy (described under fine-grained rocks) sandstone. Sandstone with 50 percent or more quartz, feldspar, or rock fragments may be termed **quartz sandstone**, **feldspar sandstone**, or **rock fragment** (or **lithic**) **sandstone**. Other minerals, too, if conspicuous, may enter into the rock name; the abundance of mica, for example, gives rise to a mica or **micaceous** sandstone. Quartz is the most common mineral of sandstones and may constitute 90 percent or more of such rocks. Feldspar in appreciable amounts is uncommon; sandstone with 25 or 30 percent or more feldspar, however, may also be called **arkose** (ARE-kohse). Another sandstone name, in disfavor with some, is **graywacke**, (GRAY-whack or GRAY-whack-ee), which denotes a "dirty" or muddy (15% or more mud) sandstone of angular particles of quartz, feldspar, rock fragments, and mica that vary in their proportions.

Figure 16-3. Sandstone, of largely quartz and feldspar, from the west shore of Tomales Bay, Marin County, California. Width of specimen is 4.8 inches (12.2 cm).

As with the coarse-grained rocks, sandstone names may be as complex as you wish to make them, with modifiers given in order of increasing abundance of the contained minerals. A sandstone mainly of framework particles of quartz (40%), feldspar (20%), and rock fragments (15%), and bound together by a muddy (15%) matrix and calcite cement (10%), could be called a limy (or calcareous), muddy, rock fragment, feldspar, quartz sandstone—or simply feldspar quartz sandstone.

Sandstones form in stream and tidal channels, alluvial fans, dunes, on the tops and fronts of deltas, on beaches, and in shallow seas.

Sandstones grade into tuff as the amount of volcanic ash and dust (see chapter 15) increases. A sandstone with considerable ash or dust is a tuff (or **tuffaceous**) sandstone.

Fine-grained clastic rocks are made up of lithified **silt** or **clay**—the two together are called **mud**—particles, 50 percent or more of which are less than 0.002 inch (0.06 mm) in diameter. Silt particles are barely discernible with the unaided eye and feel slightly gritty between the fingers and teeth. (Yes, some geologists "chew" sediment to estimate the particle size!) Clay particles are indistinguishable with the unaided eye, lack grittiness between the teeth, and are smooth or slippery when rubbed between the fingers. Clay, in a size sense, refers to a sediment of clay-sized particles. But clay may consist, in part, of clay minerals along with such other minerals as quartz and feldspar. A rock rich in clay minerals sticks to the tongue and exudes a strong earthy odor after being breathed upon.

Lithified mud is **mudstone** if blocky—fragments break out of exposures in small blocks—or **shale** (Figure 16-4) if **fissile** (FISS-uhl)—fragments break out into thin sheets or plates parallel

FIGURE 16-4. Shale, from Somerville, New Jersey, showing the rock's capability of breaking into thin sheets. Width of specimen is 4.7 inches (11.9 cm).

FIGURE 16-5. Siltstone, from near Newhall, California, showing blocky character, unlike the thin-sheet fracturing of shale (Figure 16-4). Width of specimen is 4.2 inches (10.7 cm).

to the layering or bedding. Shale and mudstone are the most abundant sedimentary rocks. Silt lithifies to **siltstone** (Figure 16-5), clay to **claystone**; these rocks are generally not fissile.

In the field, fine-grained rocks are named largely on the basis of color, which reflects composition. Red shale (or mudstone) is usually colored by the iron oxide hematite. Limonite tends to produce yellow or brown shales. Green shale is often colored by other iron compounds, but here the iron ion has a charge of $+2$ instead of $+3$, and is said to be "ferrous," not "ferric." Green may also be produced by other minerals; one example is glauconite, a silicate of iron, magnesium, aluminum, and potassium, that forms in seas. Gray or black shales often contain variable amounts of organic matter; the darker the shale, the more the organic matter. (Shales rich in organic matter also tend to be more fissile.) But shales may be black from fine particles of iron sulfide. Remember that the streak, the color of the powdered mineral (see chapter 14), of the iron sulfide pyrite is greenish black.

Fine-grained rocks may also be named on the basis of coarser admixtures or composition. Appreciable amounts of gravel or sand, for example, result in conglomeratic mudstone or sandy shale. Considerable carbonate or mica produces a limy (or calcareous) or micaceous shale.

Shales, mudstones, siltstones, and claystones accumulate in a variety of quiet-water environments: the deeper parts of seas and lakes, lagoons, tidal flats, deltas, backswamps, and floodplains.

Origin of Clastic Rocks

Sediments originate at Earth's surface by the in-place breakup of rocks by chemical and physical means—weathering (see chapter 23). The loose, decayed rock debris is transported by running water but also moves via wind, and glacial ice, and is deposited in a myriad of sedimentary environments, several of which have been already mentioned. Sediments accumulate, layer upon layer, until they lithify to rock.

Lithification, which involves a reduction in the pore space between particles or crystals, is accomplished mainly by compaction or cementation. In **compaction**, which is most significant for the fine-grained sediments, pore space is reduced by pressure that results from the weight of overlying rock and sediment. Particles become packed and lithify into a tight mass. In **cementation**, spaces between particles are filled with mineral matter and particles are cemented together to a lithified whole. Mineral matter can be precipitated into pore space by either fresh groundwater or seawater. Cementation is most effective for the lithification of sand and gravel.

Nonclastic Rocks

Carbonate rocks contain 50 percent or more carbonate minerals, chiefly calcite that forms **limestone** and dolomite that forms **dolostone**. (Some geologists also use the term "dolomite" for the rock.) Both limestone and dolostone are easily scratched with a knife and come in an array of colors from white to black. Limestone bubbles with vigor when dilute acid is added; dolostone bubbles weakly or not at all. If a drop of acid is placed on the powdered dolostone grooved out by a knife blade, however, the bubbling is vigorous.

Limestone, the most abundant nonclastic rock, is more common than dolostone and may consist of several constituents: organic remains such as fossil shells or coral (see chapter 18); carbonate rock particles; oolites or pisolites; calcite crystals; and calcite cement. A limestone that contains an abundant supply of unbroken fossils is an organic or fossiliferous limestone (Figure 16-6). **Chalk**, visualized in the form of blackboard chalk, is a

Figure 16-6. Fossil-bearing or fossiliferous limestone, from near Guttenberg, Iowa, made up largely of shells of brachiopods (see Figure 18-6). Width of specimen is 5.1 inches (12.9 cm).

crumbly organic limestone made up of the limy parts of single-celled plants and animals. A rock of broken fossils or carbonate rock fragments is a **clastic limestone** (Table 16-1) and has all the characteristics of any other clastic rock. **Coquina** (koh-KEE-nuh) (from the Spanish word for "shellfish") is a clastic limestone of coarse-grained fossil fragments. **Lithographic limestone** is the lithified equivalent of lime mud precipitated from seawater, and has been used for lithography because of its fine, even grain. **Oolites** (OH-uh-lights; resemble fish eggs) (Figure 16-9), less than 0.08 inch (2 mm) in diameter, and the larger **pisolites** (PIE-suh-lights; resemble peas) are spheroidal or ellipsoidal particles formed by chemical precipitation in shallow, wave-agitated waters, such as those on the Bahama Banks. Limestones in which oolites or pisolites predominate are called oolitic or pisolitic limestones. A minor limestone precipitated from spring water, hot or cold, is **travertine** (TRAV-uhr-teen) (Figure 16-7). It includes the dripstone and flowstone found in caves (see chapter 6).

Limestones grade into dolostones, and both rocks grade into noncarbonate clastic rocks. Intermediates include dolomitic limestone, calcitic dolostone, shaly limestone (dolostone), and sandy limestone (dolostone).

Dolostone develops by direct precipitation from seawater or the later replacement of limestones.

Evaporites—the most common of which are **rock gypsum**, **rock anhydrite**, and **rock salt** (Table 16-2)—form by evaporation of brines. That is, these salts precipitate from brines that are concentrated by evaporation. A necessary requirement for evaporation is an arid climate. In addition, briny waters must be partially separated from the main ocean so the salt concentration can increase by evaporation. For example, gypsum and anhydrite precipitate today at the margins of the Persian Gulf. Evaporites also form in some lakes in arid regions.

FIGURE 16-7. Porous travertine, a variety of limestone, deposited by springs (see Figure 6-8), near Yellowstone National Park, Wyoming. Height of specimen is 5.8 inches (14.7 cm).

FIGURE 16-8. Alabaster, a fine-grained variety of rock gypsum, from Rapid City, South Dakota. Height of specimen is 4.3 inches (10.9 cm).

All of the three common evaporites are crystalline—like the igneous rocks, coarse- to fine-grained, and most commonly white, although they may have a variety of tints. Each consists almost entirely of gypsum, anhydrite, or halite, with few mineral impurities. All can be readily scratched with a knife, and rock gypsum can be scratched with a fingernail. Rock salt, of course, has a salty taste. **Alabaster** (Figure 16-8) is massive, fine-grained, white or tinted rock gypsum that may be shaped into ornamental objects.

All three evaporites are often associated with one another and with carbonate rocks, especially dolostone, and shales. Rock anhydrite alters to rock gypsum in exposures by the addition of water. Because of a tendency to dissolve, rock salt occurs at the surface only in very arid regions, such as Great Salt Lake, Utah, and Death Valley, California.

Siliceous rocks consist of silica—silicon plus oxygen (SiO_2)—in the form of quartz, which includes microcrystalline chalcedony and related minerals and noncrystalline opal. **Chert**, of microcrystalline quartz and the most common siliceous rock, is light-colored, dense, harder than a knife, and exhibits shell-like fracture. Chert may include oolites (Figure 16-9) if silica has replaced oolitic limestone. **Flint** (Figure 16-10) is dark gray to black chert that owes its color to included organic matter. Because of its hardness and durability, aboriginals have favored flint to fashion weapons and implements. **Jasper** is yellow, brown, or red chert colored by limonite or hematite.

FIGURE 16-9. Chert, with numerous oolites, from Centre County, Pennsylvania. Width of specimen is 4.0 inches (10.2 cm).

FIGURE 16-10. Flint, a variety of chert, showing shell-like fracture; Dover Cliffs, England. Width of specimen is 4.5 inches (11.4 cm).

Chert (and flint) occurs in nodules and beds. Such nodules (defined under Sedimentary Rock Structures) are discrete, often irregular, even lumpy, masses in carbonate rocks. Bedded chert is associated with shales and iron formations (described under iron-rich rocks). Chert may form by the direct, inorganic precipitation of a jellylike silica mass from seawater; replacement of other rocks, such as limestones; or by organic precipitation of silica by such organisms as diatoms (mentioned below), radiolarians (single-celled animals with siliceous shells), and certain sponges that secrete spicules or needlelike elements of opal.

Other siliceous rocks include white or gray siliceous sinter, deposited by hot springs or geysers (geyserite) (see Figure 6-7), and **diatomite** (die-AT-uh-might) (Figure 16-11), composed of the microscopic siliceous shells of single-celled plants called diatoms. Diatomite, or the more crumbly **diatomaceous** (die-uht-uh-MAY-shuhs) **earth**, is usually white, chalklike—but does not bubble in acid—is somewhat gritty when rubbed between the fingers, and generally lacks the earthy odor of clay minerals when breathed upon. Diatomites form in both fresh and marine waters.

Iron-rich rocks of sedimentary origin contain about 15 percent or more iron, which is difficult if not impossible to estimate. A little iron goes a long way, and rocks appear to contain more iron than they do.

The iron-rich rocks group into ironstone and banded iron formation. **Ironstone** (Figure 16-12) may be of almost any sedimentary rock type but especially mudstone, sandstone, and limestone; ironstone is massive to poorly banded, and almost always of Cambrian age or younger. The most common minerals of iron-

Figure 16-11. Chalklike diatomite, from Santa Barbara County, California, showing thin layering. Height of specimen is 1.1 inch (2.8 cm).

FIGURE 16-12. Ironstone, of oolitic hematite, from the Clinton Formation (Silurian) of Clinton, New York. Height of specimen is 3.1 inches (7.9 cm).

stone are hematite, limonite, and siderite (SID-uh-right). Siderite, an iron carbonate mineral, looks like brown calcite but is heavier and somewhat harder, though capable of being scratched by a knife; siderite often alters to limonite. Much of the hematitic ironstone consists of oolitic hematite or other hematite that has replaced fossils or filled spaces between them. The Silurian Clinton Formation, which extends from New York to Alabama, contains such hematitic ironstone, a commercial iron ore. Thin-bedded **banded iron formation** (Figure 16-13), also called **taconite**, most often contains layers of magnetite, hematite, or pyrite (uncommonly) that alternate with chert (jasper) or quartz. Banded iron formation is nearly always of Precambrian age. The extensive banded iron formation near western Lake Superior is renowned.

Iron-rich rocks have been formed largely in shallow seas, either by direct precipitation of iron minerals or by the later iron-replacement of other rocks. Minor iron-rich rocks (ironstones) have also formed in lakes or bogs (bog iron ore).

Carbonaceous rocks—they bear carbon—include peat (strictly a sediment rather than a rock) and coal. **Peat** (Figure 16-14) is a brown-to-black accumulation of plant matter, which resembles compressed or chewing tobacco dependent on the depth of burial. Under pressure, peat converts to **coal**—lignite, bituminous, and anthracite, in order of increasing rank created as the coal is subjected to additional pressure and heat. As carbonaceous material passes through the coalification progression, luster im-

Figure 16-13. Banded iron formation, of largely alternate bands or layers of hematite (lustrous) and jasper (iron-bearing chert; dull). Width of specimen is 7.7 inches (19.6 cm).

Figure 16-14. Peat, from Cambridge, Massachusetts, showing plant fragments on a surface of layering. Height of specimen is 2.9 inches (7.4 cm).

proves, carbon content and heating value increase, and moisture and gas content decrease. **Lignite** (Figure 16-15) is brown to black, lacks luster, often displays original wood structure, and burns readily with a smoky flame and strong odor. Lignite may contain as much as 40 percent moisture and crumbles upon exposure to the atmosphere. **Bituminous coal** (Figure 16-16) is black, has a glassy or pitchy luster evidenced in distinct bands or layers, lacks original wood structure, and does not crumble upon exposure. **Anthracite coal** (Figure 16-17) displays glassy to submetallic luster and shell-like fracture, is more difficult to ignite than lignite or bituminous coal, and burns with little smoke or odor.

Coal originates in swamps where luxurious vegetation proliferates in a humid climate. Plant matter partially decomposes in the standing water and accumulates to form peat. Burial by over-

FIGURE 16-15. Lignite coal, from southwestern North Dakota, showing cracking and crumbling upon exposure to air. Width of specimen is 4.3 inches (10.9 cm).

FIGURE 16-16. Bituminous coal, from Pittsburgh, Pennsylvania, showing pitchy luster and banding. Width of left front surface is 3.1 inches (7.9 cm).

FIGURE 16-17. Anthracite coal, from Jeddo, Pennsylvania, showing glassy luster and shell-like fracture. Height of specimen is 2.3 inches (5.8 cm).

lying sediment compresses the peat and coalification occurs. Older coals tend to be of higher rank because of the likelihood of deeper burial, but exceptions occur. Coals of higher rank also are found near intrusive igneous rock bodies and where rocks have been intensely folded. In western Pennsylvania, for example, where strata are nearly flat-lying, the coal is bituminous; in eastern Pennsylvania, mined anthracite is enclosed within folded strata that have undergone considerable deformation. Most coals are of Pennsylvanian, Cretaceous, or Tertiary age. They associate primarily with shales, mudstones, and sandstones.

Phosphate rock or **phosphorite** consists mainly of apatite, but this mineral is unrecognizable in the rock as found in the field. This rock resembles limestone, but does not bubble when acid is applied, and is heavier. Phosphate rock is often black, but may be almost any color from white to black. It frequently contains oolites, pisolites, sand-sized pellets and larger nodules, and fossil bone, fish teeth and scales, and shells. Interbedded strata often include limestone, mudstone, and chert. Much phosphate rock occurs, for example, in the Permian Phosphoria Formation of Idaho and adjacent states. Phosphate rock originated largely in the sea by direct precipitation or by later replacement of limestones. Upwelling and the consequent arrival of nutrient-rich bottom water toward the surface seem conducive to the precipitation of phosphate.

Sedimentary Rock Structures

Sedimentary rock structures are large-scale features best seen in rock exposures. They help identify sedimentary rocks and help interpret the sedimentary environment in which a sediment was laid down. Some structures were formed at the time a sediment was deposited, others originated later.

Stratification, or layering or bedding, is the most distinctive structure of sedimentary rocks, formed when a sediment is laid down and emphasized by exposure to weathering and erosion (Figure 16-18). The layers so formed may also be called **beds** or **strata** (singular, **stratum**). Certain igneous rocks, such as basalt in flows, are stratified as well but stratification is best developed in sedimentary rocks. Large-scale stratification displays changes in major rock type; small-scale stratification reflects changes in size and composition of grains that make up a sedimentary rock.

Original bedding is normally horizontal but **cross-bedding**

FIGURE 16-18. Stratification or layering of sedimentary rocks, emphasized by uneven erosion of hard and soft strata, Grand Canyon National Park, northwestern Arizona. The deeper, inner gorge is cut into metamorphic and intrusive igneous rocks. (Photograph 238-197-63 by the National Park Service.)

(see Figure 3-4 and the photograph that introduces Part IV), stratification that occurs at an angle, is produced when water or wind currents deposit sediment on a slope. Cross-bedding develops in sand ridges that orient at about right angles to a current; these ridges—dunes, sand bars, sand waves, and ripples—vary in size from less than half an inch (ripples) to several hundred feet (dunes) high. Sand ridges with cross-bedding are asymmetrical in profile; the steeper slope faces down-current. Water or wind currents carry sand grains up and over a sand ridge; the grains slide down the steeper, down-current slope and accumulate into inclined layers or cross-beds. Imagine the cross-beds (beds inside a sand dune) viewed as if the dune were sliced through vertically by a huge knife.

An understanding of the way cross-bedding forms helps us to decipher the directions of flow of ancient currents. We can measure the directions of inclination of cross-beds in rocks and plot them on maps. The compilations of measurements enable us to work out ancient current patterns (see Figure 12-5).

Another type of stratification is **graded bedding**, in which grains of sediment gradually grade in size from coarse at the bottom of a bed to fine at the top. To understand how graded bedding forms, place a half cup measure of sediment with mixed grain sizes—small pebbles to silt—in a quart jar of water. Shake the jar upside down until all the sediment is in suspension, then set the jar down upright. Watch the sediment grains settle out of suspension: pebbles first, followed by sand, then by silt—to produce a graded bed.

In nature, graded bedding is often generated by **turbidity currents**, those which flow down a slope and owe their high density to sediment carried in suspension. In the sea, turbid (muddy) water flows down the continental slope and onto the flat ocean basin floor. As velocity of the turbidity current is checked at the base of the continental slope, coarser sediment particles settle out first, followed by finer ones; when the current halts, the finest silt and clay particles are the last to settle. Each turbidity current episode produces a graded bed; stacked graded beds, one above the other, evidence several turbidity current episodes. Earthquakes and submarine landslides can generate turbidity currents in the sea. Streams can also generate such currents as they release dense, muddy water into deep lakes and reservoirs.

Other sedimentary structures that form when a sediment is deposited are such surface features as ripple marks, mud cracks, and pockmarking raindrop impressions. **Ripple marks** (Figure

FIGURE 16-19. Ripple marks, in quartz sandstone from Missouri. Length of specimen, front to back, is 11.4 inches (29.0 cm).

16-19) are tiny parallel ridges effected by the drag of currents and waves that move over sediment. Wave-produced ripple marks are symmetrical in profile and tend to parallel lake and ocean shorelines. Current-produced ripple marks are asymmetrical in profile and orient at right angles to the currents that generate them. Such ripple marks are found on sand dunes, in streambeds, on tidal flats, and on shallow bottoms of lakes and seas—shallow enough so that currents can move and shape sandy sediment. Current ripple marks often display small-scale cross-bedding. Ripple marks give clues to positions of ancient shorelines, current directions, and relative water depth.

Mud cracks, which outline mud polygons, form wherever wet, fine-grained sediment dries out when exposed to the air. When found in rocks, mud cracks signify sediment laid down on tidal flats, mud flats of shallow lakes, and muddy stream banks.

Raindrop impressions are miniature craters with raised rims, best developed in mud, that record impacts of raindrops. Larger and deeper impressions may result from the impact of hailstones. Raindrop and hailstone impressions in rocks record the same historical imprint as do mud cracks, muddy sedimentary surfaces exposed for a time to the air.

Fossils (see chapter 18) may be considered organic sedimentary structures, whether they are actual remains of organisms or such traces as tracks, trails, or borings. Both groups of fossils reflect much about the sedimentary environments that gave rise to the rocks that contain them. The trace fossils, in particular, had to have formed while sediments were being deposited or not long after.

Some sedimentary structures form, in the main, after sedi-

FIGURE 16-20. Concretions, of siltstone from near Medora, North Dakota. Width of left, broken concretion is 3.3 inches (8.4 cm).

ment is deposited by chemical action. Nodules and concretions are notable examples; both are segregations of mineral matter. Definitions of nodules and concretions vary somewhat from geologist to geologist. Here are mine. **Nodules** are regular or irregular bodies of mineral matter unlike in composition to that of the host rock in which they are found. Chert and flint nodules in carbonate rocks are examples. **Concretions** (Figure 16-20) are discrete bodies—often spheroidal, ellipsoidal, or disk-shaped—with a composition similar to that of the host rock except for the mineral cement, which is frequently calcite, silica, or iron oxide. Some people call the spheroidal types "cannonball" concretions. Concretions may have a fossil nucleus and a concentric internal structure; some concretions serve as concentrations of fossils. Oolites and pisolites may be thought of as miniature concretions, but they form at the time a sediment is deposited.

Suggested Reading

Arem, Joel. *Rocks and Minerals*. Phoenix, AZ: Geoscience Press, 1991.

Chesterman, C. W. *The Audubon Society Field Guide to North American Rocks and Minerals*. New York: Alfred A. Knopf, 1978.

Hamilton, W. R., A. R. Woolley, and A. C. Bishop. *The Henry Holt Guide to Minerals, Rocks, and Fossils*. New York: Henry Holt, 1989.

Mottana, Annibale, Rodolfo Crespi, and Guiseppe Liborio. *Simon and Schuster's Guide to Rocks and Minerals*. New York: Simon & Schuster, 1978.

Pellant, Chris. *Rocks, Minerals & Fossils of the World*. Boston: Little, Brown, 1990.

Pough, F. H. *Peterson First Guide to Rocks and Minerals*. Boston: Houghton Mifflin, 1991.

Sorrell, C. A. *A Field Guide and Introduction to the Geology and Chemistry of Rocks and Minerals*. New York: Golden Press, 1973.

Zim, H. S., and P. R. Shaffer. *Rocks and Minerals: A Guide to Familiar Minerals, Gems, Ores and Rocks*. New York: Golden Press, 1957.

17

Metamorphic Rocks

As mentioned in chapter 15, metamorphic rocks originate from the alteration of preexisting rocks—igneous, sedimentary, or other metamorphic—by the action of heat, pressure, and chemically active fluids and gases. Metamorphic rocks are exposed on the land surface to as great an extent as igneous rocks, and most of the rocks beneath sedimentary rocks on continents are metamorphic. Metamorphic rocks, therefore, deserve a close look, although, at times, they are more difficult to identify than igneous or sedimentary rocks.

Main Metamorphic Rock-Forming Minerals

Since metamorphic rocks derive from igneous and sedimentary rocks, we might suspect metamorphic rock-forming minerals to be similar to the minerals of those two rock groups. Common, therefore, are quartz, feldspars, micas, amphiboles, pyroxenes, and carbonate minerals. Other minerals, however, such as graphite (see Figure 14-1), talc (see Figure 14-14), chlorite (see Figure 14-20), serpentine (see Figures 14-22, 14-23), and garnet (see Figure 14-30), are characteristic of, but not restricted to, metamorphic rocks. Still others, such as staurolite (see Figure 17-4) and kyanite, are restricted to metamorphic rocks.

Classifying and Identifying Metamorphic Rocks

The classification of metamorphic rocks (Table 17-1) is based, first, on whether they are foliated and, second, on grain size and composition. **Foliation** (from the Latin *folium*, "leaf"; literally, "splitting into leaflike layers") is a layering in metamorphic rocks caused by the parallel arrangement of platy or elongate minerals. Micas are platy minerals, and amphiboles, for example, tend to occur as elongate crystals. Pressure-induced foliation produces **rock cleavage**, the tendency for rocks to split into sheets along well-defined surfaces. Don't confuse rock cleavage with mineral cleavage, the tendency for *minerals* to split along planes because of weaknesses in internal atomic bonding.

TABLE 17-1. Classification of Metamorphic Rocks

Foliated		Nonfoliated
Mostly from Regional Metamorphism	**From Mechanical Metamorphism**	**Mostly from Contact Metamorphism**
Slate	Fault Breccia	Metaconglomerate
Phyllite	Mylonite	Metabreccia
Schist		Quartzite
Gneiss		Marble
		Hornfels
		Serpentinite

FIGURE 17-1. Black slate, showing good slaty rock cleavage. Length of the upper (right) slab is 7.0 inches (17.8 cm).

Foliated Rocks

Slate (Figure 17-1) is a fine-grained foliated rock—the grains are invisible with the unaided eye or hand lens—that splits into thin sheets and has good slaty cleavage. Don't confuse slaty cleavage with the original bedding of the parent rock from which slate evolved; slaty cleavage is often at some angle to the original bedding. When slate is struck with a metal object, such as the handle of a pocket knife, you often hear a tinkling sound. Slate is most often gray or black but may be green, purple, red, brown, or yellow. This rock develops from the metamorphism of shale, tuff, and other fine-grained rocks.

Phyllite (FILL-ight) (from the Greek *phyllon*, "leaf") differs from slate by its coarser-grained, visible mica flakes that impart a satiny sheen on rock cleavage surfaces. This rock forms under higher pressures and temperatures than does slate.

Schist (SHIST) (from the Greek *schistos*, "that may be split") is a medium- to coarse-grained foliated rock in which the mineral grains, in particular, the micaceous ones, are eminently visible. Rock cleavage is distinct (Figure 17-2) but not as well developed as in slate and phyllite. The numerous varieties of schist, with a spectrum of colors, are named after prominent minerals. Examples include talc schist, graphite schist, chlorite schist, biotite schist,

FIGURE 17-2. Exposure of quartz biotite schist, showing distinct, steeply dipping rock cleavage. The weathered, upturned edges of the schist are bent to the right because of creep, the slow, down-slope movement of rock, soil, and sediment (see chapter 7).

garnet mica schist (Figure 17-3), and staurolite mica schist (Figure 17-4). Schist derives from a wide group of rocks that include shale, sandstone, tuff, basalt, felsite, and gabbro. Metamorphism of higher intensity is required to produce schist than to produce phyllite or slate.

Gneiss (NICE) is a coarse-grained metamorphic rock with poor foliation and rock cleavage. Minerals—more quartz and feldspar than micaceous minerals—tend to segregate into light and dark bands that are often folded or contorted as seen in exposures. Most gneiss has the composition of granite—granite gneiss—but composition varies and, therefore, so does color. Varieties of gneiss are named after rock composition (as for granite gneiss) or major minerals: Examples include mica gneiss, biotite gneiss (Figure 17-5), and hornblende gneiss. Gneiss derives from a host of rocks that include granitic rocks, diorite, gabbro, felsite, tuff, shale, and sandstone. Gneiss forms under higher pressures and temperatures than do schist, phyllite, and slate.

Fault breccia and **mylonite**, minor metamorphic rocks, form in fault zones by the mechanical mashing and pulverizing of rock against rock. Fault or crush breccia resembles sedimentary

FIGURE 17-3. Garnet mica schist—looking along the direction of well-developed foliation—from New York, showing two well-developed garnet crystals. Width of the rock specimen is 4.2 inches (10.7 cm).

FIGURE 17-4. Staurolite mica schist, from Little Falls, Minnesota, showing foliation surfaces and intergrown (crossed) staurolite crystals in the upper right. Width of the rock specimen is 4.8 inches (12.2 cm).

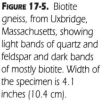

FIGURE 17-5. Biotite gneiss, from Uxbridge, Massachusetts, showing light bands of quartz and feldspar and dark bands of mostly biotite. Width of the specimen is 4.1 inches (10.4 cm).

breccia and must be recovered from a fault zone to substantiate its identity. Foliation may not always be obvious. This rock forms near the surface under low confining pressure (pressure that is equal in all directions). Mylonite (from the Greek *mylon*, "a mill") is a fine-grained, flintlike or felsitelike, tough rock that often appears streaked as if it has been smeared out. Mylonite has, literally, passed through a metamorphic mill. Depth and confining pressure are greater than for fault breccia. Both mylonite and fault breccia vary to a great degree in composition, which depends on the rocks involved in faulting.

Nonfoliated Rocks

Metaconglomerate and **metabreccia** are nonfoliated metamorphic rocks that differ from their sedimentary equivalents in being more durable, and rock fractures pass *through* particles instead of around them. The same characteristics are present in **quartzite**, metamorphosed sandstone.

Marble (Figure 17-6) is metamorphosed limestone and dolostone, and sparkles in reflected light. The sparkling results from recrystallization (discussed under Origin of Metamorphic Rocks) during the metamorphic process; the interlocked crystals that form are often larger than the grains of the original carbonate rock. Because marble consists mostly of calcite and dolomite, easy scratching by a knife and the capacity to bubble with acid identify this rock. Be aware, however, that various accessory minerals, such as garnet, feldspar, graphite, and apatite, might also be present. Marble is normally light-colored, but almost any color from white to black is possible. A "marbling" effect from impurities that stripe or blotch the rock is common.

Hornfels (HORN-felz) is a fine-grained, dense, nonfoliated rock that resembles dark chert, basalt, or nonfoliated slate. It is usually gray or black. Hornfels develops from metamorphism by

Figure 17-6. Pink marble, from Tate, Georgia, showing the sparkle of recrystallized crystal faces and cleavage surfaces. Width of the specimen is 4.1 inches (10.4 cm).

igneous intrusions; this rock usually derives from shale, but basalt and felsite are among other possible parent rocks.

Serpentinite (sir-puhn-TEEN-ite), as the name implies, is a rock composed mostly of serpentine with the general properties of that mineral. Normally green, this rock varies from yellow to black. Common associated minerals are olivine, pyroxene, and amphibole. This rock serves as a host for nickel and chromium ores. Serpentinite derives from the alteration of igneous rocks, such as peridotite and pyroxenite, and metamorphic rocks, exemplified by amphibole schist.

Origin of Metamorphic Rocks

Through metamorphism, a rock changes in texture, composition, or internal structure as it adjusts or responds to a new geologic environment. Such change, an attempt to reach equilibrium with new environmental conditions, occurs within the solid (nonmolten or nonliquid) state and is apart from the domain of igneous activity. New minerals form, but no real change occurs in the bulk composition of the rocks so affected—elements are not added or removed from the system but merely reshuffled.

Agents of Metamorphism

Agents responsible for metamorphic changes are increased *heat* and *pressure* and *chemically active fluids* and *gases*. These agents tend to work in concert more often than alone.

Greater heat increases the activity of ions and causes the breakdown of minerals; but increased heat also causes more vigorous chemical reactions and the recombination of ions to form new minerals in a new thermal environment. Heat drives off water from minerals and provides more water in the pore space between grains. The increased heat-water combination softens rocks and causes them to yield under pressure. Heat derives from (1) that released from Earth's core; (2) the decay of radioactive minerals; (3) molten rock or magma; and (4) frictional heat generated as rock masses grind against one another during large-scale Earth movements.

High pressure caused by the weight of piled rock strata makes underlying rocks more compact as pore space between grains is reduced. But this downward pressure doesn't contribute much to metamorphism; sideways-directed pressure at considerable depth, by large-scale Earth movements, is significant and causes a directional property to develop in many metamorphic rocks. Large crystals, pebbles, and fossils may be smeared out to several times their length. But more important is the development of foliation as newly formed platy or elongate minerals align themselves at right angles to sideways pressure or parallel to shearing pressure. We've already examined in chapter 12 the manner by which extensive vertically foliated rocks form from Earth-plate squeezing during mountain building. Where shearing pressures are involved, however, two opposed pressures glide past one another. To visualize this process, imagine thin plastic disks cut out with a hole puncher (to mimic mica flakes) and placed in a ball of modeling clay. As the ball of clay is sheared or smeared between two boards, which represent opposed shearing pressures, the plastic disks tend to align themselves parallel to one another and simulate foliation. Shearing in nature occurs where two opposed Earth plates slide past one another.

Chemically active fluids and gases act as solvents, speed up chemical reactions, and serve as media by which ions can be transported through pore space between grains to form new minerals. The most important fluid is water, derived from (1) original seawater trapped in sediments; (2) magmas; and (3) water molecules combined chemically in minerals.

A significant process that often involves the three metamorphic agents in combination is **recrystallization**, a change in crystal size or mineral composition as material is dissolved and removed in some places and added elsewhere. For example, solution by pressure occurs at points of greater stress, and addition or precipitation—growth of minerals—occurs in places of lesser stress. Increased heat accelerates solution and precipitation, and fluids and gases enhance solution and facilitate the recombination of ions for precipitation.

Kinds of Metamorphism

Contact metamorphism develops from a body of magma in *contact* with surrounding rocks. Increased heat is the primary cause of rock alteration, although pressure is also influential. A baked zone of contact metamorphism (see Figure 15-14) surrounds an exposed intrusive mass, often a few hundred feet wide and rarely a few thousand feet wide. The degree or intensity of metamorphism lessens gradually away from the intrusive body, and is reflected by key minerals, which depend on the rock types intruded and the temperatures reached. These minerals, and associated rocks, can be perceived to occur in concentric cylinders or zones that envelop the intrusive body. Sillimanite (SILL-uh-muh-night), for example, may occur adjacent to the intrusive, followed outward in order by kyanite, staurolite, garnet, biotite, and chlorite.

The nonfoliated rocks form mostly by contact metamorphism (Table 17-1). Rare is the rock, however, that forms strictly by this process. As an aside, the grades of nonfoliated coal may be thought of in terms of a metamorphic progression—peat, lignite, bituminous, and anthracite. Further metamorphism of anthracite may produce graphite.

Regional metamorphism, or large-scale metamorphism not linked with obvious intrusive bodies, has formed the greatest volume of metamorphic rock. This type of metamorphism involves areas of thousands of square miles, elongate regions that have undergone mountain building (see chapter 12). Tremendous pressures have caused the primary rock alteration, although high temperatures have contributed as well; both high pressures and temperatures have occurred at considerable depths—in the roots of mountain belts. As for contact metamorphism, key minerals reflect the degree or intensity of metamorphism. Staurolite schist (Figure 17-4), for example, has formed at higher pressures and temperatures than garnet schist (Figure 17-3).

Plate tectonic theory explains that huge Earth plates have slammed together to squeeze sediments and rocks between them, as in a vise. Metamorphic rocks are best developed in the roots of folded mountain belts derived from converging plates. Foliation is vertical or at a high angle and parallels the margins of the plates. As rocks of a descending plate reach a critical, hot depth, they melt, along with certain of the deepest squeezed metamorphic rocks. Lighter magma from the melted rocks rises and intrudes the shallower metamorphic rocks to produce the extensive batholiths at the cores of mountain belts. When we see extensive tracts of metamorphic rocks and associated intrusives, even where planed relatively flat, as in the great Canadian Shield of eastern and central Canada, we can conclude these rocks represent the roots of former mountain belts, brought to view by much erosion over long periods of time.

The foliated rocks originate mostly by regional metamorphism (Table 17-1). Slate, phyllite, schist, and gneiss form a metamorphic series, with gneiss produced by the greatest pressure and associated heat. In the progression from slate to gneiss, foliation and rock cleavage become poorer and grain size increases.

Mechanical or **dynamic metamorphism** occurs, in the main, by rock deformation. The type of mechanical metamorphism that produces fault breccia and mylonite merges into regional metamorphism with greater depths and associated higher pressures and temperatures. Breccia may also form by mechanical metamorphism as the pressure of an igneous intrusion fragments surrounding rock.

Another rather intriguing type of mechanical metamorphism, **shock metamorphism**, occurs by the impact of meteors or underground nuclear explosions. In a fraction of a second, shock waves produce very high pressures and temperatures. Rock is shattered to form breccia and some is fused. Shock-formed natural glass is created along with distinctive types of quartz from quartz-bearing rocks such as sandstones. On the moon and similar bodies with abundant meteoritic impact craters, shock metamorphism must be a significant near-surface metamorphic process.

Suggested Reading

Arem, Joel. *Rocks and Minerals*. Phoenix, AZ: Geoscience Press, 1991.

Chesterman, C. W. *The Audubon Society Field Guide to North American Rocks and Minerals*. New York: Alfred A. Knopf, 1978.

Hamilton, W. R., A. R. Woolley, and A. C. Bishop. *The Henry Holt Guide to Minerals, Rocks, and Fossils*. New York: Henry Holt, 1989.

Mottana, Annibale, Rodolfo Crespi, and Guiseppe Liborio. *Simon and Schuster's Guide to Rocks and Minerals*. New York: Simon & Schuster, 1978.

Pellant, Chris. *Rocks, Minerals & Fossils of the World*. Boston: Little, Brown, 1990.

Pough, F. H. *Peterson First Guide to Rocks and Minerals*. Boston: Houghton Mifflin, 1991.

Sorrell, C. A. *A Field Guide and Introduction to the Geology and Chemistry of Rocks and Minerals*. New York: Golden Press, 1973.

Zim, H. S., and P. R. Shaffer. *Rocks and Minerals: A Guide to Familiar Minerals, Gems, Ores and Rocks*. New York: Golden Press, 1957.

18

Fossils

Fossils and Fossilization

Fossils (from the Latin *fossilis*, "dug up") are any evidences of past life, plant or animal, preserved by natural means in materials of Earth's crust. The word "fossil" tends to conjure up images of a bone or shell—a **body fossil**. But indirect evidence, such as a track, trail, or burrow (Figure 18-1)—a **trace fossil**—is also included within the realm of fossils. We expect to find fossils entombed in sediment or sedimentary rock. But they also get stuck in asphalt and the resin of cone-bearing trees or are frozen in ice or permanently frozen ground. The study of fossils is known as **paleontology** (pay-lee-uhn-TAHL-uh-gee).

Most fossils are millions of years old, and purists maintain organic remains or traces must have been buried prior to written history to be called fossils. But how can you always know the age of a supposed fossil? Human remains in cemeteries are not considered fossils, but similar remains in other contexts might be called fossils. To qualify for designation as a fossil, having been buried might be a more significant criterion than age. After all, a fossil is something "dug up," as stipulated by the literal meaning of the word "fossil."

To visualize the creation of fossils, consider a scenario from an organism's death to eventual burial and preservation—**fossilization**—to discovery of the fossil. A clam that lives at the edge of a sea will be the catalyst for this mental journey. The clam dies when a snail bores a hole through the clam's shell and feasts on the flesh. The shell opens and gets knocked around by waves and currents for a time. Before being broken, the shell is buried by sand during a storm. Encroachment of the sea over the land ensues, and layer upon layer of marine sediment pile over the clam. Thousands of years pass, then millions. The weight of the overlying sediment compacts the sand, with the enclosed clam, into sandstone. Earth movements raise the land, and the final sea withdraws; a river carves a deep valley through the thick sequence of sedimentary rocks and exposes the clam-bearing sandstone.

223

Figure 18-1. Trace fossil, a presumed burrow filling (*Ophiomorpha*) of a marine ghost shrimp, showing the characteristic knobby surface; Cretaceous; near Rhame, North Dakota. The burrow may branch vertically or horizontally. Length of the specimen at the base is 5.7 inches (14.5 cm).

One hot, summer afternoon, a tired backpacker ambles along the river, his mind preoccupied with his heavy pack and the ache in his shoulders. He nearly topples as one of his boots hooks the sharp broken edge of a sandstone block. He turns to look back at the obstruction and sees a white shell in the reddish rock. The block has broken around half the shell, and the shell's impression is left in one of the rock fragments. He kneels down for a closer look, notices a small, neat hole in one part of the shell. He looks up, traces the sandstone layer from which the block has fallen—and ponders his lucky find, the ache in his shoulders forgotten.

Our imaginary clamshell could have done worse. If acid-bearing groundwater had percolated through the sandstone, the shell would have been dissolved. A less drastic change may have been the replacement of the shell by, say, silica or pyrite or the later filling of a shell cavity in the rock by the same materials. The shell could also have been distorted by recrystallization (see chapter 17) or misshaped or even destroyed by metamorphism of the sandstone.

We might infer from the clam incident that *hard parts* and *rapid burial* of an organism are conducive to fossil preservation and later recovery. Both conditions resist decay and destruction. Soft parts, however, are sometimes preserved, as evidenced by elephantine mammoths preserved in ice or frozen ground in Siberia and Alaska. Rapid burial by sediment is most apt to take place in watery environments: the sea, streams, lakes, ponds, and bogs.

Oldest Fossils

The oldest known fossils fall into two groups, both of which go unnoticed by most people. One group includes microscopic filaments believed to be bacteria or blue-green algae (single-celled plantlike organisms, also called cyanobacteria). The other consists of the easily visible **stromatolites** (strow-MAT-uhl-ights), thinly layered; usually limy; domal, moundlike, or pillarlike structures that resemble sliced-through cabbage heads. Today, blue-green algae produce stromatolites along the margins of some warm seas and may have formed the oldest known of these structures. The oldest known organic filaments and stromatolites are dated at about 3.5 billion years and have been recovered from Western Australia.

Earliest life must have originated prior to 3.5 billion years ago (because the oldest known fossils likely do not evidence the earliest life) but after about 4.5 billion years ago (see chapter 11), generally considered by geologists as the time of Earth's origin.

Classifying, Identifying, and Naming Fossils

To classify fossils (or any objects for that matter) is to arrange them within a previously devised system. With fossils, the classification system consists of several categories. Classifying fossils is often more complex than classifying rocks and minerals. The customary procedure is to assign an identified **species** (SPEE-sheez), the basic kind of organism, or a **genus** (GEE-nuhs) to higher, more inclusive categories. Classification of the human species, *Homo sapiens*, illustrates this approach (Table 18-1). A primary goal of biologic classification is to portray relationships among similar animals and plants.

To identify fossils is to assign individual specimens into pre-established categories of classification, proceeding from higher-level to lower-level categories—the opposite of classification. To identify the clam I had in mind in the imaginary incident above, I would proceed from the Phylum Mollusca (assumed) to the Class Bivalvia (the class to which all clams belong), to the Family Arcticidae (ark-TISS-uh-dee), to the Genus *Arctica* (ARK-tih-kah), and to the species *Arctica ovata* (oh-VAY-tuh). I disregard the category of Order, which is of lesser importance in the study of clams. Paleontologists are more often concerned with identification than classification but classification is, at the least, always assumed or implied. Identification precedes classification. Only preliminary identification is an aim of this chapter; for more specific identification, consult the readings at the end of this chapter, explore the numerous others available in libraries, or, if you are particularly serious, acquire the aid of a paleontologist at a university, museum, or geological survey.

TABLE 18-1. General Classification of the Human Species

Kingdom ANIMALIA: Many-celled organisms that obtain complex organic food by consuming other organisms and are capable of voluntary movement.

Phylum CHORDATA (core-DAY-tuh): *Animals*, at some state of development, with an upper, lengthwise support, the **notochord**; an upper nerve cord and brain; and gill arches and pouches.

Class MAMMALIA: *Chordates* with hair and mammary glands for suckling the young.

Order PRIMATES (pry-MAY-teez): *Mammals* with four generalized limbs, each with five fingers or toes that bear nails.

Family HOMINIDAE (hahm-IN-uh-dee): *Primates* (PRY-mates) with humanlike features, and a larger and more functional brain than the apes and gibbons.

Genus HOMO: Hominids (HAHM-uh-nihds) unlike other genera in the family.

Species: *Homo sapiens.* A member of the genus *Homo* unlike other species in the genus.

Why is each fossil, or living organism, given a separate, often long, and seemingly unpronounceable "scientific" name? Paleontologists and biologists everywhere must be able to communicate worldwide, and a single, *Latinized* name for each organism provides this means of communication. Regardless of the scientist's native language, the scientific name is always the same.

As for the use of so-called "common" names instead of scientific names, many organisms don't have common names, and some organisms may have several, which depend on peoples' whims. Consider, for example, a bush with edible fruit, *Amelanchier alnifolia*, which has at least four common names: juneberry, serviceberry, sarviceberry, and saskatoon. The single scientific name tends to eliminate any possible confusion.

Granted, the Latinized scientific names are often long and may, at times, be awkward to pronounce. But the presumed awkwardness often dissipates with familiarity and frequent use. Do most children find the scientific dinosaur names *Triceratops, Tyrannosaurus,* and *Stegosaurus* difficult to prounounce? And, are the names *Hippopotamus, Rhinoceros, Chrysanthemum,* and *Delphinium* difficult to pronounce? For the last four organisms, the scientific and common names of the two animals and two plants are the same. One final point: Scientific names often tell something about an organism. *Triceratops*—formed by the Greek *tria,* "three"; *kerat,* "horn"; and *ops*, "eye"—names and describes a Cretaceous plant-eating dinosaur that had a long horn above each eye and a shorter horn on its nose.

Scientific names are best learned through constant use and total immersion, two habits you'll acquire if you develop a serious interest in fossils. Such names appear in this chapter mostly in the figure captions.

Main Fossil Groups

Fossils can be grouped into three categories: invertebrates, vertebrates, and plants. **Invertebrates** are "animals without backbones," those that lack interlocked vertebrae to form a backbone or segmented spinal column, such as the clams, snails, or lobsters. **Vertebrates**, which have vertebrae and a vertebral column, include the fishes, amphibians, reptiles, birds, and mammals. Man, of course, is a vertebrate; this would have been clear if "Subphylum Vertebrata" had been included under Phylum Chordata in Table 18-1.

More than 250,000 species of fossils are known, three-fourths of which are invertebrates. New species are discovered each year, and perhaps several million will eventually be known. By comparison, about 2 million living organisms have been named, and biologists estimate that 10 to 50 million species remain to be discovered. Most living organisms are invertebrates, chiefly insects from tropical regions.

Because of the great number of fossils, only a few, on a larger group basis, can be mentioned in this chapter. Since most fossils found are invertebrates, I will allocate more space to them. By the way, if you have forgotten the geologic time designations, you might wish to slip a bookmark in chapter 11 for easy referral. They will be referred to often in the rest of this chapter.

Invertebrates

We will examine only those invertebrates that are obvious and most apt to be seen by the traveler. For example, **protozoans** (prote-uh-ZOH-uhnz)—single-celled animals—are not described because they are mostly microscopic, although tens of thousands of species exist as fossils.

Sponges (Precambrian to present) are evidenced in rocks most often by microscopic, limy or siliceous, needlelike elements, but occasionally as globular, cylindrical, vaselike, or saucerlike impressions (Figure 18-2). **Stromatoporoids** (stroh-muh-TAH-

Figure 18-2. Impressions of sponges of Silurian (left; saucerlike *Astraeospongia* from Decatur County, Tennessee) and Devonian (right; knobby *Hydnoceras* from near Alfred, New York) age. Height of *Hydnoceras* on the right is 5.3 inches (13.5 cm).

puh-roydz) (Ordovician to Cretaceous) are sponges whose thinly layered structure somewhat resembles that of stromatolites; they formed reefs during the Silurian and Devonian. Most sponges are marine today and are presumed to have been so in the past.

Corals (Ordovician to present) have generally limy skeletons that, from Paleozoic rocks, are usually hornlike (Figure 18-3) or resemble many-sided prisms (Figure 18-4) or cylinders, often grown together to form a tight, rounded mass. Both growth forms are usually partitioned lengthwise in radial fashion as well as crosswise. Many-tentacled animals, like sea anemones, sat at the ends of the horns, prisms, or cylinders and secreted the hard parts. Living corals, and those from younger rocks, have assumed branchlike forms, those that resemble convoluted brains, and others. Today, corals live only in marine waters. The grown-together or colonial types form reefs in warm seas, and similar types must have done so in the past.

Bryozoans (bry-uh-ZOE-uhnz) (Ordovician to present), pinhead-sized animals with tentacles and more complex than corals, secrete mostly limy colonies that are encrusting, stemlike or branching-twiglike, and lacy (Figure 18-5). The stemlike or branching-twiglike—or stony—bryozoans, found mostly in Ordovician and Silurian rocks, may have bumps or ridges on the colonies. *Archimedes* (ar-kuh-MEED-eez), a screwlike fossil about

FIGURE 18-3. Solitary hornlike corals of Devonian age, showing radial partitions. At the top is *Heliophyllum*, at the bottom is *Zaphrentis*. Length of *Zaphrentis* is 3.4 inches (8.6 cm).

FIGURE 18-4. Colonial coral *(Lithostrotionella)* of many-sided prisms showing crosswise and radial partitions; Mississippian; Keokuk, Iowa. Width of the specimen on the right is 3.1 inches (7.9 cm).

FIGURE 18-5. Bryozoans. Clockwise, from the lower right , are *Fenestella* (Devonian; White Mound, Oklahoma), *Archimedes* (Mississippian; Logan County, Kentucky), *Dekayella* (Ordovician; Cincinnati, Ohio), and *Hallopora* (Ordovician). *Archimedes* is 0.9 inches (2.3 cm) high.

which a lacy colony grew spirally wrapped, characterizes Mississippian rocks in central North America. This fossil was named after the Greek, Archimedes, who invented the water screw for raising water. Most bryozoans favor marine waters today and must have done so in the past.

Brachiopods (BRACK-ee-uh-podz) (Cambrian to present) generally have limy shells of two parts that differ in size and shape (Figure 18-6). This implies that a plane of symmetry, an imaginary plane that divides the shell as equally as possible, would pass *across* the two parts and not between them, along the midline. The shells vary in shape and may be smooth or ornamented with ridges, grooves, spines, and growth lines. Most brachiopods are marine today and must have been so in the past; more species, however, occurred in the past than now, and most are collected from Paleozoic rocks.

Of the **mollusks** (MAHL-uhsks), soft-bodied invertebrates usually with a shell and more complex than brachiopods, those most often found as fossils are snails, clams, and cephalopods. **Snails** (Figure 18-7) (Cambrian to present) usually have a limy, coiled shell that is not partitioned. They may be smooth or possess an ornamentation similar to that of brachiopods. Most live today in shallow seas, but many live in freshwater and on land. They probably occupied similar habitats in the past. Many freshwater shells tend to be thinner than marine shells and lack ornamentation.

Clams (Figure 18-8) (Cambrian to present) have two-part limy shells somewhat similar to those of most brachiopods, but the plane of symmetry most often passes *between* the two shell parts. The two parts, therefore, are usually of similar size and shape. If the two shell parts are dissimilar, clams may be distinguished on the inside of the shell from brachiopods by rather large, shallow, oval or circular depressions; these depressions represent attachment scars of muscles that, upon contraction, close the two parts of the shell. Clams are most frequent in Mesozoic and Cenozoic rocks, whereas brachiopods are most abundant in Paleozoic rocks. Clams today prevail in shallow seas but they are common in brackish water, which is less salty than seawater but more so than freshwater—and freshwater as well. This pattern, presumably, is an extension from the past. Oysters, for example, exemplify clams generally characteristic of brackish water, as found in bays and estuaries.

Cephalopod (SEF-uh-luh-pahd) mollusks (Cambrian to present) today include few species of squids, cuttlefish, the chambered

FIGURE 18-6. Brachiopods. Clockwise, from the upper right, are *Oleneothyris* (Paleocene; New Egypt, New Jersey), *Dictyoclostus* (Pennsylvanian; Wichita, Kansas), *Platystrophia* (Ordovician), and *Mucrospirifer* (Devonian; near Sylvania, Ohio). *Oleneothyris* is 1.9 inches (4.8 cm) long.

FIGURE 18-7. Snails. Clockwise, from the right, are *Turritella* (Eocene; near Ariton, Alabama), *Volutospina* (Eocene; near Jackson, Alabama), *Fasciolaria* (Pliocene; near Clewiston, Florida), *Campeloma* (Paleocene; McKenzie County, North Dakota), and *Oliva* (Miocene; near Magnolia, North Carolina). All are marine except *Campeloma*, which is freshwater. Height of *Turritella* is 3.4 inches (8.6 cm).

FIGURE 18-8. Clams, *Crassatellites* (left; Cretaceous; near Enville, Tennessee) and *Pecten* (right; Miocene; Jones Wharf, Maryland). *Pecten* is 3.1 inches (7.9 cm) high.

nautilus, octopuses, and related groups, usually with poorly developed or no shells. But cephalopods of the past were numerous and had well-developed limy shells, straight or coiled, external or internal, with partitions (Figure 18-9). External-shelled **nautiloid** (NAWT-uh-loyd) cephalopods (Cambrian to present) possessed straight or slightly curved partitions, seen where the shell is stripped away, and **ammonoid** (AM-uh-noyd) cephalopods (Devonian to Cretaceous) had wrinkled partitions. The chambered nautilus is the only living nautiloid. The extinct **belemnites** (BELL-uhm-nights) (Devonian to Eocene), related to squids, had cigar-shaped internal shells. All cephalopods are marine today and most likely were marine in the past.

Arthropods (AR-thruh-podz), such as crabs, lobsters, shrimp, and insects, are the most numerous of invertebrates today, especially the insects, but not all groups left a good fossil record. The **trilobites** (TRY-luh-bytes) (Figure 18-10) (Cambrian to Permian), however, did leave a good record. Segmented, like all ar-

Figure 18-9. Cephalopods. Clockwise, from the upper right, are two ammonoids, a belemnite, and a nautiloid: *Scaphites* (Cretaceous; near Linton, North Dakota), *Baculites* (Cretaceous; near Belle Fourche, South Dakota), *Belemnitella* (Cretaceous; near St. Georges, Delaware), and *Michelinoceras* (Devonian; Cayuga Lake, New York). *Baculites* (lower right) and *Michelinoceras* (upper left) show the distinctive wrinkled or relatively straight partitions of ammonoids and nautiloids. Length of *Belemnitella* (extreme left) is 3.8 inches (9.6 cm).

thropods, they are also tri- or three-lobed lengthwise, with a central lobe flanked by two side lobes. Although they occur throughout the Paleozoic, most trilobites are found in Cambrian, Ordovician, Silurian, and Devonian rocks. Paleontologists believe trilobites were probably all marine because of their association with other marine fossils.

Echinoderms (ih-KYE-nuh-durmz), or "spiny-skinned" animals, include the living starfishes, sea cucumbers, sea urchins, and others. Three groups of echinoderms are common as fossils: blastoids, crinoids, and sea urchins.

Blastoids (BLASS-toydz) (Figure 18-11) (Ordovician to Permian) have budlike skeletons of limy, fused plates with five distinct, radial, depressed areas bisected by food-gathering grooves. Most were attached to segmented stalks or columns that anchored to the sea bottom.

Crinoids (CRY-noydz) (Figure 18-12) (Cambrian to present), also known by the misleading term "sea lilies," have cuplike skeletons that contain more numerous plates than those of blastoids, and the plates are arranged in circlets. Branched, armlike append-

FIGURE 18-10. Trilobites, *Peronopsis* (left; Cambrian; Jince, Bohemia) and *Paedumias* (right; Cambrian; near York, Pennsylvania). Specimen on the left is 1.8 inches (4.6 cm) long.

FIGURE 18-11. Blastoids, two species of *Pentremites* from Mississippian rocks at Monroe County, Illinois. Specimen at the left, 0.7 inch (1.8 cm) long, shows the point of attachment of a segmented stalk on the right edge.

Figure 18-12. *Crinoids, on bedding surface of limestone (Mississippian; LeGrand, Iowa). At least eight crowns—cups-with-arms—and several segmented stalks are visible. Length of the largest crown in the lower right, excluding the stalk, is 2.9 inches (7.4 cm).*

ages extend upward. Most fossil crinoids had stalks, as did the blastoids. Disklike or star-shaped stalk segments are found more frequently than the crowns (cups-with-arms). Both crinoids and blastoids are abundant in Mississippian rocks. Paleontologists conceive crinoid "gardens" (Figure 18-13) on limy, Mississippian seafloors; the numerous individuals gathered food with their outspread, armlike structures and swayed on flexible stalks in the waves and currents. Upon preservation, their remains are seen scattered on bedding surfaces of limestone (Figure 18-12).

Sea urchins (Ordovician to present) have globelike, heart-shaped, or disklike limy skeletons and lack stalks and armlike structures. "Regular" urchins display fivefold, radial symmetry, emphasized by top-to-bottom-trending bands of numerous plates. "Irregular" urchins (see Figure 21-3), which include heart urchins and sand dollars, display bilateral symmetry. Petal-like impressions on the upper surfaces, through which breathing structures extend, characterize many irregular urchins. Sea urchins, and all other echinoderms today, are marine; presumably those of the past were as well.

Figure 18-13. Reconstructed crinoid "garden" on a Mississippian seafloor. (Courtesy of Field Museum of Natural History, Chicago; photograph GEO-80871.)

Figure 18-14. Grapto-lites, in limestone (Ordovician; near Overbrook, Oklahoma). Largest, isolated branch in the lower left is 0.6 inch (1.5 cm) long.

Graptolites (GRAP-tuh-lights) (Figure 18-14) (Cambrian to Mississippian) appear as long, dark, carbon films in fine-grained clastic or carbonate rocks. They resemble narrow, saw-blade impressions with "teeth" on one or both sides. The "saw-blades" or branches occur singly, in groups, or in a netlike arrangement. "Teeth" on the branches are in reality tubes or cups in which tiny animals presumably lived and, together, formed colonies. The colonies either floated in Paleozoic seas or were attached to sea bottoms. Graptolites, most often found in Ordovician and Silurian rocks, may be related to a group close to the vertebrates.

Vertebrates

Less common than invertebrates, vertebrates are most often evidenced as scattered teeth, skeletal bones, bony plates, spines, and scales. Study of these remains is detailed and complex, and the amateur paleontologist may find it difficult to place them, at times, into even one of the five major groups (Table 18-2).

Fish remains are most frequent in Mesozoic and Cenozoic rocks, but rarely are complete skeletons found (Figure 18-15). **Ostracoderms** (AHS-truh-coh-dermz; Cambrian to Devonian) and **placoderms** (PLACK-uh-dermz; Silurian to Devonian) are two groups of extinct primitive fishes. Both possessed an armor of bony plates; the ostracoderms lacked jaws and the placoderms were the earliest fishes known to have had them. Sharks and their relatives (Silurian to present), with skeletons mostly of cartilage, are usually represented as fossils by teeth (Figure 18-16). Fossil bony fishes have left behind numerous scales, more abundant than their bones; thick, rhomboid scales covered the primitive

TABLE 18-2. Selected Characteristics to Distinguish Major Groups of Fossil Vertebrates

Characteristic	Fishes	Amphibians	Reptiles	Birds	Mammals
Joint bone at back of skull	Single	Single in early forms, double in later forms	Single	Single	Double
Shallow grooves or pits on side of skull	Yes	Early forms only	No	No	No
Cheek openings in skull back of eye orbits	No	No	1 or 2 in later forms	No	No
Teeth	Alike	Alike	Alike	——	Unlike
Roots of rear teeth	Single	Single	Single	——	Divided
Scales	Most	Rare or lacking	Yes	No	No

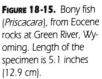

FIGURE 18-15. Bony fish (*Priscacara*), from Eocene rocks at Green River, Wyoming. Length of the specimen is 5.1 inches (12.9 cm).

types—such as the present-day gar—and thin, circular scales prevailed in the remainder. **Acanthodians** (ack-uhn-THOH-dee-uhnz; Silurian to Permian) are extinct bony fishes with conspicuous spines.

Amphibians reached their heyday during the late Paleozoic. The earliest, extinct group, the **labyrinthodonts** (lab-uh-RIHN-thuh-dahnts; Devonian to Jurassic), had an intricate folding of the dentine of their teeth that, when cut, resembles a labyrinth. Am-

FIGURE 18-16. Shark teeth, from middle Tertiary rocks. Height of the tooth on the right is 1.6 inches (4.1 cm).

phibians are believed to have evolved from one of the fleshy-finned or lobe-finned bony fishes during the Devonian.

Reptiles occur mostly in Mesozoic rocks: marine, freshwater, and terrestrial. Among the extinct groups are the flying **ptero-saurs** (TARE-uh-soarz; Triassic to Cretaceous), crocodilelike **phytosaurs** (FIGHT-uh-soarz; Triassic), dolphinlike **ichthyo-saurs** (ICK-thee-uh-soarz; Triassic to Cretaceous), sea serpentlike **plesiosaurs** (PLEE-see-uh-soarz; Triassic to Cretaceous), **notho-saurs** (NO-thuh-soarz; Triassic), **mosasaurs** (MOH-zuh-soarz; Cretaceous), and **dinosaurs** (Triassic to Cretaceous). The notho-saurs were smaller precursors of plesiosaurs, and the mosasaurs had spindle-shaped bodies. Skeletal remains of ichthyosaurs might be confused with those of huge fish. All these groups except pterosaurs and dinosaurs were adapted for swimming in the sea. Bone fragments of the land-dwelling dinosaurs are common in Jurassic and Cretaceous rocks in places. Reptiles are believed to have evolved from an amphibian ancestor during the Pennsylvanian.

Birds are the rarest of vertebrate fossils; their characteristic, relatively light, hollow bones and skulls with large eye sockets occur mostly in Cenozoic rocks. Reptilian characteristics, such as teeth and a backbone that extends into the tail, of the earliest Jurassic bird imply a reptilian ancestor for this group.

Mammal fossils are found mostly in Cenozoic rocks. Besides the characters given in Table 18-2, other characteristics aid to separate mammals from fossil reptiles: (1) a single opening in the skull for the nostrils as compared to two for the reptiles; (2) a bony roof of the mouth, lacking in reptiles except for certain groups such as the crocodiles; and (3) each half of the lower jaw is a single bone, compared to multiple bones in reptiles. These and other differences only partly aid in the indistinct separation of gradational, latest Paleozoic mammal-like reptiles from reptiles and

Figure 18-17. Under view of a reconstruction of the long-necked, long-tailed, Jurassic dinosaur *Apatosaurus* (= *Brontosaurus*). Calgary Zoo, Botanical Gardens and Prehistoric Park, Calgary, southern Alberta, Canada. Height of the person is 5.5 feet (1.7 m).

Figure 18-18. Plaster cast of a Pleistocene mastodon tooth, from Big Bone Lick, Kentucky, showing the high points or cusps on the upper surface, here considerably worn. Length of the tooth is 6.7 inches (17.0 cm).

mammals. Such a problem, however, seems to clearly indicate that mammals arose from reptiles, during the Triassic.

Among the extinct groups of mammals are the **condylarths** (KAHN-duh-lahrths; Cretaceous to Miocene), piglike **entelodonts** (en-TELL-uh-dahnts; Eocene to Miocene), **chalicotheres** (KAL-ih-cuh-thearz; Eocene to Pleistocene), rhinoceroslike **brontotheres** (BRAHN-tuh-thearz; Eocene to Oligocene), elephantlike **mammoths** and **mastodons** (both Eocene to Pleistocene), and **saber-toothed cats** (Oligocene to Pleistocene). The condylarths were primitive hoofed mammals and the chalicotheres were horselike but with claws on their limbs.

From the fossil evidence, although sometimes meager, vertebrate paleontologists flesh out and reconstruct extinct vertebrates (Figure 18-17), and speculate on their behavior and diet. For example, the teeth of mastodons (Figure 18-18) have high points or cusps and those of mammoths possess a flat grinding surface of folded enamel. These features of the teeth imply that mastodons were leaf-chomping browsers and mammoths were grass-grinding grazers.

Plants

Plants occur more commonly as fossils than do vertebrates: Those most frequently found are algae, lycopods, arthophytes, ferns and seed-ferns, cycads and cycadeoids, ginkgoes, conifers, and flowering plants.

Algae (AL-gee) (Precambrian to present), the simplest of green plants that lack true roots, stems, and leaves, are typified by the scumlike masses in ponds and by the seaweeds. As fossils, they are commonly preserved as stromatolites (mentioned under Oldest Fossils) and similar thinly layered masses. Diatomite (see chapter 16) consists of the siliceous-secreting algae called diatoms.

Lycopods (LIE-cuh-podz) (Devonian to present), with true roots, stems, and leaves, are represented today by such small, inconspicuous plants as the club mosses, also known as ground pines. But in the late Paleozoic they assumed tree size and were the main contributors to the vegetation of coal-forming swamps. These "scale trees" have rhomboid or circular leaf-attachment scars on the trunks that resemble scales.

Arthrophytes (ARE-thruh-fights) (Devonian to present), also known as **sphenopsids** (sfee-NAHP-suhdz), get their name from the Greek *arthron*, "joint" and *phyton*, "plant." Who hasn't sat on a stream bank or railroad embankment and pulled apart the finely ribbed stems of horsetails or scouring rushes at their joints? Arthrophytes, with circlets of leaves and branches at the stem joints, grew treelike on higher ground but also existed in the late Paleozoic coal-forming swamps.

Ferns (Devonian to present) and **seed-ferns** (Figure 18-19) (Devonian to Jurassic) are similar with their usual feathery leaves of many leaflets; but ferns reproduce by spores and seed-ferns developed from pollen and seeds. Both small and tree-sized representatives of both groups grew in late Paleozoic coal-forming swamps.

Cycads (SIGH-cadz) (Permian to present) and **cycadeoids** (sigh-CAD-ee-oydz) (Permian to Cretaceous) are similar in that both have palmlike leaves and rhomboid leaf-attachment scars on the trunks. But cycads, most often with columnlike trunks, reproduce by male and female cones on separate plants. Cycadeoids,

FIGURE 18-19. Impressions of leaflets of a frond of a seed-fern (*Pecopteris*), in a split concretion (Pennsylvanian; Mazon Creek, Illinois). Height of the concretion on the right is 5.2 inches (13.2 cm).

FIGURE 18-20. Impression of a ginkgo (*Ginkgo*) (right) of Paleocene age (near Almont, North Dakota) compared with a leaf of the sole living species (*Ginkgo biloba*). Consider the similarity in spite of a time separation of 60 million years! Length of the fossil leaf plus leafstalk is 3.3 inches (8.4 cm).

on the other hand, developed from cones with both male and female organs embedded in squat trunks on the same plants; the trunks resemble large pineapple fruits. Both groups are most common in Mesozoic rocks.

Ginkgoes (GINK-gohz) (Permian to present) (Figure 18-20) have fan-shaped leaves, divided or not, with veins that radiate out from the point of attachment to the leafstalks. Prominent during the Mesozoic, only a single species survives today.

Conifers (KAHN-uh-furz) (Pennsylvanian to present), cone-bearing plants with needlelike or scalelike leaves such as the pines, firs, and spruces, probably reached their maximum numbers during the Mesozoic, but are significant plants now as well. The best-

Figure 18-21. Petrified tree trunks of a fossil forest buried by volcanic breccia, ash, and dust about 50 million years ago; Specimen Ridge, Yellowstone National Park, northwestern Wyoming. Height of the person is 5.5 feet (1.7 m).

known conifer fossils are the silicified logs in Petrified Forest National Park, Arizona (see Figure 13-2).

Flowering plants, also called **anthophytes** (AN-thuh-fights) or **angiosperms** (AN-gee-uh-spermz) (Cretaceous to present) have dominated plant life on Earth since the late Cretaceous. They include two major groups: **monocots**, with one seed leaf and parallel-veined leaves—such as the grasses and lilies; and **dicots**, with two seed leaves and net-veined leaves—such as most deciduous trees and other broad-leaved plants. Most leaves and petrified wood (Figure 18-21) from late Cretaceous and younger rocks are of dicot flowering plants.

Uses of Fossils

Perhaps the most apparent use of fossils is to date, or determine the age of, rocks that contain them. For example, I mentioned that the bryozoan *Archimedes* is an index of Mississippian age in central

North America. Identification to genus or species is normally necessary for specific age determination, but knowing general groups, their age ranges, and their times of greatest abundance allows general age assignment. Trilobites are Paleozoic—most are Devonian and older—and graptolites, in most cases, signify an Ordovician or Silurian age for a rock. In related fashion, fossils help determine the equivalence or correlation (see chapter 11) of rock layers in widely separated places.

Fossils may be so abundant as to form rocks exclusively, or nearly so, of their hard parts, analogous to rock-forming minerals. Coquina, chalk, diatomite, and coal are examples.

Together with sedimentary rocks, fossils aid to decipher environments of the past (see chapter 12). Some people may have difficulty believing that seas covered North America several times since the beginning of the Cambrian. But rock layers with marine fossils, stacked one above the other, tell us this is so. You may recall that corals, brachiopods, cephalopods, blastoids, crinoids, graptolites, and trilobites likely all lived in saline (or brackish) water during their existence, and are generally good marine indicators. Certain snails (Figure 18-7) and clams, however, serve to distinguish freshwater environments. In related fashion, fossils are good indicators of past climates. Silurian coral reefs in the now temperate east-central United States, for example, signify previous tropical conditions there.

Fossils also document the progression of life through time, which generally has gone from simple to complex and from less varied to more varied. The order of coverage of fossil groups in this chapter—invertebrates, vertebrates, and plants—is toward more complexity for each group. To most paleontologists and biologists, the progression of life is explained by the concept of **evolution**: that later organisms develop or evolve from earlier organisms as their continually changing genetic makeup interacts with changing environments and a continual selecting of the better fit goes on. In marked contrast is the concept of **creationism**, that all organisms were created by an omnipotent Creator. Granted that the fossil record documents the **extinction**, dying out, of several organisms at different times and the later appearance of new organisms, creationism implies the creation of organisms several times. I'll leave you to ponder the validity of both concepts. But keep in mind the existence of certain "intermediates," such as the mammal-like reptiles and the oldest fossil bird. The mammal-like reptiles possessed different tooth types, a mammalian characteristic, and the earliest known bird has reptilelike teeth. If organic evolution did not take place in the past, why should intermediates exist in the fossil record?

Suggested Reading

Arduini, Paolo, and Giorgio Teruzzi. *Simon & Schuster's Guide to Fossils.* New York: Simon & Schuster, 1986.

Cvancara, A. M. *Sleuthing Fossils: The Art of Investigating Past Life.* New York: John Wiley, 1990.

Murray, J. W. *Atlas of Invertebrate Macrofossils.* New York: Halsted Press, 1985.

Rhodes, F. H. T., P. R. Shaffer, and H. S. Zim. *Fossils: A Golden Guide.* Racine, WI: Western Publishing, 1990.

Stearn, C. W., and R. L. Carroll. *Paleontology: The Record of Life.* New York: John Wiley, 1989.

Thompson, Ida. *The Audubon Society Field Guide to North American Fossils.* New York: Alfred A. Knopf, 1982.

Tidwell, W. S. *Common Fossil Plants of Western North America.* Provo, UT: Brigham Young University Press, 1975.

19

The Geologist's Approach

Basic Premise: Uniformitarianism (Actualism)

Most geologists, in their attempt to unscramble geological puzzles, adhere to a basic premise (introduced in chapter 11): that physical and chemical laws of nature have remained constant—invariant through time. Because natural laws have not changed, natural processes governed by those laws have not either; processes that shape Earth and determine events today are continuations from the past. So, for example, geologists assume erosion by running water and wind took place in previous times as we witness these processes today.

That natural laws and processes have been continuous and *uniform* through time has led to the term "uniformitarianism" for the basic premise, championed and developed by the Scottish geologist James Hutton (1726–1797). But a uniformity of causes does not imply a uniformity of rates, intensities, conditions, or results. Why should the rate of erosion on a mountain slope or the rate of sediment buildup in an ocean basin today, for example, equal that of a million years ago? Remember, too, that the present is but a geological instant, and can hardly encompass all events of the past. The extensive cold climate and continental glaciers of 18,000 years ago that occurred in presently temperate regions are no longer with us. The last Ice Age is but one instance of events that have occurred on Earth during the past but do not exist today.

Some people consider **actualism** a better term than uniformitarianism. Processes that *actually* operate now, or those inferred to operate, can explain features and events of the past. The term "actualism" is less apt to mislead; actualism does not imply uniformity of anything other than processes and natural laws.

By either designation, uniformitarianism or actualism, geology can hardly be accomplished without its basic premise: that "the present is the key to the past."

OVERLEAF. Cross-bedding in Permian sandstone, Canyon de Chelly National Monument near Chinle, northeastern Arizona. The cross-bedding records parts of many lithified wind-blown dunes stacked on one another.

How Do Geologists Think?

Geologists are scientists, and one may expect them to think creatively like other scientists. But all scientists do *not* think alike. How do geologists differ?

Anne Roe, in *The Making of a Scientist*, analyzed the thinking processes of three groups of research scientists: biologists, physicists (both experimental and theoretical), and social scientists (psychologists and anthropologists). Four types of creative thinking emerged: thinking in terms of pictures or symbols ("visual imagery"), favored by biologists and experimental physicists; thinking in terms of unspoken words ("auditory-verbal"), used especially by theoretical physicists and social scientists; just knowing by a feeling of relationships ("imageless thought"), used mostly by experimental physicists and social scientists; and thinking through feelings of muscular tension ("kinesthetic thinking"), mentioned only by the social scientists.

Because most geologists deal or have dealt with natural objects in the field—like most biologists—we might infer that geologists often think in terms of pictures or symbols. A nearly universal behavior of geologists is their constant use of maps, cross sections (see chapter 20), and diagrams to help convey or confirm ideas, either in discussions or in published writings. This behavior has evolved from exposure to a multitude of graphic aids during their training. Sophisticated graphics, in particular, are utilized to portray such Earth features as folds amd fractures in three dimensions. These graphics, quite naturally, lead to three-dimensional thinking. Who can always say when illustrations convey ideas or prompt their birth?

How to Mentally Attack a Geological Problem

Imagine you are flying over a broad stream valley in the U.S. Southwest. Below, you spot what appear to be broad, flat-topped benches that flank the valley on both sides—and at least at three levels. You speculate: Are they lava flows through which the stream has cut? Human-made features? Do they relate directly to the stream in some way? You make a mental note of their location.

Weeks later, you drive through the valley. Upon examining road-cut exposures, you discover the steplike benches to consist of sand and gravel. That rules out lava flows. You see no evidence of humans having cut these extensive benches along the valley walls or having formed them by fill from the surrounding terrain.

What a massive project either would have been! And for what purpose? You observe that the stream now occupies a wide, flat valley floor, similar in relief to that of the flat-topped benches, and the sediment in the stream is of sand and gravel. You surmise that these benches are likely linked to the past behavior of the stream.

After reading about the geology of streams (see chapter 2), you realize that the flat-topped benches in question must be stream terraces, remnants of former valley floors or floodplains into which the stream has incised (see Figures 2-4, 9-15). Possible causes for incision are an increase in stream discharge, perhaps because of a change in the regional climate or overgrazing of the slopes and greater runoff from the watershed, or an increase in the gradient or slope of the streambed. The gradient might be increased by the lowering of a feature that controls base level, such as a reservoir, natural lake, or resistant rock layer. Or the gradient might be increased by uplift of the region. Uplift? Hmm. Unable to relate to uplift, you decide that hypothesis need not be considered seriously.

Back in the valley, you observe the terraces more closely, and this time you take notes on what you observe. You've brought along a detailed topographic map of the valley and you begin to outline the terraces on the map. Armed with several hypotheses for the origin of terraces, you apply them to "your" valley and begin to test them, one by one. Your favorite, an increase in gradient by a lowering of base level, is shot down when you cannot substantiate a former higher base level downstream. Other modes of genesis succumb to your rigorous analysis until you are left with one: uplift, the seemingly implausible explanation.

The way you have mentally attacked this geological problem is really *the* scientific method: You observed and gathered facts, and formulated and tested hypotheses that may fit those facts. The scientific (geological) approach can be elaborated by the following steps, not necessarily listed in the order in which they are pursued:

1. State the problem clearly.

2. Reconnoiter the area or situation.

3. Review any previous study on the problem by others; this step may precede the reconnaisance.

4. Observe, collect, and record facts.

5. Compile and synthesize the recorded facts.

6. Formulate multiple working hypotheses; this activity may break loose soon after you become aware of the problem; always attempt to formulate more than a single hypothesis.

7. Test the hypotheses.

8. Select the hypothesis that best interprets the gathered facts.

9. Apply the selected hypothesis to predict solutions to similar problems.

Two classic writings on the scientific method by T. C. Chamberlin and G. K. Gilbert are listed at the end of this chapter.

But you've wondered: What produced the uplift that resulted in the formation of the stream terraces? Whoops! You're snagged by *another* geological problem! And the process of the geological approach begins once again.

The Geologist's Approach to Finding Oil and Gas

Many geologists are concerned with finding crude oil and natural gas, major sources of energy for our society. A petroleum geologist's approach is on the line when pure economics is involved. The geologist must explore creatively and make sound decisions if his or her company is to survive.

How Oil and Gas Form

An understanding of the way petroleum (from the Latin *petra*, "rock" and *oleum*, "oil") and gas form helps us to better appreciate how they are discovered. Microscopic plants and animals accumulate in lake or sea muds for long periods, maybe thousands of years. The organic-rich muds are covered by other sediments, all of which, in time, lithify to rock. Once deeply buried, say at least 1,600 feet (500 m), heat and pressure transform the organic matter in a shale or limestone into the **hydrocarbons**, organic compounds of hydrogen and carbon, that make up petroleum and gas. This heat-pressure transformation, which may be thought of as organic metamorphism, may take millions of years.

Once formed, the oil and gas, being lighter, migrate upward from the organic-rich **source bed** into a **reservoir rock** that stores the oil and gas. This reservoir rock, highly porous and permeable, is most often of sandstone or porous limestone and dolostone.

What the Geologist Looks For

In the search for a **prospect**, a geological condition that shows promise of containing oil and gas, an exploration geologist first seeks a thick sequence of sedimentary rocks in which organic matter could have accumulated and later transformed into hydrocarbons. (Igneous or metamorphic rocks rarely produce oil and gas.)

An automatic second basic step is the search for a **trap** (Figure 19-1), a geological condition that confines oil and gas to a part of the reservoir rock. **Seeps** are places where oil, not entrapped, spills out on the surface of the ground. Traps may be structural or stratigraphic. **Structural traps** are those whereby rocks are folded into anticlines or faulted. In **stratigraphic traps**, tilted reservoir rocks "pinch out" into impermeable rock or are covered by an unconformity. Both types of traps require an overlying capping seal of impermeable rock, most often a shale.

Assume that the geologist has located a prospect and has garnered evidence for its existence. The next step is to engage in a different kind of search, a way to sell the prospect to the company's management. Million-dollar oil or gas wells are common, and some may cost $10 million or more to drill to 30,000 feet (9,000 m) or deeper. To drill oil or gas wells is a risky business; 80 percent or more of the **wildcats**, exploratory wells drilled in untried or unproven regions, result in **dry holes** (wells that fail to strike oil or gas). We might conclude that the oil-finding geologist plays two roles: that of trap locator and prospect salesperson.

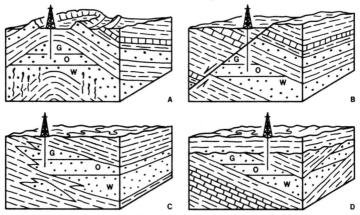

Figure 19-1. Some kinds of traps that confine oil and gas. Structural traps are shown in *A* (anticline) and *B* (fault), stratigraphic traps in *C* (pinch out) and *D* (unconformity). In *A*, oil and gas migrate from the shale source bed to the sandstone reservoir rock. In all diagrams, gas, oil, and water occupy pore space within the sandstone reservoir rock. Dots = sandstone, dashed lines = shale, brick pattern = limestone, *G* = gas, *O* = oil, and *W* = water.

Some Tools of the Exploration Geologist

Many exploration tools are available to the petroleum geologist. I'll touch on a few.

Although seeming perhaps inappropriate at first, remote sensing of the land surface can be a useful approach to oil-finding. **Remote sensing** includes, along with other techniques, the use of aerial photographs, radar images, and infrared images received by both aircraft and satellites. Infrared images, which are based on heat radiated from Earth's surface, often record features that are obscure on photographs and on the ground. The techniques of remote sensing detect drainage patterns, topography, tonal patterns, and **lineaments**—linear features on Earth's surface, many of which are caused by faults and joints. A critical scrutiny of surface features gives clues to the presence of anticlines and faults that may serve as possible traps.

Another useful exploration tool is the **seismic survey**. The seismic reflection survey is the most widely used by the petroleum industry. Shock waves, set off by vibrator trucks or explosives, are sent into the subsurface rock layers. Each rock layer reflects some of the sound wave energy back to the surface where it is recorded by geophysicists. Received data are processed by computers to produce an image, most graphic in a seismic cross section, that reveals the thickness of subsurface layers, folds and faults, and buried landforms.

Electrical well logs have proved a real boon to the explorationist. These are wiggly lines or strip graphs, records of the electrical properties of rock formations in a borehole as an instrument is let down on a cable. Because electricity travels faster through fluids than through rock, information on the fluid content of the rocks is also gained. From the logs, the trained geologist recognizes rock types and porosity and permeability of the rocks, and acquires some idea of the types of fluids in the formations. Other, nonelectrical logs record information useful to the petroleum geologist.

To work up a prospect, the oil-finder obtains electrical and other logs of wells in the vicinity of the prospect. From the logs, the geologist constructs cross sections and contour maps. Two basic contour maps are structure contour and isopach (EYE-suhpack) maps. **Structure contour maps** depict the varying elevation of a rock surface at depth and, thereby, reveal such rock structures as anticlines and faults. **Isopach maps** portray the varied thickness of a rock layer or formation; an isopach map of a reservoir rock is often essential.

The geologist records specific information as a well is drilled. From examination of the rock chips or **cuttings** cut by the drill bit and brought to the surface by circulating drilling mud, the geologist compiles a **sample log**. Under fluorescent light the chips will often appear green if hydrocarbons are present. At selected depths, **cores** or cylinders of rock may be cut to obtain a better idea of the rocks drilled and what fluids they contain. Fossils in the cuttings or cores help identify the rock formation and its age.

Although mentioned last, a creative mind is likely the most significant tool of the exploration geologist. Most participants in the oil industry recognize that petroleum exploration is an art as much as a science or business. Creativity will be called upon more and more as the easier found structural traps become history. A challenge remains for locating much undiscovered petroleum in stratigraphic traps shrouded beneath thrust-faulted rocks, volcanic rocks, or other concealments.

A creative thinker is unconventional and strives to ask the right questions. This person functions best within a free-to-experiment environment. Wise company management allows a creative thinking geologist some latitude within which to ply the search for oil and gas.

The creative mind as a foremost exploration tool was well expressed by Wallace E. Pratt ("Toward a Philosophy of Oil-finding," *Bulletin of the American Association of Petroleum Geologists* 36, no. 12 (1952): 2236):

> Where oil is found, in the final analysis, is in the minds of men. The undiscovered oil field exists only as an idea in the mind of some oil-finder. When no man any longer believes more oil is left to be found, no more oil fields will be discovered, but so long as a single oil-finder remains with a mental vision of a new oil field to cherish, along with freedom and incentive to explore, just so long new oil fields may continue to be discovered.

All I would add to this perceptive quotation, written more than 40 years ago, is to point out that female geologists now also share in the challenging search for oil and gas.

Suggested Reading

Chamberlin, T. C. "The Method of Multiple Working Hypotheses." *Journal of Geology* 5 (1897): 837–848.

Curtis, D. M., P. W. Dickerson, D. M. Gray, H. M. Klein, and E. W. Moody. *How to Try to Find an Oil Field*. Tulsa, OK: PennWell, 1981.

Foster, N. H., and E. A. Beaumont, compilers. *Oil Is First Found in the Mind: The Philosophy of Exploration*. Treatise of Petroleum Geology Reprint Series, No. 20. Tulsa, OK: The American Association of Petroleum Geologists, 1992.

Gilbert, G. K. "The Inculcation of Scientific Method by Example, with an Illustration Drawn from the Quaternary Geology of Utah." *American Journal of Science* (3rd ser.) 31 (1886): 284–299.

20

How to Read Geologic Maps and Cross Sections

Most maps locate places. They may also locate products, animals, and plants, and portray land surface configuration, as do topographic maps (see chapter 1). **Geologic maps** are different: They portray rocks. Besides the occurrence and extent of rock types, though, these maps indicate ages of rocks and depict any rock deformation. Geologic maps often exhibit the so-called **bedrock** as if loose, surface sediment and soil were stripped away. On other geologic maps, the surface geology is shown with all surface materials intact. Some surface geologic maps may evaluate environmental hazards; others, the engineering properties of rock materials. These maps may answer such questions as: Where are landslides likely to occur? Where should you construct sewage lagoons? At what depth can you expect to find the water table? Other geologic maps, the **tectonic maps**, concentrate on large-scale deformational features—folds, faults, joints. And **paleogeologic maps** portray land surfaces at former times.

Cross sections show us how rocks would appear at depth along the side of an imaginary trench cut straight down through Earth's surface, similar to the side view of a cut layer cake. Cross sections complement what we can see on geologic maps.

Geologic maps and cross sections are of special importance in that they allow us to predict what we can expect to find along new roads, excavations, tunnels, and in wells. And so they help us to locate oil, water, coal, iron ore, and other materials vital to our society.

Reading Geologic Maps and Cross Sections

Rock and sediment layers and rock bodies shown on geologic maps are those readily identified and traced. If such features cannot be traced, they cannot be mapped. Drawn on geologic maps are the boundaries or **contacts** between **formations**, the most frequently mapped rock or sediment units. Subdivisions (members or beds) or groups of formations are mapped on occasion.

Let's examine a geologic map and cross section to understand how they are read. On Figure 20-1 the geologic map has been superimposed on a topographic map. Formations are emphasized on geologic maps by color, pattern, or both, and labeled by a symbol. The formation that holds up V-shaped Cove Mountain is the largely sandstone Pocono Formation; the symbol used for the formation reflects its age and name: *Mpo*; *M* = Mississippian, *po* = Pocono. Age relationships are summarized along a side or on the bottom of a map by stacking all the rock or sediment units in their correct order with the oldest at the bottom. Colors for rocks of various ages are fairly standard: for example, green for Cretaceous and yellow for Tertiary. Formations are named, in North America, after places at or near where they were first identified. The overlying, younger Mississippian Mauch Chunk Formation (*Mmc*), of shale, siltstone, and sandstone, which forms a triangular lowland below and within the arms of Cove Mountain, was named after Mauch Chunk, Pennsylvania.

Rock deformation is clearly delineated on geologic maps. On Figure 20-1, the banding of the formations indicates tilted rock layers that have been eroded to parallel ridges and intervening valleys (see chapter 9). Several formations parallel V-shaped Cove Mountain and the Pocono Formation that forms the mountain. This configuration is part of the zigzag pattern of ridges and valleys (and formations) of plunging folds (see Figure 9-5). But is this fold a plunging anticline or syncline? A dashed line that runs along and near the middle of the Mauch Chunk Formation says "Cove Syncline." But let's check this: The easiest way is to glance at the cross section, which displays a distinct syncline. We can also identify the fold from the map. A V-shaped notch (see Figure 9-1) above point A causes indentations of formation contacts that point and dip toward the fold axis, only true for a syncline. Another clue to the type of fold is given by the relative age of the eroded formations. In eroded synclines, younger formations are closer to a fold axis as seen on a map; remember that Mauch Chunk, which straddles the fold axis, is younger than Pocono. The opposite relationship is true for anticlines. Notice, too, how the stream drainage, a part of a trellis drainage pattern (see Figure 9-9), reflects the structure. Near the south (bottom right) edge of the map is an east-west line—heavier than a contact line—with *D* (down) on the north side and *U* (up) on the south; the heavier line

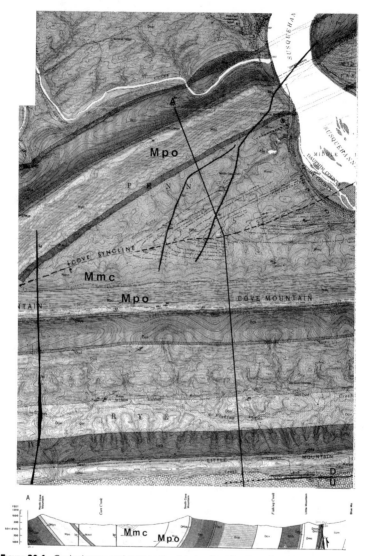

FIGURE 20-1. Geologic map and cross section (along a bent line from *A* to the bottom of the map) of strata within a plunging syncline cut by basaltic dikes; south-central Pennsylvania. The beds are faulted near the bottom (southern) edge of the map. (From *Pennsylvania Geological Survey Atlas* 137 cd by J. L. Dyson, 1967.)

indicates a fault and the two letters signify relative movement along that fault. The cross section shows this fault as a high angle reverse fault (see chapter 9).

Three, heavy, dark lines are evident on the map; the one along the left edge varies in width. They represent basaltic dikes that transect the formations of the plunging syncline. On the cross section these dikes are depicted by heavier vertical lines.

Geologic maps and cross sections enable us to read the geologic history of a region. For the region in Figure 20-1, you first assume that the folded beds were originally flat-lying. Fossils reveal that the oldest formations were laid down in the sea but those north of a line about halfway between Cove and Little Mountains were deposited on land. This change in formation origin implies uplift of the land, a drop in sea level, or perhaps some combination of the two. Some time after the Mauch Chunk Formation was laid down in streams and lakes, all the formations were squeezed together and folded to form a plunging syncline. Since the basaltic dikes transect the Mauch Chunk, they must have been intruded after the folding (see Figure 11-2). From the cross section we can tell that faulting followed folding, but did it occur after or before the intrusion of the dikes? We would require a fault in contact with a dike to determine this. After faulting and and emplacement of the dikes, stream erosion dissected the land surface and formed linear ridges in resistant sandstones and linear valleys in weaker shales and limestones. The Susquehanna River, though, cuts *through* resistant ridges like Cove Mountain, and its downcutting must have kept up with uplift of the land after folding. Besides downcutting, present streams have deposited sediment in their valleys.

Constructing Geologic Maps and Cross Sections

Let's say you've roamed central Pennsylvania for considerable time and decide to try to construct a geologic map somewhere in that region. You select an area of about 6 square miles (16 km^2)— the smaller the better for a first attempt—that straddles New Lancaster Valley (Figure 20-2). You obtain a topographic map (see chapter 1) and use this as a base map; a good aerial photograph of a suitable scale could work as well.

First, you reconnoiter the region to find out how much walking will be required, where the best exposures are located, and what rock types are present. Be prepared to expend some footwork. On the other hand, some geologic maps can be constructed remotely from maps and photographs with only strategic ground-

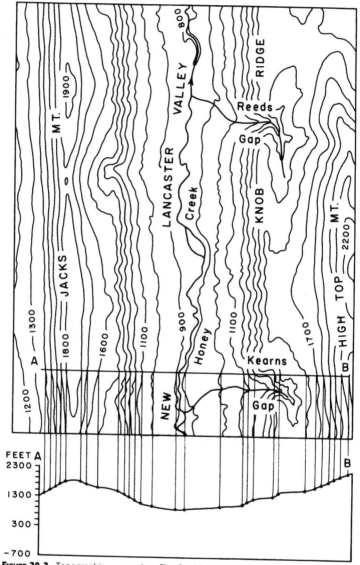

Figure 20-2. Topographic map and profile of a ridge and valley region in central Pennsylvania. For the profile along line A-B, drop a point on the elevation scale below wherever line A-B crosses a contour; connect the points with curved line segments. (Map is modified from *Pennsylvania Geological Survey Atlas* 126 by R. R. Conlin and D. M. Hoskins, 1962.)

checks (or few or no ground-checks, as for geologic maps of the moon or Mars). From the map and terrain, you realize the region is one of linear ridges and an intervening linear valley. These land-forms suggest folded or fractured rock layers that vary in resistance to erosion (see chapter 9). Now, you get serious.

Because this region is within a humid climate, vegetation obscures much of the rock, and the ridges, in particular, are heavily forested. Your best bet for exposures is to search first along gaps in the ridges, such as Reeds Gap and Kearns Gap, and other gaps between New Lancaster Valley and Jack Mountain. You discover at Reeds and Kearns Gaps that Knob Ridge is held up by a sandstone with conglomerate. (You learn later that the same rock holds up a similar ridge across New Lancaster Valley.) At each good exposure you record characteristics of a rock formation: rock type, color of freshly broken and weathered surfaces, predominant minerals, any fossils and their abundance, and anything else that would enable you to consistently identify a formation. Pay attention to the vegetation, which may help you recognize a formation. Plot the examined exposures on the field map with rock symbols and sketch in formation contacts where possible (Figure 20-3). (Normally you would plot directly on the topographic map. A separate map is used for illustration here to lessen confusion from overlapped lines and symbols.)

Take strike and dip readings where inclined rock layers are well exposed. Geologists use a Brunton compass (Figure 20-4) for these readings. Perhaps the easiest method is to place your notebook on an inclined rock surface and take the readings off the even surface of the notebook. Adjust the compass to true north before you take any readings. To measure strike, the direction of a horizontal line on an inclined rock surface, place an edge of the opened compass on the notebook with the window and mirror face up; maneuver the instrument until the level bubble is centered. Read the compass direction on the outermost scale. Now, place the instrument side down on the notebook at right angles to strike (Figure 20-5). Adjust a lever in the back of the instrument until another level bubble is centered. Read the dip value—in degrees from the horizontal, less than 90—on the innermost scale. To partly compensate for the unevenness of a rock surface, you might take three readings and accept the average value. Note the general direction of dip and plot a T-shaped dip-strike symbol—the shorter stem of the T points in the direction of dip—with a protractor on the field map. Write the value of dip next to the symbol.

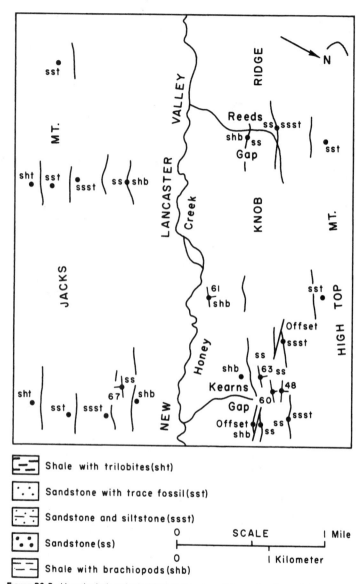

FIGURE 20-3. Hypothetical geological field sketch map of the region shown in Figure 20-2. (Based on data modified from the same source as for Figure 20-2.)

Figure 20-4. One method of measuring strike of a sandstone bed, with a Brunton compass, by placing the instrument on a notebook and leveling it. The sandstone surface dips to the lower right at right angles to strike.

Figure 20-5. One method of measuring dip, with a Brunton compass, on the same sandstone surface as in Figure 20-4. The dip value in this case, read off the inner scale, is 14°. The level bubble at the top center of the instrument face is centered.

Brunton compasses are expensive, but you can achieve reasonable dip/strike results with equipment of less cost. (You can purchase a relatively inexpensive version of the Brunton compass from Ward's Natural Science Establishment, Inc., 5100 West Henrietta Road, P.O. Box 92912, Rochester, NY 14692-9012.) An inexpensive, fluid-filled compass mounted on a straight-sided base is useful for strike readings, more so if an air leak has created an automatic leveling bubble. For dip, cut or file a notch at the center of the base of a protractor. Lay a string with an attached weight in the notch and hold the string in place. Align the straight base of the protractor parallel with the surface of an inclined rock layer at right angles to strike. Read the dip angle from the horizontal where the taut string meets the arc of the protractor.

Continue with your observations until you've examined all the exposures or the time allotted for the project is consumed. Don't forget to check stream cuts, road cuts, and other human-made excavations. Geologists would also examine any information about the rocks beneath the surface from water or oil wells.

In the vicinity of Kearns Gap the rocks are offset (Figure 20-3), at first glance by a strike-slip fault. But at one place where the fault is partly exposed, the block toward High Top Mountain has moved up relative to the other to substantiate a reverse fault. You can only estimate the value of the steeply dipping fault, greater than that of the rock layers.

You notice Jacks and High Top Mountains are held up by the same sandstone with an intertwined, tubelike trace fossil; New Lancaster Valley is underlain by a shale with brachiopods; and a shale with trilobites overlies the sandstone of Jack Mountain. Other areas intermediate in relief between prominent ridges and the valley are underlain by the same sandstone and siltstone formation. With the topographic contours as guides, you draw in all contacts. At ridge gaps the contacts indent away from New Lancaster Valley, and follow broad V-shaped notches (see chapter 9) that point in the direction of dip of the rock layers. You draw the fault with a heavier line than that drawn for contacts. Fill in the formation areas with the rock symbols or use patterns or colors.

Your map shows five rock units that may be called formations (Figure 20-6). You recall which formation underlies another and arrange all the formations in their correct order, the oldest at the bottom (Figure 20-3). If time allows, you might try to identify the fossils and assign a real age to the formations.

Now, you draw a cross section at right angles to the strike of the formations where you have the most dip and strike readings. A logical choice is along line A-B. First, draw a cross profile from the topographic map (Figure 20-2). Set up a vertical scale along one margin for elevations; this scale may or may not equal the

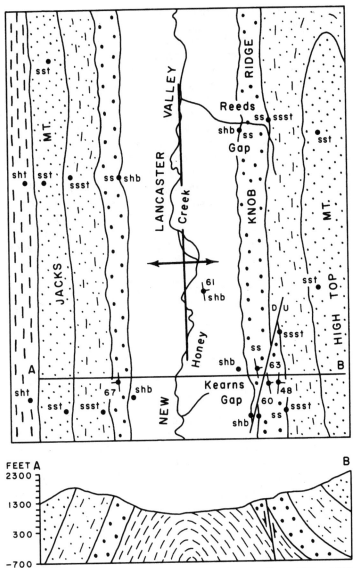

FIGURE 20-6. Completed geologic map and cross section based on Figures 20-2 and 20-3. For the cross section, drop a point on the cross profile wherever line *A-B* crosses a formation contact; show the formations dipping at those angles depicted on the map, and draw in the fault and rock symbols. Rock symbols are explained and arranged according to relative age in Figure 20-3. (Based on data modified from the source as for Figure 20-2.)

horizontal scale. If the vertical scale is greater, the vertical dimensions are drawn upward unnaturally high and the vertical scale is said to be exaggerated. Wherever a contour line intersects line A-B, project its value straight down onto the vertical scale below and plot the position with a point. Connect all points with a smooth, curved line, and keep in mind the contour interval when you extrapolate above the highest or below the lowest points. Now project on the cross profile every formation contact that intersects line A-B. With a protractor, plot the dip values and watch for the correct dip direction. Maintain the formation thicknesses as you extend them deeper. Caution: Don't extend your cross section any deeper than the observations warrant. The opposed dips show that an anticline dominates the region; its axis, shown by a heavy long line crossed by a shorter double-barbed line, runs along the center of New Lancaster Valley. High Top Mountain rests along the axis of an adjoining syncline. Show the formations in the cross section with rock symbols, and align any linear symbols parallel to the layering. Depict relative movement on opposite sides of the fault with opposing arrows.

There, the project's done (Figure 20-6). And you have the feeling of intimate knowledge of a region. Sometime later a geologist friend shows you a published geologic map that includes your mapped area. Your map is very similar to that shown on the published version—you did a good job! Your formations, from oldest to youngest, are called Reedsville, Bald Eagle, Juniata, Tuscarora, and Rose Hill; the first three are Ordovician in age, the other two are Silurian.

With this brief tutorial under your belt, you have the means to understand and appreciate the regional geological highway maps, with accompanying cross sections, listed in Appendix C.

Should you wish to obtain detailed geologic maps, contact the appropriate state geological survey (Appendix B) or the U.S. Geological Survey (USGS). From the USGS request a geologic map index for the state in question and an order form; send your request to: USGS Map Distribution, Box 25286, Denver, CO 80225 (Phone: 303-236-7477).

Suggested Reading

Barnes, J. W. *Basic Geological Mapping.* New York: Halsted Press, 1991.
Compton, R. R. *Geology in the Field.* New York: John Wiley, 1985.

How to Make a Mineral, Rock, or Fossil Collection

Why Collect Minerals, Rocks, or Fossils?

Minerals, rocks, and fossils are the stuff of geology—that of which Earth is made. A collection of these materials allows you to handle them at will, pore over them, become intimate with the basic components of your natural physical surroundings. To collect such materials, you survey the natural world outdoors and visit places not regularly tramped.

Although professional mineralogists, petrologists, and paleontologists make most discoveries in their specialty, an amateur collector can unearth equally significant finds. Amateurs have made important discoveries.

The collection and maintainance of a collection is a fun, interesting hobby. But this endeavor may also lead to a career in the natural sciences or related fields.

Collecting

Ethics of Collecting

Up front must be the ethics of collecting. To collect minerals, rocks, and fossils should be considered a privilege rather than a right. Don't abuse that privilege and ruin the possibility for further collecting by yourself or for others that follow you. Collecting ethics include at least the following:

1. Always make a reasonable attempt to gain authorized access to any property, private or public. If you lack permission to enter a property, you violate the common law of trespass. Private landowners may be reluctant to grant you permission because of their responsibility for any injury you might sustain, unless their state has an owner-release law that relieves them of such responsibility.

Collecting on federal land, except in national parks and similar prohibited areas, has been generally allowed for the noncommercial, avocational collector who takes a few specimens without the

265

use of motorized excavating devices. But the laws are changing. Check with such agencies as the U.S. Forest Service or the Bureau of Land Management to determine if collecting is permissible and if a collecting permit is required. What you wish to collect may make a difference. Rocks cause less concern than minerals, and minerals may be less of a concern than fossils, in particular, vertebrate fossils.

Similar leniency for collecting on most state land has existed as on federal land as far as the avocational collector is concerned, but new regulations in some states have come into play. Contact an appropriate state agency, such as a state geological survey (Appendix B), for information on any such regulations.

2. Once your entrance has been authorized, behave as an honored guest on the property. Close any gates you have opened, and remain on established roads or trails with your vehicle. Do not disturb crops, buildings, or other personal property. Remove litter, even some you didn't create. Don't start fires. If you must excavate, fill in all holes. And, in particular on private property, avoid the use of alcohol and drugs, and don't make unnecessary noise. To ensure future visits by you and others, and in common fairness, return the landowner's favor with a gesture of your own: Present the owner with a fine specimen from your collection, a book, food, or drink.

3. Practice restraint in collecting. Specimen hogs are as bad as fish- and game-hogs. Collect only those specimens that will enhance your collection and you will definitely use. If a specimen is apt to decorate the mantelpiece for a time, but will eventually be thrown out, leave that specimen at the exposure. And don't collect specimens for later sale, which leads naturally to overcollection—and exploitation.

Where to Look

Whether you pursue minerals, rocks, or fossils, the general approach is similar: You seek out exposures of rocks, natural or human-made. Natural exposures include stream cutbanks or valley walls, cliffs, caves, or hillsides—in particular where masking vegetation is scarce. Absence of soil, sediment, or ice may expose rocks in terrain of little slope. Human-made exposures are more numerous: quarries; pits; mines; excavations for dams, buildings, pipelines, and cables; tunnels; canals; and road and railroad cuts. Many such exposures can be located on detailed topographic maps. Quarries, mines, and gravel pits, especially, are plotted on these maps.

Don't neglect the use of geologic maps (see chapter 20 and Appendix C) in your quest. A knowledge of where rocks of a given age or fossil-bearing formations might be exposed narrows your search.

For known specific localities, consult collectors' magazines and books, publications of state geological surveys or the U.S. Geological Survey, and other professional geological publications. *An Illustrated Guide to Fossil Collecting* by R. L. Casanova and R. P. Ratkevich contains many fossil localities listed by state, and J. R. MacDonald's *The Fossil Collector's Handbook* provides general suggestions for collecting in the United States. For a more direct approach, ask local collectors, museum personnel, or geology professors. Many are willing to share collecting localities if they know you are a serious collector who collects conservatively for learning and enjoyment.

Collecting Equipment

Useful collecting equipment includes: hammer; a cold chisel or two; steel wrecking bar; goggles; old pocketknife or sturdy kitchen knife; awl; fossil hardener; hand lens; notebook and pencil; marker pen; slips of paper for labels; newspaper; tape; toilet tissue; small boxes, cans, and jars; knapsack or backpack; maps; and perhaps an acid bottle. The hammer helps free a specimen from enclosing rock. A geologist's or mason's hammer is most often used. The pounding end of a geologist's hammer (Figure 21-1) is squarish; the chipping or picking end tapers to a point if the hammer is the "hard-rock" type or a chisel edge if the "soft-rock" type. A mason's hammer resembles the soft-rock type, useful to split apart shaly rocks. The longer, tapered end of either type of hammer helps pry out specimens from cracks and cavities. The wrecking bar is another good prying tool. Use a cold chisel to free specimens when a hammer itself won't work. An extra, heavier sledgehammer to break up the occasional larger rocks can be carried in your vehicle. CAUTION: Watch out for flying rock chips when you whack rocks with hammers or chisels, not only for yourself but also for others nearby. Here's where goggles come in handy; if you lack goggles, at least turn your head away from the source of the rock shrapnel. Old knives enable you to pry apart the weaker shales, and an awl assists you to extricate fossils from poorly lithified shales and sandstones.

Now for the nonextractive equipment. The fossil hardener is used to impregnate and harden crumbling or flaking fossils, or the rock they are in, before you collect the fossils. Elmer's glue, thin-

FIGURE 21-1. Cretaceous ammonoid cephalopod broken out from a concretion with a geologist's hammer.

ned with water; Duco cement and clear fingernail polish, both soluble in acetone; and shellac, thinned with alcohol, are all good fossil hardeners. Allow the fossils to dry before you apply a hardener. Fragile leaf and insect fossils in split shales may also be slightly hardened with a plastic spray. A 5-to-10-power hand lens or magnifying glass is useful to view mineral grains, small crystals, and small fossils or the details of larger ones. Pack out your specimens in a knapsack or backpack. I'll discuss the other items in the next section.

How to Collect

Don't rush your collecting; be prepared to expend *time*. How much time is enough? At least continue your search until better specimens no longer come into view.

Examine an exposure in systematic fashion, left to right, bottom to top (if the slope is not too steep). But first, look over weathered rock accumulated at the base of a slope. Turn over rock fragments. Look for associations of minerals and fossils with particular rock types. When you find a desired mineral, rock, or fossil, trace its source upslope.

Minerals and rocks are best sought from fresh exposures, little altered by the action of weathering. You don't want iron oxide–stained or partly dissolved specimens for your collection. Walk into the sun to better detect translucent or transparent minerals in rock rubble. Agates, for example, are easily seen along beaches or in dry streambeds by this tactic.

Fossils of good quality can be taken from both fresh and weathered exposures. Those preserved as carbonized films or thin impressions, such as leaves, are best collected by splitting fresh shales. Others, such as brachiopods or blastoids with thicker hard parts, often are set free as shales and limestones weather and can be easily collected. Fossils, as a rule, are best preserved in shales and limestones; shales, in particular, allow for the most detailed preservation. Break concretions apart in your search for fossils (Figure 21-1). For serious study, collect also the impressions contained in the enclosing fragments. Concretions are often jammed with fossils, although the enclosing rock may be barren or rarely contains them.

As you work an exposure, set specimens aside. Moist or wet fossil specimens require time to dry and harden up before they are wrapped. When you are finished at an exposure, select only the best specimens from those accumulated to become part of your collection.

For minute and microscopic fossils, collect bags of crumbly rock and sediment. Later, you can soak, wash, and sieve the bagged material to concentrate and recover the fossils.

If you come upon part of a vertebrate skeleton that seems to continue into the exposure (Figure 21-2), *do not* begin to dig! Notify a vertebrate paleontologist at the nearest university, museum, or geological survey. Record the position of any bones you can see. If possible, take a few photographs for the paleontologist's perusal. You might have discovered a significant find that a trained and well-equipped expedition can properly excavate for later study and display.

A pertinent rule for the serious collector might be: If you haven't recorded the locality for a specimen, don't collect that specimen. Similar is the adage: A specimen is as good as its label. Comparison of specimens from different localities is meaningless without good locality data, and a collection donated to a university or museum will have limited use without such information.

Record the locality in your field notebook, and be as precise as you can: ideally so precise that another collector, upon reading your description, could find the spot. A locality description might

FIGURE 21-2. Middle Cenozoic mammal bones partly weathered out of mudstone. Length of the incomplete lower jaw at the left is 6.3 inches (16 cm).

read: "East road cut South Dakota (Highway) 63, 16.4 air miles southwest of Timber Lake, South Dakota." Access to a map with legal land divisions may allow you to prefix this description with "NE1/4NE1/4SW1/4 Sec. 32, T. 15 N., R. 24 E.," for a more detailed location. And, if possible, localize the exposure further by reference to a mileage marker.

Of special importance when collecting fossils is to record their stratigraphic position or level of occurrence within layered strata. Once you've pinpointed a locality on a geologic map you can determine the formation and its age. But you must also position collected fossils within a formation to add further significance to your collection. Relate them to the distance in feet or meters above or below an obvious "marker bed," such as one of coal, limestone, or sandstone.

Assign a field number to each collecting locality for easy reference to that locality. Place this number in your field notebook and next to a plot of the locality on a map. If you are rushed, the field number can substitute for a description on the locality label tucked in with a specimen. A simple system I use is a two-digit number for the year of collecting followed by a consecutive number for each locality visited during that year: 95-23, 95-24. If necessary, the field number may be modified for specimens collected from a single locality but from different rock layers or different positions within the same rock layer: 95-23-1, 95-23-2, 95-23-3.

Other entries in the notebook include date, a description of the rock from which fossils or minerals were collected, an estimate of abundance of the collected specimens—abundant, common, rare—and associated rocks, minerals, or fossils. The recommended acid bottle will enable you to recognize calcareous shales and sandstones and help you distinguish limestones and dolostones.

Now some techniques to bring the collected specimens home. Use newspaper to wrap specimens, mainly so they don't rub and deface each other during transport. For the larger and more durable specimens, chip off unnecessary sharp edges. Larger, broken fossils can be assembled and pressed together with aluminum foil before being wrapped. Lay a specimen on a few thicknesses of newspaper ripped to an appropriate size. Insert a locality label. Pass a corner of the newspaper over the specimen and snug it underneath. Fold the newspaper tightly against the specimen, left to right and right to left, and fold further any projecting corners. Roll the specimen toward the remaining corner and fold this corner in toward yourself. Seal the folded corner to the rest of the tight package with a small piece of tape; any kind will do, but filamentous tape is strongest. Write the field number on the package with a marker pen.

Fragile specimens require different treatment. Wrap somewhat fragile specimens in toilet tissue before you wrap them in newspaper. Especially delicate specimens should also be wrapped in toilet tissue and then placed with a snug fit in a rigid box, can, or jar. Some fossil or mineral specimens should be left in the rock, wrapped, and removed from the rock at home. Transport fragile fossils from sand or silt in a protective cushion of these sediments in bags, boxes, or cans.

Preparing Specimens

Most specimens benefit from a good wash with detergent. Scrub with an old toothbrush. Stubborn dirt may require considerable soaking or even boiling. Don't wash fragile or cracked specimens, which may crumble in water, or water-soluble minerals such as halite. If you're unsure of the water treatment, test any expendable fragments first.

You have several methods at your disposal to remove unnecessary rock material. Break away thicker rock masses with a hammer and chisel. First, however, study the rock to see if natural cracks might separate the rock around a specimen. Wear goggles for this hammer-and-chisel operation as you would in the field. You might have to cut a channel around the specimen until it rests on a pedestal. Then chisel the pedestal free. For thin, slabby rock, nibble away with pliers or cut the rock with an old hacksaw. You can work faster with silicon carbide cutoff disks or grinding wheels and brass brushes mounted in power drills. Better still is the use of a special table-mounted saw with a diamond blade. Again, don't forget to wear protective goggles.

For detailed rock removal, resort to old dental tools and crochet hooks with their ends modified to points and tiny chisels. Scrape and flake with care, and wash the cleaning area often. A vibrating-point engraving tool speeds up the fine work. For better control of the specimen, hold it against a sandbag or some other means of support.

Some fragile fossils require that you impregnate them with hardener before you remove the containing rock. Experiment until you determine which dilution of a hardener works best. You might begin with one part hardener and one part thinner.

You might try to dissolve unwanted carbonate minerals or rocks with acetic or hydrochloric acid, diluted with five to ten parts water. Always test a small fragment first before you decide on the type and strength of acid. Acetic acid, the gentler of the two, is present in vinegar; concentrated glacial acetic acid, used in the stopbath for photograph processing, can be bought at a photographic supply store. Hydrochloric acid is known commercially as muriatic acid and is used in the geologist's acid bottle. The acid treatment works best to clean and free siliceous materials. CAUTION: When you work with acid, use nonmetallic containers and wear goggles and gloves.

More detailed information on the preparation and cleaning of fossils is given in *Fossils for Amateurs, A Guide to Collecting and Preparing Invertebrate Fossils* by Russell P. MacFall and Jay Wollin.

Samples of sediment or crumbly rock collected for minute fossils or microfossils should first be soaked. If breakup of the sediment or rock doesn't occur, try boiling. Wash easily handled amounts of broken-up material in a small pot until the water is clear. Dry the material and pass it through several fine sieves. Retrieve minute fossils from the sieve concentrates with tweezers and a large magnifier; recover microfossils with a fine brush and a microscope.

Identifying, Cataloging, Storing, and Displaying Specimens

Once minerals, rocks, and fossils are prepared, you are better able to see the features useful for identification. Chapters 14 through 18 help you begin to identify minerals, rocks, and fossils. If the collection bug bites hard, consult your nearest library for the numerous publications available on Earth materials or request interlibrary loans if your library is small. Join a mineral, rock, or fossil club for help with some of your identification problems as you interact with those who have larger collections. And university, museum, and geological survey staff are usually willing to help if you request only occasional aid and don't overpower them with too many specimens. Reciprocate their aid with an offer of specimens they consider of value to their collections.

Cataloging is the assignment of numbers to collected and prepared specimens. If a label is lost or the specimen is displayed without one, such a specimen can be readily identified and its locality recovered by a catalog number. The easiest system assigns "1" to the first specimen and numbers others consecutively. Assign a number to each specimen or a group of similar specimens (Figure 21-3) of the same kind of mineral, rock, or fossil from the same level in a rock layer at a given locality. So specimens of the same mineral, rock, or fossil from the same locality but from different rock layers or different levels in the same rock layer should be assigned different catalog numbers.

Print the catalog number in an inconspicuous place on the specimen with a fine, black, waterproof marker pen or with a fine drawing pen and waterproof black ink. On light-colored specimens the number will appear clearly; for dark-colored specimens, dab on a spot of white paint before you write the number. Smooth out rough surfaces with hardener before you apply a number.

For the actual catalog you might begin with a card file. In reality, such a file may consist of two: one alphabetic, the other numeric. If you replace specimens with others of better quality, it's simple to replace cards. The catalog bears what is given on the specimen label but often more: for example, catalog number and number of specimens, name, perhaps age and rock formation, locality, collector, date of collecting, and perhaps donor, identifier, field number, and remarks, such as position of specimens in a rock layer or formation. Inclusion of the field number cross-references your catalog with your notebook(s).

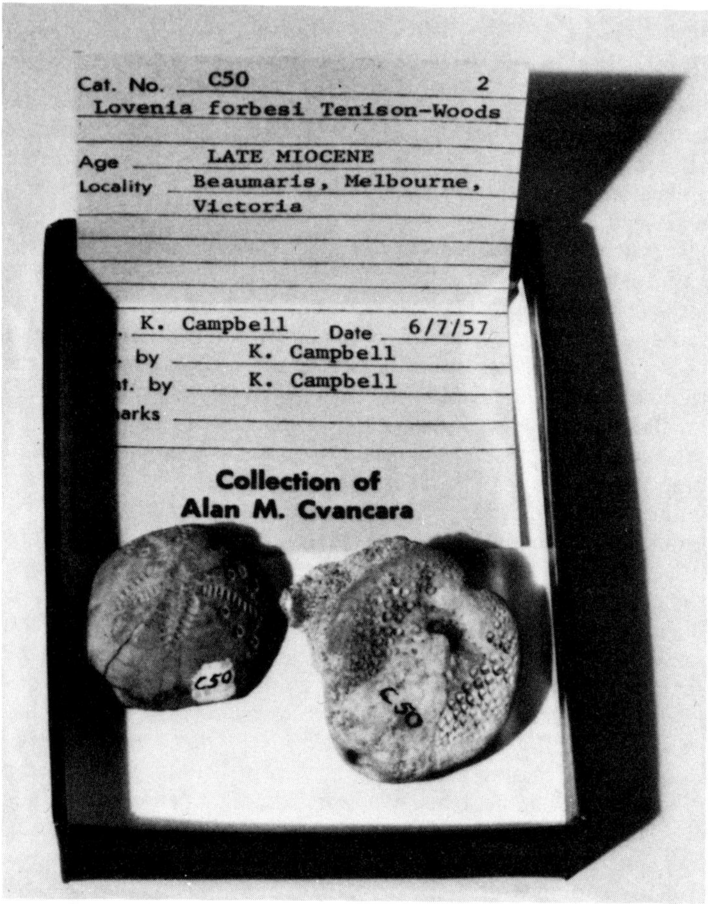

Figure 21-3. Cataloged specimens of a Miocene sea urchin in a specimen tray with a label. The catalog number (C50) may be inked directly on a specimen (right) or over a dab of white paint (left).

If your collection grows beyond what you had first imagined and you desire rapid retrieval of information about your collection, you may wish to transfer your card file to a computer database. Computer-generated labels for your specimens are a logical next step.

Cabinets with shallow drawers are ideal places to store specimens. You might acquire these cabinets at garage sales, used-furniture stores, or build them yourself. The most expensive cabinets are those from geological or biological supply firms. If you must store specimens in boxes, select those of the same size that stack well.

Place specimens that bear the same catalog number in separate cardboard or plastic trays. Add labels to the trays with information from the catalog. If the label is folded at 90°, with the catalog number and name on the vertical part (Figure 21-3), it is easy to locate a specimen from the front of a cabinet drawer.

The way you organize the specimens within your collection depends on personal preference. But minerals are often grouped by chemical composition, such as sulfides, oxides, and silicates; rocks by their classification, such as conglomerates, sandstones, and shales; and fossils by group, such as sponges, corals, and bryozoans. As you specialize with your collection, as most collectors do, your organization will become more specialized. Whatever the organization, arrange the specimen trays in cabinet drawers or boxes alphabetically by kind of mineral, rock, or fossil and numerically by catalog number.

For ideas on how to display specimens, visit museums, shows, or the homes of experienced collectors. Display only your best and larger specimens. A good display case is glass-fronted; its use is enhanced if the sides and top are also of glass. If you can't acquire one of these cases, you might try an old glass-fronted china cabinet. Place specimens directly on glass shelves or on raised wooden, plastic, metal, or Styrofoam bases. Accompany each specimen with an attractive label. Give some thought to special lighting and the way light may enhance the beauty of your displayed specimens.

Suggested Reading

Casanova, R. L., and R. P. Ratkevich. *An Illustrated Guide to Fossil Collecting*. Happy Camp, CA: Naturegraph, 1981.

Cvancara, A. M. "Curating Your Rocks, Minerals, and Fossils." *Earth* 1 (4) (1992): 62–66.

MacDonald, J. R. *The Fossil Collector's Handbook: A Paleontology Field Guide*. Englewood Cliffs, NJ: Prentice-Hall, 1983.

MacFall, R. P., and Jay Wollin. *Fossils for Amateurs: A Guide to Collecting and Preparing Invertebrate Fossils*. New York: Van Nostrand Reinhold, 1983.

Parker, Steve. *The Practical Paleontologist*. New York: Simon & Schuster, 1990.

Pellant, Chris. *Rocks, Minerals and Fossils of the World*. Boston: Little, Brown, 1990.

22

How to Sleuth Stone

A stone is not a stone is not a stone. To a geologist a **stone** usually means a loose mineral or rock fragment shaped by natural processes and derived from a larger rock mass; sand grains may be included. R. V. Dietrich's interesting little book, *Stones*, is devoted to them; tidbits of information include stones' therapeutic value, such as the palming of smooth stones for their tranquilizing effect.

To those in the stone industry, stone is natural hard rock material quarried or mined largely for constructional or industrial use and altered only by shaping or sizing. But gemstone, precious or semiprecious stone used as a gem when cut and polished, is also within the realm of stone. **Construction stone**, used for construction without chemical or heat treatment, includes crushed or broken stone and dimension stone. **Crushed stone** is used for riprap on breakwaters, piers, and similar places; concrete aggregate; cement; highway base; railroad ballast; and a myriad of other uses. **Dimension stone** is cut into blocks and slabs for a variety of purposes.

Stone? Rock? Rock to the stone industry is stone still in place. To a geologist, rock is an aggregate of minerals (see chapter 14) or a relatively hard, coherent, naturally formed mass of minerals.

I hope this stone-rock discourse has enlightened and not confused you, for such confusion is frequent. In the Viking cartoon, *Hagar the Horrible*, for example, a jewelry merchant attempts a sale to a reluctant Hagar for his wife. The persistent merchant asks Hagar for his wife's birthstone. Hagar conceives a hard, strong, "stone" appropriate for his domineering wife and replies: "Granite."

Stone sleuthing, the tracking down of the source of stone utilized by humans, is a conscious or subconscious pastime of many geologists. This activity may never develop into an overwhelming craze, but it intrigues those who savor a little detective work now and then. And the challenge provides an easy way to learn more geology. If we restrict our sleuthing to dimension stone, the pieces tend to be large, and cut or polished surfaces better reveal the features of the stone. For useful background, though, we might first examine the kinds and uses of dimension stone.

Kinds of Dimension Stone

The rock classification of the dimension stone industry is much simplified compared to that of the petrologist. Six basic groups are recognized by the stone industry: granite, traprock, limestone, marble, sandstone, and slate.

Granite includes all granitic rocks (see chapter 15) and also gneiss. The geologic definition is stretched further to allow the inclusion of diorite, gabbro, and similar dark rocks—the **black granite** of the dimension stone industry. Color is of utmost importance for more specific names, such as "Georgia Gray," "Mahogany," "Wausau Red," and "Wyoming Raven."

Traprock encompasses all dark igneous rocks finer grained than black granite: basalt and fine-grained diorite, gabbro, pyroxenite, hornblendite, and peridotite. Even darker felsite, such as andesite, may be called traprock.

The stone industry's **limestone** generally agrees with the geologist's concept of that rock (see chapter 16), but also includes dolostone. **Marble**, though, translates to any limy, crystalline rock or serpentinite that will take a polish. **Onyx** (AHN-icks) **marble** or **Mexican onyx**—most comes from Mexico—is dense, banded, translucent, and unmetamorphosed and formed by cold-water precipitation. Dripstone (see chapter 6) is called **cave onyx**. Porous travertine, if banded and dense enough to accept a polish, is also called marble. Green to nearly black **verde antique** (vuhr-dan-TEEK) or **serpentine marble** consists of serpentine (see chapter 14) intersected by small veins of lighter-colored minerals. This rock is marble to the stonecutter because of the marblelike veining and the capability to take a good polish.

Commercial **sandstone** includes also the conglomerate, breccia, siltstone, and quartzite of the geologist. Other names used by the stone industry are: **puddingstone**, colloquial for certain conglomerates; **bluestone**, a hard, dark or slate gray, feldspar sandstone that splits easily into slabs; **brownstone**, a brown to reddish-brown feldspar sandstone, typified by those from the northeastern United States; **freestone**, one that slabs in any direction; and **flagstone**, a sandstone or slate that splits into large, thin slabs.

Slate, a fine-grained rock that cleaves into thin sheets, is essentially as the geologist conceives it.

Many other varieties of stone, the so-called **miscellaneous stone**, may be used, at times, for dimension purposes. Examples include soapstone (rich in talc), greenstone (green from chlorite and epidote), schist, pumice, fieldstone (of cobbles and boulders), pegmatite, and petrified wood.

Uses of Dimension Stone

The uses for a dimension stone depend on a stone's strength, durability, hardness, and color. Strength refers to a stone's resistance to crushing or bending. A stone's durability is defined by maintenance of strength with time, and resistance to weathering (see chapter 23), impact, and abrasion. Hardness relates somewhat to durability but also to the ease of workability or shaping. Dimension stone may be classified according to its use as building stone, ornamental stone, monumental stone, paving blocks, curbing, flagging, roofing slate, and millstock slate.

Building stone incorporates a large variety of stone for exterior (Figures 22-1) and interior construction. Included is stone for bridges, sea walls, and the facing of levees and dams. The use of massive blocks in buildings today is rare because of high cost, but stone blocks and slabs in such places as cornices and trim around doors and windows are common. Thin veneer slabs may cover walls or parts of them.

Most **ornamental stone**, valued for its markings or color, is used for interior finishing. Marble in thin slabs is a favorite, but limestone, sandstone, granite, and slate are also used. A famous building and ornamental stone is the Indiana Limestone (Figure 22-2), trade name for a limestone from the Mississippian Salem Formation and quarried in south-central Indiana. This limestone has been used in the construction of such buildings as the Pentagon, Empire State Building, and the Washington Cathedral.

Monumental stone must meet more exacting requirements than building stone, and to some extent, ornamental stone. It should, for example, be uniform in color and texture, be free of flaws, and allow a good contrast to lettering when polished. Another important quality is the lack of such minerals as pyrite that may cause rust stains upon weathering. Tombstones (Figure 22-3) fit into this category of dimension stone. A variety of monumental stone is **statuary stone**, with the added requirements of easy workability and lack of chipping when carved. Granite and marble constitute most of the monumental stone. A fuzzy line may exist between building and monumental stone. The Lincoln

FIGURE 22-1. Church walls constructed (1949) of split fieldstone of glacial cobbles and boulders; Salem Lutheran Church, Hitterdal, northwestern Minnesota.

Memorial in Washington, D.C., for example, is a building constructed of monumental stone.

Paving blocks, most often of granite, are rectangular blocks once used for areas subjected to heavy, abrasive traffic such as that in city streets and freight yards. Their use has largely diminished to patios, borders for walks and gardens, and similar uses.

Curbing is stone in long, thin slabs for edging streets and roadways. Granite, quartzite, and certain types of sandstone provide the most resistance to abrasion and weathering, and so are used mainly for curbing.

FIGURE 22-2. A Pleistocene mammoth constructed of Indiana Limestone and set into an exterior brick wall of Leonard Hall, a geology and geological engineering building at the University of North Dakota at Grand Forks. The marine Mississippian limestone, from the Salem Formation, is clastic, oolitic, and bears fossils; this limestone was quarried in south-central Indiana. (From Alan M. Cvancara, 1990, *Sleuthing Fossils*, Fig. 2-5; with permission, © 1990 by John Wiley & Sons, Inc.)

FIGURE 22-3. Granite tombstone, a kind of monumental stone. This rock is resistant to weathering (see chapter 23) and receives lettering, carving, and polishing well.

Flagging or flagstone is made of thin, easily split slabs for lining walks, patios, courtyards, and the like. Mostly sandstone and slate are used, but certain types of limestone may be suitable.

Roofing slate must be easily cleavable, smooth, and lack imperfections. The availability of other, cheaper, roofing materials has drastically diminished the use of roofing slate. But some persons still favor the attractiveness and unusual durability of roofing slate in spite of the cost.

Millstock slate includes blocks and slabs for sills, switchboards, billiard tables, blackboards, and the like. It must be even-grained but not all that fissile (splits readily into thin sheets). The best blackboard slate comes from Lehigh and Northhampton Counties, Pennsylvania.

Dimension stone has a myriad of other minor uses. A sampling includes: grindstones (sandstone); tubs, sinks, and tanks (soapstone, slate); shower and toilet stalls (limestone, marble); and fireplaces, chimneys, and decorative walls—sandstone, pegmatite, petrified wood, and slate and related rocks.

Practicing the Art of Stone Sleuthing

Armed with knowledge of the main kinds and uses of dimension stone, you can restrict the number of stone possibilities somewhat as you sleuth. And, to know the main producing states and exporting countries (Table 22-1) helps narrow down the choices for the United States. Yes, we must keep in mind exporting countries, too, wherever we are. More than three decades ago, I stood at the edge of a small rural cemetery in eastern New South Wales, Australia. My professor pointed out a dark, pillarlike grave marker that rose above an overgrowth of bracken. Imagine my surprise when I learned the stone was laurvikite (or larvikite), a quartz-free granitic rock with pyroxene, from southern Norway!

In the United States, granitic and metamorphic rocks are extracted from mountainous belts and nearby regions of the Appalachians, Rockies, and Pacific mountain belt. Granite of the Lake Superior region, chiefly from Minnesota and Wisconsin, derives from eroded mountain roots in a southern extension of the Canadian Shield. Marble is extracted from both eastern and western states in both metamorphic and nonmetamorphic terrane. Limestone and sandstone are produced mainly from the interior states, where igneous intrusive and metamorphic rocks are scarce or absent, and the interior parts of coastal states. Slate is quarried from metamorphic terrane of eastern states. Traprock is mainly pro-

TABLE 22-1. Main Producing States and Major Countries Exporting Dimension Stone to the United States

Dimension Stone	Main Producing States and Countries Exporting to the U.S.
Granite	California, Colorado, Connecticut, *Georgia*, Maine, Maryland, *Massachusetts*, Minnesota, Missouri, New Hampshire, New York, North Carolina, Oklahoma, Pennsylvania, Rhode Island, South Carolina, South Dakota, Texas, *Vermont*, Virginia, Washington, Wisconsin; Argentina, Brazil, Canada, China, India, Italy, Portugal, Spain
Limestone	Alabama, Arkansas, California, *Indiana*, Iowa, Kansas, Minnesota, New Mexico, New York, Ohio, *Texas*, *Wisconsin*; France, Mexico
Marble	Alabama, Arkansas, *Colorado*, *Georgia*, Idaho, Massachusetts, Montana, New Mexico, Puerto Rico, Tennessee, *Vermont*, China, France, Greece, Italy, Mexico, Portugal, Spain
Sandstone	Alabama, *Arizona*, Arkansas, California, Colorado, Indiana, Maryland, Michigan, Missouri, *New York*, North Carolina, *Ohio*, Oklahoma, Pennsylvania, Tennessee, Virginia; Canada
Slate	Maine, New York, Maryland, *Pennsylvania*, *Vermont*, Virginia; Italy, Spain
Traprock	Hawaii, Oregon, Washington

Primary source: U.S. Bureau of Mines' *Minerals Yearbook, Volume I, Metals and Minerals, 1991.*
States italicized were leading producers in 1991.

duced from a few western states that have been subjected to relatively young extrusive igneous activity. Table 22-1 tends to reflect these generalities about rock sources.

Now, for the actual sleuthing. First, identify the suspect stone to the best of your ability (see chapters 14 to 17). Pay attention to accessory, or unusual, features such as bedding, mottling, foliation, fossils, and weathering effects. Take some time with your scrutiny, and don't worry if, say, passersby stare suspiciously as you snuggle up to the wall of a bank building with your hand lens. Don't trust your memory; take good notes. Photograph the stone if you have the equipment; watch for the best light, if you have the time, to emphasize the stone's diagnostic qualities.

Once you've identified the stone, proceed in much the same manner as a detective who sleuths a human. Ask questions. Interview. A tombstone? Consult cemetery caretakers and dealers of tombstones. Most will probably be glad to help once they realize you are serious. Stone in a building? Interrogate companies that sell construction materials and construction firms. Should this lead nowhere, locate the builder, perhaps through the owner if the two are not the same. For older buildings, where builders have left or are deceased and present owners lack knowledge of building materials, your job becomes more involved. You might have to pore over city or county records. Don't become discouraged if the desired results take some time to surface.

For a traveler, stone sleuthing is also possible, but answers may materialize less often because of less intensive searches. Keep an eye out for dimension stone quarries, and attempt to solve stone sources in those cases where a stone is distinctive even from a distance. If you suspect a local source for a stone in a building, tombstone, or monument, ask residents about quarries—and seek out the quarries for your verification.

Here's a specific example of stone sleuthing while traveling. Imagine you're on an automobile trip through north-central Kansas; in a daydream, you stare ahead as your vehicle seems to drive itself. After a time, though, the mile-after-mile parade of squarish fenceposts along the highway snatches your attention. You realize there's something different about them. Well, of course, they're made of *stone*! You screech to a stop, run to the nearest fencepost for a closer look. The fenceposts are of tan, clastic limestone with marine fossils—clams and ammonoid cephalopods (see chapter 18). At the next town you inquire to discover the fenceposts derive from local quarries in a bed of "fencepost" limestone used, primarily during the late 1800s but also later, for clothesline poles, flagpoles, tombstones, stepping stones, watering troughs, and buildings, as well as fenceposts.

And now for a final, but significant point: Always verify any testimony or story about a stone source you have garnered. Don't antagonize, but analyze and confirm. A careful sleuth is a more accurate sleuth.

Suggested Reading

Barton, W. R. "Dimension Stone." *U.S. Bureau of Mines Information Circular* 8391 (1968): 1–147.

Dietrich, R. V. *Stones: Their Collection, Identification, and Uses.* San Francisco: Freeman, 1989.

Taylor, H. A., Jr. "Dimension Stone," in U.S. Bureau of Mines, *Minerals Yearbook, Volume I, Metals and Minerals, 1991.* Washington, DC: U.S. Department of the Interior, 1993.

23

How to Read Rock Weathering from Tombstones

Rock Weathering and Its Results

Weathering is natural decay. We see the effects as paint cracks and peels, bricks and concrete crumble, and metals rust and corrode. Rock weathering is the in-place breakup of rocks as they interact with the atmosphere, in particular with water, oxygen, and carbon dioxide. Given sufficient time, all rocks succumb and crumble to form that most vital of Earth materials that supports life—**soil**. Mixed with organic matter, soil differs from sediment, which has been moved and later deposited or precipitated. Rock weathering also provides the loose material from which sediments and sedimentary rocks are made.

Rocks weather both physically and chemically. **Physical weathering** is the breakup of rock into smaller fragments by physical, nonchemical means. Chief processes are **ice wedging**, already mentioned in chapter 3, and sheeting. Water seeps into cracks, expands its volume by 9 percent upon freezing to ice, and wedges apart rock blocks and particles. In loose sediment, water freezes to cause ice heaving, evidenced by tilted sidewalks and raised areas in roads that develop into chuckholes as ice melts. Ice wedging is most evident in regions of repeated freezing and thawing.

Sheeting or unloading breaks rocks into sheets or slabs, not by ice wedging but by release of pressure. Massive igneous rocks form at depth under high temperature and high pressure—confining pressure from all directions. Erosion removes the overlying rocks and lessens pressure. The massive igneous rock, brought toward the surface, expands upward with the release of pressure and forms expansion fractures parallel to its exposed surface. Quarry workers witness the formation of these fractures, often accompanied by loud noises, after rock is removed. Sheeting also causes rock bursts in some mines and tunnels during their excavation.

Minor mechanical weathering also occurs by other means. Plant roots wedge apart rock and sediment, and forest and grass fires may cause rocks to fracture and flake as they cool. Burrowing animals mix soil and rock particles.

Chemical weathering is rock decay caused by changes in chemical composition and the internal structure of minerals that make up the rocks; new minerals are created by these changes. Rocks fragmented by physical weathering are more susceptible to attack by chemical weathering: The smaller the particle, the greater is the surface area for chemical reaction.

First, rocks weather chemically by dissolving. The most notable rocks that dissolve are the carbonate rocks—limestone, dolostone, and marble. (This process was described in chapter 6.) Partly dissolved rocks display rough surfaces, often pitted, grooved, or fluted (Figure 23-1). Since the onset of industrialization and the expansion of fuel-driven vehicles, burned fuels have released copious amounts of carbon dioxide and sulfur dioxide into the atmosphere. These gases combine with precipitation to form carbonic and sulfuric acid, released as acid rain, fog, and snow—prevalent in such places as the northeastern United States. These added acids speed up the solution of rocks, and also injure the life of natural waters.

Second, rocks weather chemically as minerals combine with oxygen—**oxidize** to form such oxides as hematite and limonite (see chapter 14). The rusting of iron is oxidation. Oxidation is most prevalent with minerals rich in iron, such as amphibole and pyroxene.

And, third, rocks weather chemically when minerals unite in a chemical fashion with water or are said to **hydrolyze**. Water is not simply absorbed but distinct chemical changes occur and new minerals are formed.

To visualize how chemical weathering accomplishes rock decay, imagine a granite that both hydrolyzes and oxidizes. Remember granite (chapter 15)? It is a coarse-grained, igneous rock of mostly feldspar with quartz and iron- and magnesium-bearing minerals such as biotite and amphibole. The feldspar combines with water and carbonic acid (from carbon dioxide and rainwater) to form clay minerals, salts in solution (mostly carbonates and bicarbonates of sodium, calcium, and potassium) that are flushed away, and silica, some of which is removed in solution and some of which may remain behind as quartz. Likewise, the ferromagnesian minerals combine with water and carbonic acid to form products similar to those for the weathered feldspar. The removed

Figure 23-1. Fluted and pitted surface of dissolved limestone. The flutes at least partly follow fractures. The widest flute is about 0.6 inch (1.5 cm).

salts, however, are carbonates and bicarbonates of iron, magnesium, and calcium. And the oxidation of iron produces iron oxides. Quartz grains of the granite, very resistant to weathering, may be somewhat dissolved and rounded, but remain behind as little-changed grains of sand. Just think: A mighty rock—granite—reduced to a rusty, sandy, clay soil! The only requirements for this drastic transformation are air, water, and time. And Earth's surface provides plenty of all three.

Prior to the formation of soil, an intermediate state of weathering occurs called **spheroidal weathering**, the creation of rounded or spherical surfaces on weathered rock and the reduction of rock blocks to spheres or ellipsoids. Spheroidal weathering, well displayed in coarse-grained igneous rocks, is initiated by intersecting joints. Chemical weathering attacks the rock along joint surfaces but does more damage on the corners and edges of the rock blocks. In time, the blocks assume a rounded or spherical form.

A related process is **exfoliation**, the breaking of rock into concentric sheets, shells, or slabs. Exfoliation may result from sheeting, ice wedging, chemical weathering, or a combination of all three processes. Through chemical weathering, the expansion caused by an increase in volume as feldspar weathers to clay minerals may be significant. Exfoliation forms rounded hills called **exfoliation domes**, well exhibited in the granitic rocks of Yosemite National Park, California (see Figure 3-6).

Intersecting joints in sedimentary strata also allow physical and chemical weathering, in concert with other processes of erosion, to sculpture fascinating rock fins, arches, and columns or pinnacles. These features are well displayed in such places as Arches (see Figure 13-1) and Bryce Canyon National Parks, Utah.

What affects the rate at which rocks weather? Chiefly climate, followed by rock type. Water is a vital ingredient in any kind of weathering, and high temperatures speed up chemical reactions. Chemical weathering, therefore, occurs fastest in wet, hot climates in which thicker soils form and slowest in dry, cold climates where thinner soils result. In dry or cold climates, chemical weathering is minor or insignificant, and physical weathering dominates. Temperate climates induce intermediate rates of weathering and soil thicknesses, and a more even mix of chemical and physical weathering.

Rocks made up of soluble minerals, such as limestone, dolostone, marble, rock salt, and rock gypsum, weather or dissolve at a rapid pace in wet climates, slowly in dry climates. Expect, for example, that a limestone in New York will weather faster than one in Utah.

Rocks of silicate minerals (see chapter 14)—quartz, feldspar, olivine, and the like—weather in relation to how distant their conditions of formation were from those at Earth's surface. Dark minerals, such as olivine (least resistant to weathering), pyroxene, and amphibole, have crystallized from molten rock material under high temperatures and pressures. Light minerals, such as muscovite and quartz, have crystallized at lower temperatures and pressures. So, dark, coarse-grained igneous rocks, at the surface and far from their conditions of formation, weather much faster than do light-colored ones. Quartz is one of the most resistant minerals to weathering, and rocks largely of this mineral—quartzite or quartz sandstone—are, therefore, resistant too; unless, of course, the grains are cemented together by calcite or some other similar soluble mineral.

Reading Rock Weathering from Tombstones

What we can read from tombstones—and other similar kinds of dimension stone (see chapter 22) used for monumental, ornamental, and building purposes—are *dated* effects and rates of weathering. As already mentioned, both effects and rates relate largely to climate and rock type.

Most tombstones are of granite and related rocks, marble, limestone, sandstone, and slate. Marble and sandstone, because of the ease with which they could be carved and engraved, were the rocks of choice in the past; now granite prevails.

Marble weathers chiefly by dissolving, and does so more in wetter climates. Solution is evidenced first by a dulling of polished surfaces; later, these surfaces become roughened and, in extreme cases, pitted and grooved. Roughened surfaces provide more exposed surface area and come under greater attack by further weathering. If lichens, incompatible with polluted atmospheres, grow on a marble tombstone, solution is enhanced. Lichens retain moisture in their vicinity and secrete acids. Marble tombstones that receive prolonged precipitation that drips from overhanging trees are also more susceptible to solution. And areas of frequent fog accelerate the weathering of marble because water droplets remain suspended for a long time.

Try to measure the thickness of surface removed from marble tombstones by solution to arrive at a rate of weathering. Required for accurate measurement is a resistant, almost insoluble mineral within the marble. A quartz vein, cut and polished within a flat surface of the marble and that now remains above a dissolved surface, is ideal. Professor E. M. Winkler, in the 1960s, measured such a projecting vein at the top of a Vermont marble tombstone in humid South Bend, Indiana; he obtained an average reduction of the marble surface of .06 inch (1.5 mm) in 43 years or 0.14 inch (3.5 mm) in 100 years. Professor A. Geikie, in the late 1800s, calculated a rate of lowering of about a third of an inch (8.5 mm) per century for marble tombstones in another humid region: Edinburgh, Scotland. In 1983, in subhumid Grand Forks, North Dakota, I arrived at a conservative weathering rate of about 1 mm in 97 years or 0.04 inch (1.0 mm) in 100 years for the lower marble part of a marble-granite tombstone (Figure 23-2). Conservative rate, I say, because I measured the relief of narrow ridges presum-

FIGURE 23-2. Comparison of the weathering effects of two rocks in a 97-year-old tombstone (1886 to 1983) in subhumid Grand Forks, northeastern North Dakota. The lower, inscribed part of fine-grained marble shows obvious effects of solution; the fine, diagonal ridges and crack (left) seem to follow foliation of the marble. The upper granite pillar is essentially un-weathered except for barely discernible iron oxide staining (not evident in the photograph).

ably caused by foliation, and the ridges were partly dissolved. Keep in mind that the rate of solution depends on the surface measured (lower versus upper) and the direction of exposure. More solution tends to occur on the side from which rain is most often wind-driven.

Physical weathering of marble is evidenced by cracks and rock flakes. Most of these features result from ice wedging in the higher latitudes. Southern exposures of tombstones tend to show more cracks and flakes because of more frequent freezing and thawing on these surfaces. Rock flakes may also form by the expansive force of newly formed minerals that occupy a greater volume than the original minerals. In a polluted, sulfur-dioxide atmosphere, sulfuric acid reacts with marble to form calcium sulfate or gypsum. This newly formed gypsum, with about a twofold increase in volume, may force calcite crystals apart and cause the marble to flake.

Granite tombstones are much more resistant to weathering than are marble tombstones. Rock flakes, though, may be evident and perhaps iron oxide stains from the chemical weathering of the ferromagnesian minerals; again, the degree of weathering depends on the climate and the time involved. Professor Geikie saw no apparent sign of decay of granite in the Edinburgh churchyards after 20 years. I saw only barely evident tinges of iron oxide on polished granite in the Grand Forks example (Figure 23-2). Careful observers have been surprised to find that some polished granite weathers faster than unpolished granite.

An extreme case of granite's resistance to weathering is found in monuments along the Nile in arid Egypt which date back to 2850 B.C. In 1916, D. C. Barton, an American geologist, estimated the average rate of disintegration of these monuments as only about .04 inch to .08 inch (1 mm to 2 mm) in 1,000 years, which equates to about 0.006 inch in 100 years; the greatest rate he found was only about 0.02 inch (0.5 mm) per 100 years.

Of the other rocks used for tombstones, limestone weathers much the same as does marble. Sandstone is highly resistant to weathering if the grains are largely of quartz and cemented by silica. Look for weathering in sandstone tombstones where the grains are cemented by soluble carbonate minerals or iron oxides. G. F. Matthias, a New York high school instructor, examined tombstones, in humid Middletown, Connecticut, of reddish brown feldspar-quartz sandstone ("brownstone," see chapter 22) cemented by calcite and hematite. In the 1960s, he measured chemical weathering by using the depth of inscriptions, based on an assumed standard depth of 0.16 inch (4.1 mm) on slate tombstones. The slate tombstones displayed no obvious weathering. Result: an average rate of weathering of about 0.03 inch (0.8 mm) in 145 years or 0.02 inch (0.5 mm) in 100 years. Also in the 1960s, in nearby West Willington, Connecticut, Professor P. H. Rahn discovered that brown sandstone weathers faster than marble, followed by schist and granite.

Accessory structures in sedimentary rocks such as fossils, concretions, or nodules (see chapter 16) may cause accelerated weathering. And if the rock is well bedded and cut so the beds are directed upward, weathering attack may be intense if other resistive qualities are lacking.

Slate offers great resistance to weathering because, most often derived from metamorphosed shale, this rock consists in large part of stable clay minerals already derived by weathering. You are apt to see, within a humid climate, perfectly legible 200-year-old slate tombstones in the same graveyard with younger, illegible marble tombstones.

Since we are all mortal, why not apply our knowledge of tombstone weathering to personal practical use? To choose a tombstone for yourself or others, you realize that a marble or limestone tombstone just doesn't have the permanence of one of granite, silica-cemented sandstone, or slate. The choice of marble or limestone is even less wise if the tombstone remains within a humid climate. But the final choice also depends on cost and attractiveness to the beholder.

Suggested Reading

Geikie, Archibald. "Rock-Weathering, as Illustrated in Edinburgh Churchyards." *Proceedings of the Royal Society of Edinburgh* 10 (1880): 518–532.

Matthias, G. F. "Weathering Rates of Portland Arkose Tombstones." *Journal of Geological Education* 15 (1967): 140–144.

Ollier, C. D. *Weathering*. New York: Wiley, 1986.

24

How to Prospect for Gold

A similar approach is used to prospect for useful Earth materials whether the desired material is uranium, copper, coal, water—or gold. You must learn ways to recognize the sought-after mineral and be aware of the kinds of rocks that contain the mineral. We've already seen how geologists prospect for oil and gas (see chapter 19). In this chapter you will learn how to prospect for gold.

In prospecting, science—based on careful observations and organization and analysis of facts—is of foremost importance. But art is also important, in the sense of a feel where discovery may occur and the predisposition to dare try a theory or supposition.

To prospect for gold is desirable for three reasons: (1) It excites the thrill of discovery in most of us; (2) in our day of sophisticated equipment and big business, gold, as a useful Earth material, can still be sought by the individual with limited equipment and funds; and (3) any gold discovered in sediment can be extracted and easily sold.

Recognizing Gold

As almost everyone knows, gold is yellow, glitters, and is heavy. These are all the characteristics you need to recognize gold, right? Not quite. Gold is gold- or sun-yellow in its native or chemically uncombined state, but may be pale yellow to silver-white if the combined silver, with which it often alloys, is appreciable. Gold glitters because of a metallic luster, but so do many other metallic minerals. Be aware of the metallic fool's gold minerals, pyrite and chalcopyrite (see chapter 14), which are brittle and yield a blackish powder (streak) when scratched; pyrite is harder than a knife and chalcopyrite is somewhat softer. Gold, on the other hand, is malleable (readily pounded into thin sheets) and displays its own color when most easily scratched by a knife. Oxidized, iron-stained biotite mica flakes are often confused for flakes of gold. The mica flakes, however, are crushed with a knife or needle, and float away with water currents. Gold is heavy, about 19 times heavier than water, and tends to remain behind as other materials are swept away. To visualize the heftiness of gold, conceive a pure cube of the precious metal 12 inches (30 cm) on a side—one cubic foot. Weight: a little more than 1,200 pounds (544 kg)!

Expect to find native gold in rock as feathery leaves, wires, crystals, or plates. In sediment, gold occurs as flakes, grains, or larger nuggets.

Gold, although durable in nature, dissolves in some substances. Gold dissolves in mercury to form an amalgam or alloy, utilized as a tooth filling. Only one acid—a mixture of three parts hydrochloric acid and one part nitric acid—will dissolve gold. Another commercial solvent, sodium or calcium cyanide, dissolves gold. The cyanide process is one of several commercial processes used to free and concentrate finely disseminated gold from pulverized rock.

This brings us to a related point. Gold may be present in a rock and not visible. Such is the case of gold that combines chemically with tellurium to form tellurides. Or gold may be so finely disseminated in the ore as to be invisible. Although unrecognizable, such gold can be mined at a profit if the ore is suitably processed.

Where to Look

Gold originates at considerable depth, carried upward by hot fluids, from magma, that force their way into rock fractures. Crystallization, most often in quartz veins, occurs as the fluids cool and pressures diminish. The ultimate source, therefore, of rock-borne or **lode gold** is igneous rocks. But just any igneous rocks won't do. The most favorable ones are light-colored, fine-grained rocks or felsites (see chapter 15) emplaced as flows, sills, and dikes (see Figure 15-14), and light-colored porphyritic rocks. Borders of granitic masses may be productive. Other rocks, igneous, metamorphic, or sedimentary, tend to contain little gold unless transected by felsite rock bodies. Your best bet, though, is to search quartz veins.

Although lode gold is most often invisible, that doesn't mean you should forego its search. Examine abandoned mine dumps for lode gold to gain a good feeling for suitable rock associations.

As lode deposits break up by weathering, such materials are carried downslope and accumulate as gold-bearing sand or gravel in streams, along beaches, in front of melting glaciers, and in sand dunes. **Placer** (PLASS-uhr) **gold**, in sand and gravel, is the most ready source for the recreational prospector.

Placer gold is best sought in stream deposits. Emphasize your search in streams where both erosion and deposition (see chapter 2) take place. Gold, heavier than most materials, concentrates wherever stream flow slackens—the downstream sides of boulders, bedrock outcrops, and submerged logs; the insides of stream bends on bars; and widened areas or pools just downstream from rapids and riffles. Focus, too, on smaller gold traps: cracks in bedrock, in particular those at right angles to stream flow; irregular surfaces of bedrock streambeds, such as foliation surfaces of slate and schist that act as natural riffles; potholes and other depressions in bedrock; and tangles of tree roots. Don't forget to prospect stream terraces: They represent former stream deposits. In like manner, examine dry streambeds and stream sediment above the present water level.

Where possible, follow gold-bearing streams to a lake or sea. Here, along beaches, wave action winnows sand and sorts and concentrates gold and other heavy minerals (see Figure 4-3).

To zero in on the search, look in places where gold has been found or mined in the past. Most of the gold retrieved in the United States has come from seven states, listed in order of declining production: California, Nevada, Colorado, South Dakota, Alaska, Utah, and Montana. But many more states have produced gold. Check with J. E. Ransom's *The Gold Hunter's Field Book* for hundreds of gold-producing localities in 32 states as well as the Canadian provinces. Another source is the U.S. Geological Survey's Professional Paper 610, *Principal Gold-Producing Districts of the United States*. Use topographic maps (see chapter 1) to help find suitable localities and abandoned mines, and geologic maps (see chapter 20) to locate suitable rock types. Generally, unreserved federal land, such as that not used for parks and military purposes, and much state land is open to prospecting, but always check with the appropriate agency, such as the Bureau of Land Management (BLM), to make sure. National forests are often likely places to prospect; detailed maps of national forests are available from ranger stations and similar outlets. Always gain permission to prospect on private land; lack of such permission may result in loss of any subsequent access for you or other recreational prospectors. Respect, too, the other ethics of collecting covered in chapter 21.

Panning

Panning is the easiest and cheapest method for an individual to extract placer gold on a small scale. Other methods of gold recovery for the recreational gold-finder include the aid of a small sluice, rocker box, hydraulic concentrator, and dredge with the use of wet suits for the operators.

Equipment

Desirable equipment for panning includes a gold pan, gold pan sieve, small shovel, geologist's hammer or small pick or mattock, wrecking bar or pry bar, crevice tool or long screwdriver, pail (to carry the smaller equipment), old spoon, whisk broom, magnet, hand lens, tweezers, and vial or small bottle.

Gold pans, constructed of steel or plastic, range up to 18 inches (46 cm) in diameter and have a broad, low-sloping brim. Easier-to-handle 12- or 14-inch pans are good sizes to begin with. Purists prefer steel pans but plastic pans are lighter and have riffles, gold traps, molded inside. You can usually pick up a gold pan from a hardware store in mining areas. If you lack a gold pan, try a frying pan from which any grease has been removed. A large plastic salad bowl will also do in a pinch. A gold pan sieve fits inside or over the pan. This accessory separates the larger gravel particles and reduces panning time.

To work rock crevices, several tools are useful. With a geologist's hammer or pick, scrape out sediment and sweep the last bit of sediment with a whisk broom. Transfer the sediment to the pan with a shovel or old spoon. For narrower crevices, dig sediment with a long screwdriver or crevice tool, made of a thin rod with a pointed hook at one end. Pry the crevices open with a pick or mattock, wrecking bar, or other pry bar. Remember that the heavy gold is apt to have settled to the bottom of a crevice.

The remaining equipment listed is for the final stage of gold recovery. A hand lens is handy to spot any fine gold traces in the pan. With tweezers transfer gold flakes and grains to a vial or small bottle for storage. Separate the dry, heavy mineral concentrate, "black sand," from the gold with a magnet. If the pan is plastic, you can make the separation by passing the magnet beneath the bottom of the pan.

The Panning Process

To become an efficient panner faster, watch an experienced panner. If this is not possible, begin this way. Fill the pan half or two-thirds full of stream sand and gravel. Submerge the pan in water, break up any clumps, and shake the pan from side to side and front to back to settle the gold. (Where water is scarce, fill a tub with water and pan in the tub.) Remove any large gravel particles. Tilt the edge farthest away from you slightly down, and shake the pan in a circular motion; this allows the lighter materials to wash away. Shake or rap the rims of the pan to resettle the gold and continue the circular motion. Slow down as black sand begins to accumulate in the bottom of the pan, and watch for any gold that might move up toward the rim of the pan.

Much of the concentrate tends to be dark gray or black because of such minerals as magnetite, platinum, and stream tin. Magnetite, especially common, is black, metallic, brittle, and attracted by a magnet. Platinum is gray-white, metallic, malleable like gold, and may be attracted by a magnet. Stream tin or cassiterite is gray, has a greasy appearance, and is brittle.

When the contents of your pan have been reduced to a tablespoon or so of black sand, remove the pan from the water. Allow just enough water in the pan to move the sand. Swirl the sand into a thin layer on the bottom of the pan, and look for "colors"—flakes or grains of gold.

To evaluate the efficiency of your panning, practice at home. Drop a known number of buckshot or other tiny, heavy objects into the sand in your pan. The number of objects you recover can be converted to a percentage of efficiency.

If water is unavailable, try dry panning or winnowing. Handpick or screen out the coarser particles. Place the fine fraction on a blanket and have a partner help you shake the blanket in a wind. The gold and other heavy minerals remain on the blanket and the finer and lighter particles are blown away.

One last point about panning or winnowing. I've emphasized placer gold because it is most readily seen. If, however, you strongly suspect gold in a well-weathered lode deposit, by all means try to pan or winnow the loose, weathered lode material.

Selling (Any of) Your Gold

Unusual gold in rock, including large flakes, wires, leaves, crystals, and large or unusual nuggets, is usually sold as specimen gold to museums or private collectors. Price is negotiable and depends on what a buyer is ready and willing to pay. Other gold, in the finer sizes, usually must be assayed before sale because gold is never

100 percent pure. For very small amounts, the assay costs could consume most of your profit.

You are apt to find several private gold buyers in mining areas. Spend time to locate one who is fair and trustworthy. You might also sell through banks, which can be relied upon and maintain good records of transactions. Whatever the outlet, keep a close eye on world gold prices—they fluctuate daily—to assure yourself a fair price. The present record gold price is $880 per troy ounce struck in 1980.

Suggested Reading

Koschmann, A. H., and M. H. Bergendahl. "Principal Gold-Producing Districts of the United States." *U.S. Geological Survey Professional Paper* 610 (1968): 1–283.

Petralia, J. F. *Gold! Gold! Beginner's Handbook: How to Prospect for Gold.* San Francisco, CA: Sierra Trading Post, 1991.

Ransom, J. E. *The Gold Hunter's Field Book: How and Where to Find Gold in the United States and Canada.* New York: HarperCollins, 1980.

West, J. M. "How to Mine and Prospect for Placer Gold." *U.S. Bureau of Mines Information Circular* 8517 (1971): 1–43.

A canyon cut into granite; Fremont Canyon near Alcova, southeastern Wyoming. The canyon walls are vertical because the granite is fractured by vertical joints but also by near-horizontal, intersecting cross-joints. Preformed granite blocks topple to the floor of the canyon.

Main Museums with Geological Materials in the United States and Canada

(Exclusive of Those in Parks and Similar Places)

The primary sources for this list of museums are: *The Official Museum Directory 1992* (by The American Association of Museums; published by the National Register Publishing Company, 1991) and *The Directory of Museums & Living Displays* (edited by Kenneth Hudson and Ann Nicholls; published by Stockton Press, 1985). As you travel, keep in mind that geology departments at universities and colleges may have museums; they may be small but are often worthwhile. Seek them out.

United States

ALABAMA
Anniston: Anniston Museum of Natural History
Birmingham: Red Mountain Museum
Tuscaloosa: Alabama Museum of Natural History

ALASKA
Anchorage: Alaska Museum of Geological & Petroleum History
Fairbanks: University of Alaska Museum

ARIZONA
Bisbee: Bisbee and Mining and Historical Museum
Flagstaff: Museum of Northern Arizona; Museum of Astrogeology,
    Meteor Crater
Mesa: Mesa Southwest Museum
Page: Carl Hayden Visitor Center
Phoenix: Arizona Mining and Mineral Museum
Tempe: Center for Meteorite Studies
Tucson: Arizona-Sonora Desert Museum; University of Arizona Mineral
    Museum; Old Pueblo Museum

ARKANSAS
Arkadelphia: Henderson State University Museum
Fayetteville: The University Museum
Jonesboro: Arkansas State University Museum
Smackover: Arkansas Oil and Brine Museum

CALIFORNIA
Aliso Viejo: The Museum of Natural History and Science
Berkeley: Museum of Paleontology

Claremont: Raymond M. Alf Museum
Los Angeles: Natural History Museum of Los Angeles County
Oakland: The Oakland Museum
Pacific Grove: Pacific Grove Museum of Natural History
Palm Springs: Palm Springs Desert Museum, Inc.
Randsburg: Randsburg Desert Museum
Redlands: San Bernadino County Museum
Riverside: Riverside Municipal Museum; World Museum of
    Natural History
Sacramento: Sacramento Science Center
San Diego: Allison Research Center: Geology and Paleontology;
    San Diego Natural History Museum
San Francisco: California Academy of Sciences
San Jacinto: San Jacinto Valley Museum
Santa Barbara: Santa Barbara Museum of Natural History
Santa Rosa: Codding Museum of Natural History
Yucaipa: Mouseley Museum of Natural History
Yucca Valley: Hi-Desert Nature Museum

COLORADO
Boulder: University of Colorado Museum
Canon City: Canon City Municipal Museum
Colorado Springs: May Natural History Museum
Cripple Creek: Cripple Creek District Museum, Inc.
Denver: Denver Museum of Natural History
Golden: Colorado School of Mines Geology Museum
Grand Junction: Museum of Western Colorado
Gunnison: Gunnison County Pioneer and Historical Society
Idaho Springs: Clear Creek Historic Mining and Milling Museum
Rifle: Rifle Creek Museum
Sterling: Overland Trail Museum
Telluride: San Miguel Historical Society Museum

CONNECTICUT
Greenwich: The Bruce Museum
New Haven: Peabody Museum of Natural History
Stamford: Stamford Museum and Nature Center
Westport: Nature Center for Environmental Studies, Inc.

DELAWARE
Wilmington: Delaware Museum of Natural History

DISTRICT OF COLUMBIA (Washington)
National Museum of Natural History
United States Department of the Interior Museum

FLORIDA
Bradenton: South Florida Museum & Bishop Planetarium
Daytona Beach: Museum of Arts and Sciences, Inc.

DeLand: Gillespie Museum of Minerals, Stetson University
Gainesville: Florida State Museum of Natural History
Miami: Museum of Science
Mulberry: Mulberry Phospate Museum
Sanibel: The Shell Museum & Educational Foundation, Inc.

GEORGIA
Athens: University of Georgia Museum of Natural History
Atlanta: Fernbank Science Center
Buford: Lanier Museum of Natural History
Elberton: Elberton Granite Museum and Exhibit
Statesboro: Georgia Southern Museum

HAWAII
Hilo: Lyman House Memorial Museum
Honolulu: Bishop Museum

IDAHO
Pocatello: Idaho Museum of Natural History
Sandpoint: Bonner County Historical Museum
Wallace: Wallace District Mining Museum
Weiser: Intermountain Cultural Center & Museum

ILLINOIS
Carbondale: University Museum
Chicago: Museum of the Chicago Academy of Sciences; Field Museum
    of Natural History
Elgin: Elgin Public Museum
Elmhurst: Lizzadro Museum of Lapidary Art
Quincy: Quincy Museum of Natural History and Art
Rock Island: Fryxell Geology Museum
Rockford: Burpee Museum of Natural History
Springfield: Illinois State Museum
Urbana: Museum of Natural History, University of Illinois

INDIANA
Evansville: Evansville Museum of Arts & Science
Indianapolis: The Children's Museum; Indiana State Museum
New Harmony: Historic New Harmony Inc.
Richmond: Joseph Moore Museum

IOWA
Cedar Falls: University of Northern Iowa Museum
Cherokee: Sanford Museum and Planetarium
Davenport: Putnam Museum
Des Moines: Science Center of Iowa; State Historical Society of Iowa
Iowa City: University of Iowa Museum of Natural History
Iowa Falls: Ellsworth College Museum
Sioux City: Sioux City Public Museum
Waterloo: Grout Museum of History and Science

KANSAS
Hays: Sternberg Memorial Museum
La Crosse: Post Rock Museum
Lawrence: KU Museum of Natural History; Museum of
    Invertebrate Paleontology
McPherson: McPherson Museum
Oakley: Fick Fossil & History Museum

KENTUCKY
Berea: Berea College Museums
Louisville: Museum of History and Science
Owensboro: Owensboro Area Museum

LOUISIANA
Baton Rouge: Louisiana State University Museum of Geoscience
Ruston: Louisiana Tech Museum
Shreveport: Grindstone Bluff Museum and Environmental
    Education Center
Sulphur: Brimstone Museum

MAINE
Augusta: Maine State Museum
Caribou: Nylander Museum
Castine: Castine Scientific Society

MARYLAND
Baltimore: Cylburn Nature Museum
Solomons: Calvert Marine Museum

MASSACHUSETTS
Amherst: The Pratt Museum of Natural History
Boston: Museum of Science
Cambridge: Mineralogical Museum of Harvard University
Lincoln: Drumlin Farm Educational Center
Pittsfield: The Berkshire Museum
Springfield: Springfield Science Museum
Worcester: New England Science Center

MICHIGAN
Alpena: Jesse Besser Museum
Ann Arbor: The University of Michigan-Exhibit Museum
Battle Creek: Kingman Museum of Natural History
Bloomfield Hills: Cranbrook Institute of Science
Chelsea: Gerald E. Eddy Geology Center
East Lansing: Michigan State University Museum
Houghton: A. E. Seaman Mineralogical Museum
Mount Pleasant: Center for Cultural and Natural History
Ossineke: Dinosaur Gardens, Inc.
Traverse City: Great Lakes Area Paleontological Museum

MINNESOTA
Granite Falls: Yellow Medicine County Historical Museum
Minneapolis: James Ford Bell Museum of Natural History
Red Wing: Goodhue County Historical Society
St. Paul: The Science Museum of Minnesota

MISSISSIPPI
Flora: Mississippi Petrified Forest
Hattiesburg: John Martin Frazier Museum of Natural Science
Jackson: Mississippi Museum of Natural Science
Mississippi State University: Dunn-Seiler Museum

MISSOURI
Fayette: Stephens Museum of Natural History & The United Methodist
    Museum of Missouri
Joplin: Tri-State Mineral Museum
Kansas City: The Kansas City Museum
Rolla: Ed Clark Museum of Missouri Geology; University of
    Missouri-Rolla Minerals Museum
St. Louis: St. Louis Science Center

MONTANA
Bozeman: Museum of the Rockies
Butte: Mineral Museum
Choteau: Old Trail Museum, Inc.
Ekalaka: Carter County Museum
Fort Peck: Fort Peck Museum
Lewistown: Central Montana Museum
Roundup: Musselshell Valley Historical Museum
Superior: Mineral County Museum & Historical Society

NEBRASKA
Chadron: Chadron State College Earth Science Museum
Hastings: Hastings Museum
Kearney: Fort Kearney Museum
Lincoln: University of Nebraska State Museum

NEVADA
Carson City: The Nevada State Museum
Las Vegas: Marjorie Barrick Museum of Natural History; Las Vegas
    Natural History Museum
Reno: Mackay School of Mines Museum
Overton: Lost City Museum

NEW HAMPSHIRE
Dover: Annie E. Woodman Institute

NEW JERSEY
Morristown: The Morris Museum
Mountainside: Trailside Nature and Science Center

Newark: The Newark Museum
Paramus: Bergen Museum of Art & Science
Paterson: Paterson Museum
Princeton: Princeton University Museum of Natural History
Rutherford: Meadowlands Museum

NEW MEXICO
Albuquerque: Institute of Meteoritics Meteorite Museum
Carlsbad: Carlsbad Museum & Art Center
Los Alamos: Los Alamos County Historical Museum
Portales: Miles Museum
Socorro: New Mexico Bureau of Mines Mineral Museum

NEW YORK
Albany: New York State Museum
Buffalo: Buffalo Museum of Science
Granville: Pember Museum of Natural History
Hicksville: The Gregory Museum: Long Island Earth
     Science Center
Ithaca: Paleontological Research Institution
New York: American Museum of Natural History
Niagara Falls: Schoellkopf Geological Museum
Richfield Springs: Petrified Creatures Museum of Natural History
Rochester: Rochester Museum and Science Center
Schenectady: Schenectady Museum and Planetarium
Stony Brook: Museum of Long Island Natural Sciences
Syosset: Nassau County Museum, Division of Museum Services,
     Department of Recreation and Parks

NORTH CAROLINA
Asheville: Colburn Gem & Mineral Museum, Inc.
Charlotte: Discovery Place
Durham: North Carolina Museum of Life and Science
Gastonia: Schiele Museum of Natural History and Planetarium, Inc.
Greensboro: The Natural Science Center of Greensboro, Inc.
Raleigh: North Carolina State Museum of Natural Sciences
Spruce Pine: Museum of North Carolina Minerals
Winston-Salem: Nature Science Center

NORTH DAKOTA
Bismarck: North Dakota Heritage Center
Epping: Buffalo Trails Museum
Grand Forks: Department of Geology and Geological Engineering
     Museum, University of North Dakota

OHIO
Cincinnati: Cincinnati Museum of Natural History & Planetarium
Cleveland: Cleveland Museum of Natural History

Columbus: Orton Geological Museum, Ohio State University
Dayton: Dayton Museum of Natural History
Glenford: Flint Ridge Memorial Museum
Toledo: Toledo Zoo Museum of Science

OKLAHOMA
Alva: Northwestern Oklahoma State University Museum
Duncan: Stephens County Historical Museum
Norman: Oklahoma Museum of Natural History
Stillwater: Oklahoma State University Museum of Natural and
    Cultural History
Tonkawa: The A. D. Buck Museum of Natural History & Science
Tulsa: Tulsa Zoological Park

OREGON
Eugene: University of Oregon Museum of Natural History
Portland: Oregon Museum of Science and Industry

PENNSYLVANIA
Ashland: Museum of Anthracite Mining
Lancaster: The North Museum of Franklin and Marshall College
Harrisburg: Pennsylvania Historical & Museum Commission
Philadelphia: Academy of Natural Sciences of Philadelphia;
    Wagner Free Institute of Science
Pittsburgh: The Carnegie Museum of Natural History
Scranton: Everhart Museum
Titusville: Drake Well Museum
West Chester: West Chester State College Museum
Wilkes-Barre: Wyoming Historical and Geological Society

RHODE ISLAND
Providence: Roger Williams Park Museum of Natural History

SOUTH CAROLINA
Charleston: The Charleston Museum
Columbia: The University of South Carolina McKissick Museum
Greenwood: The Museum
Spartanburg: Spartanburg Science Center

SOUTH DAKOTA
Hill City: Black Hills Institute of Geological Research, Inc.
Hot Springs: Mammoth Site of Hot Springs, Inc.
Kadoka: Badlands Petrified Gardens
Piedmont: Black Hills Petrified Forest
Rapid City: Museum of Geology, South Dakota School of Mines
    and Technology

TENNESSEE
Nashville: Cumberland Science Museum

TEXAS
Austin: Texas Memorial Museum
Beaumont: Texas Energy Museum
Brazosport: Brazosport Museum of Natural Science
Bryan: Brazos Valley Museum
Dallas: Dallas Museum of Natural History; Southwest Museum of
    Science and Technology, The Science Place
El Paso: The Centennial Museum at the University of Texas at
    El Paso
Fort Worth: Forth Worth Museum of Science and History
Houston: Environmental Science Center; Houston Museum of
    Natural Science
Iraan: Iraan Museum
Lubbock: Museum of Texas Tech University
McKinney: Heard Natural Science Museum and Wildlife
    Sanctuary, Inc.
Midland: The Petroleum Museum
Sequin: Fiedler Memorial Museum
Waco: Strecker Museum

UTAH
Lehi: John Hutchings Museum of Natural History
Moab: Dan O'Laurie Museum
Price: College of Eastern Utah Prehistoric Museum
Salt Lake City: Utah Museum of Natural History

VERMONT
Norwich: Montshire Museum of Science, Inc.

VIRGINIA
Blacksburg: Museum of the Geological Sciences
Harrisonburg: D. Ralph Hostetter Museum of Natural History
Lynchburg: Museum of Earth and Life History
Martinsville: Virginia Museum of Natural History
Richmond: Lora Robins Gallery of Design from Nature; Science Museum
    of Virginia; Virginia Division of State Parks
Roanoke: Science Museum of Western Virginia

WASHINGTON
Port Angeles: Pioneer Memorial Museum
Seattle: Pacific Science Center; Thomas Burke Memorial
    Washington State Museum

WEST VIRGINIA
Charleston: Sunrise Museums, Inc.
Huntington: Geology Museum

WISCONSIN
Green Bay: Neville Public Museum of Brown County
Kenosha: Kenosha Public Museum

Madison: University of Wisconsin Zoological Museum
Milwaukee: Green Memorial Museum, University of Wisconsin-
Milwaukee; Milwaukee Public Museum
New London: New London Public Museum
Platteville: Platteville Mining Museum
Stevens Point: The Museum of Natural History

WYOMING
Casper: Tate Mineralogical Museum
Greybull: Greybull Museum
Laramie: The Geological Museum, The University of Wyoming
Rock Springs: Western Wyoming College Museum

Canada

ALBERTA
Calgary: Glenbow-Alberta Institute
Drumheller: Drumheller and District Fossil Museum; Tyrrell
Museum of Paleontology
Edmonton: Mineralogy and Paleontology Museum of the
University of Alberta; Provincial Museum and Archives of
Alberta; University of Alberta Geology Museum

BRITISH COLUMBIA
Falkland: Valley Museum
Kamloops: Kamloops Museum
Nelson: Kootenay Museum
Vancouver: University of British Columbia: M. Y. Williams
Geological Museum
Victoria: British Columbia Mineral Museum

MANITOBA
Brandon: B. J. Hales Museum of Natural History
Morden: Morden District Museum
Winnipeg: Manitoba Museum of Man and Nature; University of
Manitoba Mineralogy Museum

NEW BRUNSWICK
St. John: New Brunswick Museum

NEWFOUNDLAND
St. John's: Memorial University of Newfoundland, Department
of Geology

NOVA SCOTIA
Halifax: Nova Scotia Museum
Parrsboro: Mineral and Gem Geological Museum

ONTARIO
Cobalt: Northern Ontario Mining Museum
Kingston: Geological Museum

Oil Springs: Oil Museum of Canada
Ottawa: Geological Survey of Canada; National Museum of
     Natural Sciences
Toronto: Royal Ontario Museum
Waterloo: University of Waterloo: Biology and Earth
     Sciences Museum

QUEBEC
Bonaventure: Acadien Museum
Malartic: Mining Museum
Montreal: Redpath Museum
Nouvelle: Miguasha Natural History Museum
Quebec: Laval University: Museum of Mineralogy
     and Geology
Rigaud: Bourget College Museum
Saint-Laurent: Museum of the Nuns of the Holy Cross
Thetford Mines: Museum of Minerals

SASKATCHEWAN
Marshall: Delp's Mineral Museum
Regina: Saskatchewan Museum of Natural History
Saskatoon: University Geological Museum

YUKON TERRITORY
Yellowknife: Prince of Wales Northern Heritage Center

APPENDIX B
United States State and Canadian Provincial Geological Surveys

The source for this appendix is the October 1994 issue of *Geotimes* published by the American Geological Institute.

United States State Geological Surveys

Geological Survey of Alabama
Box 0, 420 Hackberry Lane
Tuscaloosa, AL 35486-9780
(205) 349-2852

*Alaska Division of Geological and
   Geophysical Surveys*
Suite 200, 794 University Avenue
Fairbanks, AK 99709-3645
(907) 474-7147

Arizona Geological Survey
Suite 100, 845 North Park
   Avenue
Tucson, AZ 85719
(602) 628-5106

Arkansas Geological Commission
Vardelle Parham Geology Center
3815 West Roosevelt Road
Little Rock, AR 72204
(501) 663-9714

*California Division of Mines
   and Geology*
Department of Conservation
801 K Street, MS 12-30
Sacramento, CA 95814-3531
(916) 445-1923

Colorado Geological Survey
Department of Natural Resources
Room 715, 1313 Sherman Street
Denver, CO 80203
(303) 866-2611

*Connecticut Geological and Natural
   History Survey*
79 Elm Street
Hartford, CT 06102
(203) 566-3540

Delaware Geological Survey
DGS Building, University of
   Delaware
Newark, DE 19716-7501
(302) 831-2833

Florida Geological Survey
903 West Tennessee Street
Tallahassee, FL 32304-7700
(904) 488-4191

Georgia Geologic Survey
Department of Natural Resources
Room 400, 19 Martin Luther
   King Jr. Drive S.W.
Atlanta, GA 30334
(404) 656-3214

*Hawaii Department of Land and
   Natural Resources*
Division of Water and Land
   Development
Box 373
Honolulu, HI 96809
(808) 587-0230

Idaho Geological Survey
Room 332, Morrill Hall
University of Idaho
Moscow, ID 83843
(208) 885-7991

Illinois State Geological Survey
Natural Resources Building
615 East Peabody Drive
Champaign, IL 61820
(217) 333-4747

Indiana Geological Survey
611 North Walnut Grove
Bloomington, IN 47405
(812) 855-9350

*Iowa Department of Natural
   Resources*
Geological Survey Bureau
123 North Capitol Street
Iowa City, IA 52242
(319) 335-1575

Kansas Geological Survey
1930 Constant Avenue
West Campus, University of
   Kansas
Lawrence, KS 66047
(913) 864-3965

Kentucky Geological Survey
228 Mining and Mineral
   Resources Building
University of Kentucky
Lexington, KY 40506-0107
(606) 257-5500

Louisiana Geological Survey
Box G, University Station
Baton Rouge, LA 70893
(504) 388-5320

Maine Geological Survey
Department of Conservation
State House Station 22
Augusta, ME 04333
(207) 287-2801

Maryland Geological Survey
2300 St. Paul Street
Baltimore, MD 21218-5210
(410) 554-5559

*Massachusetts Office of
   Environmental Affairs*
Room 2000, 20th Floor
100 Cambridge Street
Boston, MA 02202
(617) 727-9800

Michigan Geological Survey Division
Box 30256
Lansing, MI 48909
(517) 334-6907

*Minnesota Department of Natural
   Resources, Minerals Division*
Box 567, 1525 East Third Avenue
Hibbing, MN 55746
(218) 262-6767

Minnesota Geological Survey
2642 University Avenue
St. Paul, MN 55114-1057
(612) 627-4780

Mississippi Office of Geology
Box 20307
Jackson, MS 39289-1307
(601) 961-5500

*Missouri Department of Natural
   Resources*
Division of Geology and Land
   Survey
Box 250, 111 Fairgrounds Road
Rolla, MO 65401
(314) 368-2100

*Montana Bureau of Mines
   and Geology*
Montana College of Mineral
   Science and Technology
1300 West Park Street
Butte, MT 59701-8997
(406) 496-4181

*Nebraska Conservation
   and Survey Division*
University of Nebraska
113 Nebraska Hall
Lincoln, NE 68588-0517
(402) 472-3471

*Nevada Bureau of Mines
    and Geology*
Stop 178, University of Nevada
Reno, NV 89557-0088
(702) 784-6691

New Hampshire Geological Survey
Department of Environmental
    Services
Box 2008
Concord, NH 03302-2008
(603) 271-3406

New Jersey Geological Survey
CN-427
Trenton, NJ 08625
(609) 292-1185

*New Mexico Bureau of Mines and
    Mineral Resources*
Campus Station
Socorro, NM 87801
(505) 835-5420

New York State Geological Survey
3136 Cultural Education
    Center
Empire State Plaza
Albany, NY 12230
(518) 474-5816

North Carolina Geological Survey
Environment, Health and
    Natural Resources
Box 27687
Raleigh, NC 27611-7687
(919) 733-2423

North Dakota Geological Survey
600 East Boulevard
Bismarck, ND 58505-0840
(701) 224-4109

Ohio Division of Geological Survey
Department of Natural
    Resources
4383 Fountain Square Drive
Columbus, OH 43224-1362
(614) 265-6576

Oklahoma Geological Survey
Room N-131, Energy Center
100 East Boyd
Norman, OK 73019-0628
(405) 325-3031

*Oregon Department of Geology and
    Mineral Industries*
Suite 965
800 N.E. Oregon Street #28
Portland, OR 97232
(503) 731-4100

*Pennsylvania Bureau of Topographic
    and Geologic Survey*
Department of Environmental
    Resources
Box 8453
Harrisburg, PA 17105-8453
(717) 787-2169

*Puerto Rico Geological Survey
    Division*
Department of Natural Resources
Box 5887, Puerta de Tierra
    Station
San Juan, Puerto Rico 00906
(809) 722-2526

Rhode Island State Geologist
Department of Geology,
    University of Rhode Island
Kingston, RI 02881
(401) 792-2265

South Carolina Geological Survey
5 Geology Road
Columbia, SC 29210-9998
(803) 896-7700

South Dakota Geological Survey
Science Center, University of
    South Dakota
Vermillion, SD 57069-2390
(605) 677-5227

Tennessee Division of Geology
L&C Tower 13th Floor
401 Church Street
Nashville, TN 37243-0445
(615) 532-1503

Texas Bureau of Economic Geology
University of Texas
Box X, University Station
Austin, TX 78713-7508
(512) 471-1534

Utah Geological Survey
2363 South Foothill Drive
Salt Lake City, UT 84109-1491
(801) 467-7970

Vermont Agency of Natural Resources
Vermont Geological Survey
Center Building, 103 South Main
    Street
Waterbury, VT 05671-0301
(802) 241-3601

*Virginia Division of Mineral
    Resources*
Box 3667
Charlottesville, VA 22903
(804) 293-5121

*Washington Department of Natural
    Resources*
Division of Geology and Earth
    Resources
Box 47007
Olympia, WA 98504-7007
(206) 902-1450

Geologist of Washington, D.C.
Department of Environmental
    Science
MB 44-04, University of the
    District of Columbia
4200 Connecticut Avenue N.W.
Washington, DC 20008-1154
(202) 282-7373

*West Virginia Geological and
    Economic Survey*
Mont Chateau Research Center
Box 879
Morgantown, WV 26507-0879
(304) 594-2331

*Wisconsin Geological and Natural
    History Survey*
3817 Mineral Point Road
Madison, WI 53705-5100
(608) 262-1705

Geological Survey of Wyoming
Box 3008, University Station
Laramie, WY 82071
(307) 766-2286

Canadian Provincial Surveys

Alberta Department of Energy
Mineral Resources Division,
    Minerals Disposition Branch
Department of Energy
12th Floor, South Tower,
    Petroleum Plaza
9915-108 Street
Edmonton, Alberta T5K 2C9
    Canada
(403) 427-7707

Alberta Geological Survey
Alberta Research Council
Box 8330, Postal Station F
Edmonton, Alberta T6H 5X2
    Canada
(403) 438-7615

*British Columbia Geological Survey
    Branch*
Mineral Resources Division
Ministry of Energy, Mines, and
    Petroleum Resources
Parliament Buildings
Victoria, British Columbia V8V
    1X4 Canada
(604) 387-0687

Manitoba Energy and Mines
Geological Services Branch
535-330 Graham Avenue
Winnipeg, Manitoba R3C 4E3
    Canada
(204) 945-6559

New Brunswick Minerals and Energy Division
Geological Surveys Branch, Department of Natural Resources and Energy
Box 6000
Fredericton, New Brunswick E3B 5H1 Canada
(506) 453-2206

Geological Survey Branch of Newfoundland and Labrador
Department of Mines and Energy
Box 8700
St. John's, Newfoundland A1B 4J6 Canada
(709) 729-2763

Northwest Territories Geology Division
Geology Division
Box 1500
Yellowknife, Northwest Territories X1A 2R3 Canada
(403) 920-8210

Nova Scotia Department of Mines and Energy
Box 689
Halifax, Nova Scotia B3J 2T9 Canada
(902) 424-4162

Ontario Geological Survey
Ministry of Northern Development and Mines
1121-77 Grenville Street
Toronto, Ontario P3E 6B5 Canada
(705) 670-5866

Prince Edward Island Department of Energy and Minerals
Box 2000
Charlottetown, Prince Edward Island CIA 7N9 Canada
(902) 368-5025

Quebec Ministre de l'Energie et des Ressources
5700 4e Avenue Quest, Locall A-211
Charlesbourg, Quebec G1H 6R1 Canada
(418) 646-2707

Saskatchewan Geology and Mines Division
Energy and Mines
1914 Hamilton Street
Regina, Saskatchewan S4P 4V4 Canada
(306) 787-2568

Yukon Territory Exploration and Geological Services Division
Indian and Northern Affairs
200 Range Road
Whitehorse, Yukon Territory Y1A 3V1 Canada
(403) 667-3200

United States Regional Geological Highway Maps of the American Association of Petroleum Geologists

Most of these geological maps include cross sections, a tectonic map, a landform map, and geological history of a region. Some maps provide a list of selected mineral, rock, and fossil collecting localities and places of geological interest.

Order these regional maps from: American Association of Petroleum Geologists, AAPG Bookstore, P. O. Box 979, Tulsa, OK 74101-0979 (Telephone: 800-364-2274).

Map 1   Mid-Continent Region (Revised)
Arkansas
Kansas
Missouri
Oklahoma

Map 2   Southern Rocky Mountain Region (Revised)
Arizona
Colorado
New Mexico
Utah

Map 3   Pacific Southwest Region
California
Nevada

Map 4   Mid-Atlantic Region (Revised)
Delaware
Kentucky
Maryland
North Carolina
South Carolina
Tennessee
Virgina
West Virginia

Map 5   Northern Rocky Mountain Region
Idaho
Montana
Wyoming

Map 6   Pacific Northwest Region
Idaho (in part)
Oregon
Washington

Map 7   Texas

Map 8   Alaska and Hawaii

Map 9   Southeastern Region
Alabama
Florida
Georgia
Louisiana
Mississippi

Map 10   Northeastern Region (Revised)
Connecticut
Maine
Massachusetts
New Hampshire
New Jersey
New York
Pennsylvania
Rhode Island
Vermont

Map 11   Great Lakes Region
Illinois
Indiana
Michigan
Ohio
Wisconsin

Map 12   Northern Great Plains Region
Iowa
Minnesota
Nebraska
North Dakota
South Dakota

Selected Aspects of the Regional Geology of the Coterminous United States

The coterminous United States can be divided into geologic regions that share similar landforms, rock deformation, rock types, geologic history, and climate. Such regions are called **physiographic provinces** (see Figure Appendix D-1) and are convenient to perceive and assimilate large tracts geologically.

General location, relief, predominant landforms, rock deformation, rock types, age of bedrock, selected historical highlights, and other comments is given for each province. Rock type refers to bedrock exposed at the surface. Under historical highlights pre-Paleozoic mountain building is usually not mentioned because this has occurred nearly everywhere. You will find the regional maps listed in Appendix C useful in conjunction with the information given here.

1. Coastal Plain Province
Location: Belt along Atlantic and Gulf Coasts from Cape Cod to Mexico; continental shelf is underwater extension of this belt.
Relief: Low, mostly tens of feet to few hundred feet.
Landforms: Mostly stream- and shoreline-related; also rock deformation- (cuestas), glacier- (Cape Cod and Long Island), and groundwater- (Florida, sinkholes) related.
Rock deformation: Most rock layers appear horizontal but dip gently toward sea.
Rock types: Sedimentary, mostly clastic but much limestone in Florida.
Age of bedrock: Cretaceous and Cenozoic.
Historical highlights: Sea-level rise about 10,000 years ago drowned Atlantic Coast to form major estuaries (e.g., Chesapeake Bay). Florida a submarine carbonate platform from Jurassic to late Cenozoic.
Comments: Rocks of Coastal Plain derived from erosion of Appalachian Mountains and central U.S. Much oil and gas from Cenozoic rocks of Gulf Coastal Plain.

2. Piedmont Province
Location: Borders Atlantic Coastal Plain on west, from mainly Hudson River, New York to central Alabama.
Relief: Low to moderate, up to several hundred feet.
Landforms: Mostly stream-related.
Rock deformation: Intense folding and faulting.
Rock types: Mostly metamorphic and igneous intrusive; in younger, elongate down-faulted basins, mostly reddish sandstone and shale with basalt in flows, dikes, and sills.

Figure D-1. Map of physiographic (geologic) provinces. 1 = Coastal Plain Province, 2 = Piedmont Province, 3 = Blue Ridge Province, 4 = Ridge and Valley Province, 5 = Appalachian Plateau Province, 6 = New England Province, 7 = Adirondack Mountains Province, 8 = Interior Low Plateaus Province, 9 = Interior Highlands Province, 10 = Central Lowlands Province, 11 = Superior Upland Province, 12 = Great Plains Province, 13 = Rocky Mountains Province, 14 = Columbia Plateau Province, 15 = Basin and Range Province, 16 = Colorado Plateau Province, 17 = Cascades Province, 18 = Sierra Nevada Province, 19 = Pacific Border Province. (Physiographic map by Erwin Raisz published in 1954; taken from *The National Atlas of the United States of America*, by the U.S. Geological Survey, Washington, D.C., 1970, p. 59; used with permission. Boundaries of physiographic provinces after *Field Guide to Landforms in the United States*, by J. A. Shimer, New York: Macmillan, Inc., 1972.)

Age of bedrock: Mostly Precambrian and Paleozoic; rocks of down-faulted basins Triassic and Jurassic.

Historical highlights: Mountain building during Ordovician, Devonian, and Pennsylvanian. Mostly erosion during Mesozoic and Cenozoic.

Comments: Eastern part of Appalachian Mountain system. Many falls and rapids where streams pass from more resistant Piedmont rocks to less resistant Coastal Plain rocks—along Fall Line; Fall Line cities include Philadelphia, Washington, Richmond, Columbia, and Columbus. Monadnocks (erosional remnants) near western margin include Stone Mountain, Georgia, and Brushy Mountain, North Carolina.

3. Blue Ridge Province

Location: Borders part of Piedmont on west, from southern Pennsylvania to northern Georgia.

Relief: Few hundred to few thousand feet.

Landforms: Mostly stream-related.

Rock deformation: Intense folding and faulting.

Rock types: Metamorphic and intrusive igneous.

Age of bedrock: Precambrian.

Historical highlights: Similar as for Piedmont.

Comments: Great Smoky Mountains along southwest edge. Mt. Mitchell (elevation 6,684 feet) is highest in Appalachian Mountain system.

4. Ridge and Valley Province

Location: Borders Blue Ridge on west or Piedmont where Blue Ridge missing; extends from St. Lawrence River to central Alabama.

Relief: To several hundred feet.

Landforms: Mostly rock deformation-related, of linear and zig-zag ridges and similar intervening valleys.

Rock deformation: Folding and thrust faulting, mostly folding in north, mostly thrust faulting in south.

Rock types: Sedimentary, ridges mostly of sandstone and conglomerate, valleys of shale and limestone.

Age of bedrock: Paleozoic.

Historical highlights: Mountain building during Pennsylvanian. Mostly eroded during Mesozoic and Cenozoic.

Comments: Conspicuous trellis stream drainage patterns with gaps cut through ridges (see Figures 9-8 and 9-9). Natural Bridge, in eastern part of province in west-central Virginia, formed by solution and collapse of limestone.

5. Appalachian Plateau Province

Location: Borders Ridge and Valley on west, from northern New York to northern Alabama.

Relief: Hundreds of feet to more than 1,000 feet.

Landforms: Mostly stream-related.
Rock deformation: Most rock layers seem flat-lying but actually down-folded into broad syncline.
Rock types: Sedimentary.
Age of bedrock: Paleozoic.
Historical highlights: Mountain building during Pennsylvanian. Mostly eroded during Mesozoic and Cenozoic.
Comments: Northern part glaciated—parts of New York, Pennsylvania, and Ohio; Finger Lakes of south-central New York occupy glacially scoured valleys. Much coal mined from Pennsylvanian rocks in Pennsylvania, West Virginia, and Kentucky; lower grade coal (bituminous) in western Pennsylvania than in eastern Pennsylvania (anthracite) because less rock deformation in western part. Province is westernmost belt of Appalachian Mountain system.

6. New England Province

Location: New England states. Includes extensions of Piedmont and Blue Ridge Provinces.
Relief: Less than one hundred feet to several thousand feet. Most rugged in White Mountains of northern New Hampshire and adjacent Maine; highest peak is Mt. Washington (elevation 6,288 feet).
Landforms: Mostly glacier-related, but also stream- and shoreline-related.
Rock deformation: Folding and faulting.
Rock types: Mostly metamorphic and igneous.
Age of bedrock: Mostly Precambrian and Paleozoic; Triassic-Jurassic sedimentary rocks in down-faulted basin of Connecticut River lowland.
Historical highlights: Mountain building during Ordovician, Devonian, and Pennsylvanian. Drowning of coast about 10,000 years ago formed many estuaries and islands.
Comments: Granite, marble, and slate quarried. Entire province glaciated.

7. Adirondack Mountains Province

Location: Adirondack Mountains, northern New York.
Relief: Few hundred to few thousand feet; highest point is Mt. Marcy (elevation 5,344 feet).
Landforms: Mostly glacier- and stream-related.
Rock deformation: Adirondacks a roughly circular dome; faulting.
Rock types: Mostly igneous and metamorphic.
Age of bedrock: Mostly Precambrian.
Historical highlights: Mountain building during Precambrian. Adirondack Dome uplifted several times during Paleozoic.
Comments: General stream drainage pattern radial, detailed pattern rectangular from faults and "grain" of rocks. Southern extension of Canadian Shield.

8. Interior Low Plateaus Province

Location: Borders Appalachian Plateau on west, Coastal Plain on northeast; parts of Kentucky, Tennessee, Indiana, Illinois, Ohio, and Alabama.

Relief: Similar to that of Appalachian Plateau but less.

Landforms: Mostly stream-related, also groundwater- and rock deformation-related (cuestas).

Rock deformation: Broad folding (Nashville Dome and Cincinnati Arch), also faulting.

Rock types: Sedimentary.

Age of bedrock: Paleozoic.

Historical highlights: Nashville Dome and Cincinnati Arch areas of uplift first during Devonian.

Comments: Many solution-controlled landforms in limestone terrain of southwestern Kentucky where Mammoth Cave is located (see Figure 6-2). Bluegrass region in northeastern part of province.

9. Interior Highlands Province

Location: Borders part of Gulf Coastal Plain on northwest and Interior Low Plateaus on west; includes Ozark Plateau (southern Missouri) and Ouachita Mountains (southwestern Arkansas and southeastern Oklahoma).

Relief: Tens of feet to few thousand feet.

Landforms: Mostly stream- and rock deformation-related (hogbacks, cuestas), also groundwater-related.

Rock deformation: Doming (Ozark Dome, site of Ozark Plateau) and folding and thrusting (Ouachita Mountains).

Rock types: Mostly sedimentary, igneous in core of Ozark Dome.

Age of bedrock: Mostly Paleozoic, Precambrian in core of Ozark Dome.

Historical highlights: First uplift of Ozark Dome during Ordovician. Mountain building in Ouachitas during Pennsylvanian. Ouachitas are extension of Appalachian Mountain system, similar to Ridge and Valley Province.

Comments: Many caves in carbonate rocks of Salem and Springfield Plateaus of southern Missouri. Northern edge is southern limit of continental glaciation. Significant lead and zinc mined in Ozark Plateau.

10. Central Lowlands Province

Location: Borders Adirondack Mountains, Appalachian Plateau, Interior Low Plateaus, Interior Highlands, and Coastal Plains Provinces on west and north; generally bordered by higher terrain.

Relief: Tens of feet or less to few hundred feet.

Landforms: Mostly glacier- and stream-related.

Rock deformation: Rock layers mostly horizontal except where warped by broad uplifts (e.g., extensions of Cincinnati Arch and Wisconsin Dome) and basins (e.g., Michigan and Illinois Basins).

Rock types: Mostly sedimentary, some igneous and metamorphic.

Age of bedrock: Mostly Paleozoic and Precambrian.

Historical highlights: Structural Michigan and Illinois Basins formed during Ordovician. Topographic basins of Great Lakes formed during Pleistocene as glacial ice lobes scoured former stream valleys.

Comments: Northern part of province glaciated. Stream courses (e.g., Missouri and Ohio Rivers) changed by advancing glaciers. Largest ice-margined glacial lake in North America, Lake Agassiz, evidenced by flat lake plain and shoreline features in eastern North Dakota and western Minnesota.

11. Superior Upland Province

Location: Lake Superior, northeastern Minnesota, and northwestern Wisconsin; borders Central Lowlands on north.

Relief: Tens of feet to several hundred feet.

Landforms: Glacier- and stream-related.

Rock deformation: Rock layers broadly upwarped on Wisconsin Dome (covers much of Wisconsin); Lake Superior overlies faulted syncline.

Rock types: Mostly metamorphic and igneous, some sedimentary.

Age of bedrock: Precambrian and Paleozoic.

Historical highlights: Wisconsin Dome and Lake Superior Syncline formed during early Paleozoic.

Comments: Province is southern extension of Canadian Shield. Boundary Waters Canoe Area in province. Great depth of Lake Superior (more than 1,300 feet) due to down-folding and down-faulting and scour by glacial ice.

12. Great Plains Province

Location: Borders Central Lowlands on west; eastern boundary distinct in North Dakota and Texas but generally vague elsewhere; 100th meridian is rough boundary between two provinces.

Relief: Greater (and with higher elevation) than in Central Lowlands, tens of feet to several thousand feet.

Landforms: Mostly stream-related, some glacier-related.

Rock deformation: Rock layers essentially horizontal except where warped into basins (e.g., Williston Basin of the Dakotas and eastern Montana) and uplifts (e.g., Black Hills Uplift).

Rock types: Mostly sedimentary.

Age of bedrock: Mostly Mesozoic and Cenozoic.

Historical highlights: Williston Basin formed during Ordovician. Black Hills Uplift formed during late Cretaceous and early Tertiary.

Comments: High Plains (Nebraska to Texas) flattest and least eroded of province; mostly result of sediments deposited by streams during erosion of Rockies. Many solution features in carbonates and evaporites in western Texas and southeastern New Mexico (including Carlsbad Caverns).

13. Rocky Mountain Province

Location: Borders most of Great Plains on west, from northern New Mexico to northwestern Montana and northern Idaho (and into Canada).

Relief: Frequently more than a mile, several peaks exceed 14,000 feet. Higher elevation than in provinces to east and west.

Landforms: Stream-, rock deformation-, and glacier-related.

Rock deformation: Anticlinal uplifts, down-folded and down-faulted basins, thrust faulting.

Rock types: Sedimentary, igneous, and metamorphic.

Age of bedrock: Precambrian through Tertiary.

Historical highlights: Mountain building during late Cretaceous and early Tertiary. Present elevation of Rockies from middle to late Tertiary uplift that caused dry climate in Great Plains.

Comments: Valley glacier landforms at higher elevations, few small glaciers persist. Province divided into Northern Rockies (e.g., Selkirk and Bitterroot Mountains), Central Rockies (e.g., Bighorn Mountains and Laramie Range), and Southern Rockies (e.g., Front Range and Sangre de Cristo Mountains). Wyoming Basin is extension of Great Plains through gap between Laramie Range and Bighorns; consists of group of structural basins (e.g., Wind River and Green River) between anticlinal and uplifted mountains.

14. Columbia Plateau Province

Location: Borders Northern Rockies on west and south; mostly parts of Washington, Oregon, and Idaho; cut through by Columbia and Snake River drainages.

Relief: Tens of feet to several thousand feet.

Landforms: Volcanic and stream-related.

Rock deformation: Normal faulting, jointing, and folding.

Rock types: Mostly basalt, also tuff and clastic sedimentary rocks.

Age of bedrock: Mostly Cenozoic.

Historical highlights: Basalt flows emplaced quietly from rifts or fissures during middle to late Cenozoic. Channeled Scablands, rough terrain in southeastern Washington eroded by running water, formed during late Pleistocene by catastrophic flooding of glacial meltwater.

Comments: Basalt flows, with conspicuous columnar jointing, total about 2 miles thick. Youngest flows in southern Idaho, well displayed in Craters of the Moon National Monument.

15. Basin and Range Province

Location: Borders Columbia Plateau on south and part of Rockies on west and south; most of Nevada and parts of Oregon, Idaho, California, Utah, Arizona, and New Mexico.

Relief: Tens of feet to several thousand feet.

Landforms: Mostly rock deformation- and stream-related, some volcanic and wind-related (e.g., White Sands National Monument).

Rock deformation: Normal faulting produced grabens (basins) with intervening raised blocks, now linear, generally north-south mountain ranges; also folding and thrust faulting.

Rock types: Sedimentary and igneous.

Age of bedrock: Mostly Paleozoic through Tertiary, some Precambrian.

Historical highlights: Normal faulting began during middle Cenozoic and continues today.

Comments: Mostly internal drainage.

16. Colorado Plateau Province

Location: Bordered on east and north by Rockies, on west and south by Basin and Range; covers parts of Utah, Arizona, New Mexico, and Colorado.

Relief: Tens of feet to several thousand feet.

Landforms: Mostly stream-related, also volcanic and rock deformation-related.

Rock deformation: Rock layers essentially flat-lying but broadly warped into basins and arches in places; some normal faulting.

Rock types: Mostly sedimentary, some igneous and metamorphic.

Age of bedrock: Mostly Paleozoic through Cenozoic, little Precambrian.

Historical highlights: Mile-deep Grand Canyon in southwest part of province cut by Colorado River largely during last 2 to 3 million years.

Comments: Colorado Plateau behaved as relatively rigid and little deformed crustal block. Number of plateau surfaces, held up by resistant layers, north of Grand Canyon; area of many parks.

17. Cascades Province

Location: Borders Columbia Plateau and parts of Rockies and Basin and Range on west; region of Cascade Mountains in west-central Washington and Oregon and northermost California.

Relief: Hundreds of feet to several thousand feet.

Landforms: Mostly stream-, and volcanic and glacier-related.

Rock deformation: Faulting and folding.

Rock types: Mostly igneous, some sedimentary.

Age of bedrock: Mostly Cenozoic and Mesozoic.

Historical highlights: Part of volcanic arc associated with subducting plate during middle and late Cenozoic. Many composite volcanoes formed within last 2 million years: including (north to south) Mts. Baker, Ranier, St. Helens, Hood, Crater Lake, Shasta, and Lassen Peak.

Comments: Many peaks with glaciers.

18. Sierra Nevada Province

Location: Borders part of Basin and Range on west; region of Sierra Nevada Mountains in eastern California.

Relief: Hundreds of feet to several thousand feet.

Landforms: Mostly stream- and glacier-related.

Rock deformation: Normal faulting.

Rock types: Much igneous, some sedimentary.

Age of bedrock: Mostly Mesozoic and Cenozoic, some Paleozoic.

Historical highlights: Much igneous intrusion during Mesozoic. Normal faulting produced Sierra Nevada Mountains, elevated to present height during Pliocene.

Comments: No stream breaches across mountains. Mother Lode gold belt along northwest edge of province. Sierra Nevadas in same relative position as Cascades.

19. Pacific Border Province

Location: Borders Cascades, Sierra Nevadas, and Basin and Range on west; flanks Pacific Ocean; western parts of Washington, Oregon, and California. Includes Coast Ranges on west and lowlands to east: Puget Sound, Willamette Valley, and Sacramento and San Joaquin Valleys.

Relief: Tens and hundreds of feet (lowlands) to several thousand feet (mountains).

Landforms: Mostly stream-, rock deformation-, and shoreline-related.

Rock deformation: Faulting and folding.

Rock types: Mostly sedimentary and igneous, some metamorphic.

Age of bedrock: Mostly Mesozoic and Cenozoic.

Historical highlights: Mountain building in Coast Ranges during middle to late Cenozoic, present elevation from late Cenozoic uplift. Olympic Mountains formed during early Tertiary by subduction. Movement along San Andreas fault zone, within California Coast Ranges, about 190 miles during past 15 million years.

Comments: Prehistoric coastal flooding in places (e.g., Puget Sound and San Francisco Bay), uplift of shoreline in others (e.g., Palos Verdes Hills, southern California). Many dunes in Oregon Dunes National Recreation Area. Much oil production from Sacramento and San Joaquin Valleys.

Suggested Reading

Hunt, C. D. *Natural Regions of the United States and Canada.* San Francisco: Freeman, 1974.

Shimer, J. A. *Field Guide to Landforms in the United States.* New York: Macmillan, 1972.

Selected Roadside Geology Guidebooks to Specific Regions in the United States

Listed in this appendix are roadside geology guidebooks, which are mostly nontechnical. Legions of technical field geology guidebooks have been published by such organizations as state geological societies and surveys, the Geological Society of America, and the American Geological Institute.

The Geological Society of America (GSA) Centennial Field Guide, listed here, deserves special mention. Six volumes cover six regions in the United States and a part of southern Canada. Each volume contains highlights of the 100 best and most accessible geologic features of a region for the geologic traveler, student, and professional geologist. (See the northeastern region, given below, as an example.) Six hundred prime geologic sites should more than whet the appetite of any amateur geologist!

For additional field guidebooks, contact state and provincial geological surveys (Appendix B) and peruse the references at the end of the articles in the GSA Centennial Field Guide.

Northeastern Region (CT, DE, ME, MA, MD, NH, NJ, NY, PA, RI, VT)

Roy, D. C., ed. *Northeastern Section of the Geological Society of America. Centennial Field Guide Volume 5.* Boulder, CO: Geological Society of America, 1987.

Van Diver, B. B. *Roadside Geology of New York.* Missoula, MT: Mountain Press, 1985.

———. *Roadside Geology of Vermont and New Hampshire.* Missoula, MT: Mountain Press, 1987.

———. *Roadside Geology of Pennsylvania.* Missoula, MT: Mountain Press, 1990.

Southeastern Region (AL, FL, GA, KY, LA, MS, NC, SC, TN, VA, WV)

Frye, Keith. *Roadside Geology of Virginia.* Missoula, MT: Mountain Press, 1986.

Head, C. M., and R. B. Marcus. *The Face of Florida.* Dubuque, IA: Kendall/Hunt, 1987.

Multer, H. G. *Field Guide to Some Carbonate Rock Environments, Florida Keys and Western Bahamas.* Dubuque, IA: Kendall/Hunt, 1977.

Neathery, T. L., ed. *Southeastern Section of the Geological Society of America. Centennial Field Guide Volume 6.* Boulder, CO: Geological Society of America, 1986.

Wilson, R. L. "Guide to the Geology Along the Interstate Highways in Tennessee." *Tennessee Division of Geology Report of Investigations No. 39* (1981).

North-Central Region (IA, IL, IN, MI, MN, NE, OH, MO, WI)

Biggs, D. L., ed. *North-Central Section of the Geological Society of America. Centennial Field Guide Volume 3*. Boulder, CO: Geological Society of America, 1987.

Feldmann, R. M., A. H. Coogan, and R. A. Heimlich. *Field Guide, Southern Great Lakes*. Dubuque, IA: Kendall/Hunt, 1977.

Feldmann, R. M., and R. A. Heimlich. *Field Guide, The Black Hills*. Dubuque, IA: Kendall/Hunt, 1980.

Paull, R. K., and R. A. Paull. *Field Guide, Wisconsin and Upper Michigan*. Dubuque, IA: Kendall/Hunt, 1980.

Thacker, J. L., and I. R. Satterfield. "Guidebook to the Geology Along Interstate-55 in Missouri." *Missouri Department of Natural Resources, Division of Geology and Land Survey, Report of Investigations 62* (1977).

South-Central Region (AR, KS, OK, TX)

Buchanan, R. C., and J. R. McCauley. *Roadside Kansas: A Traveler's Guide to its Geology and Landmarks*. Lawrence, KS: University Press of Kansas, 1987.

Fay, R. O. "Geology of the Arbuckle Mountains Along Interstate Highway 35, Southern Oklahoma." *Oklahoma Geological Survey, Guidebook 23* (1986).

Hayward, O. T., ed. *South-Central Section of the Geological Society of America. Centennial Field Guide Volume 4*. Boulder, CO: Geological Society of America, 1988.

Spearing, Darwin. *Roadside Geology of Texas*. Missoula, MT: Mountain Press, 1991.

Stone, C. G., and J. D. McFarland III. "Field Guide to the Paleozoic Rocks of the Ouachita Mountain and Arkansas Valley Provinces, Arkansas." *Geological Commission Guidebook 81-1* (1981).

Stone, C. G., and B. R. Haley. "A Guidebook to the Geology of the Central and Southern Ouachita Mountains, Arkansas." *Geological Commission Guidebook 84-2* (1984).

Rocky Mountain Region (AZ, CO, ID, MT, ND, NM, SD, UT, WY)

Alt, D. D., and D. W. Hyndman. *Roadside Geology of the Northern Rockies*. Missoula, MT: Mountain Press, 1982.

———. *Roadside Geology of Montana*. Missoula, MT: Mountain Press, 1986.

———. *Roadside Geology of Idaho*. Missoula, MT: Mountain Press, 1989.

Beus, S. S., ed. *Rocky Mountain Section of the Geological Society of America. Centennial Field Guide Volume 2*. Boulder, CO: Geological Society of America, 1987.

Bluemle, J. P. "Geology Along North Dakota Interstate 94." *North Dakota Geological Survey Educational Series 16* (1983).

Chronic, Halka. *Roadside Geology of Colorado*. Missoula, MT: Mountain Press, 1980.

———. *Roadside Geology of Arizona*. Missoula, MT: Mountain Press, 1983.

———. *Roadside Geology of New Mexico*. Missoula, MT: Mountain Press, 1987.

———. *Roadside Geology of Utah*. Missoula, MT: Mountain Press, 1990.

Fritz, W. J. *Roadside Geology of the Yellowstone Country*. Missoula, MT: Mountain Press, 1985.

Lageson, D. R., and D. R. Spearing. *Roadside Geology of Wyoming*. Missoula, MT: Mountain Press, 1988.

Larkin, R. P., P. K. Grogger, and G. L. Peters. *Field Guide, The Southern Rocky Mountains*. Dubuque, IA: Kendall/Hunt, 1980.

Parsons, W. H. *Field Guide, Middle Rockies and Yellowstone*. Dubuque, IA: Kendall/Hunt, 1978.

Rigby, J. K. *Field Guide, Northern Colorado Plateau*. Dubuque, IA: Kendall/Hunt, 1976.

———. *Field Guide, Southern Colorado Plateau*. Dubuque, IA: Kendall/Hunt, 1977.

Pacific Region (AK, CA, HI, NV, OR, WA)

Alt, D.D., and D.W. Hyndman. *Roadside Geology of Northern California*. Missoula, MT: Mountain Press, 1975.

———. *Roadside Geology of Oregon*. Missoula, MT: Mountain Press, 1981.

———. *Roadside Geology of Washington*. Missoula, MT: Mountain Press, 1984.

Connor, Cathy, and Daniel O'Haire. *Roadside Geology of Alaska*. Missoula, MT: Mountain Press, 1988.

Hamblin, Kenneth et al. *Roadside Geology of the U.S. Interstate 80 between Salt Lake City and San Francisco: The Meaning Behind the Landscape*. Washington, DC: American Geological Institute, 1974.

Harbaugh, J. W. *Field Guide, Northern California*. Dubuque, IA: Kendall/Hunt, 1975.

Hill, M. L., ed. *Cordilleran Section of the Geological Society of America. Centennial Field Guide Volume 1*. Boulder, CO: Geological Society of America, 1987.

Sharp, R. P. *Field Guide, Coastal Southern California*. Dubuque, IA: Kendall/Hunt, 1978.

———. *A Field Guide to Southern California*. Dubuque, IA: Kendall/Hunt, 1994.

Stearns, H. T. *Road Guide to Points of Geologic Interest in the Hawaiian Islands*. Palo Alto, CA: Pacific Press, 1978.

INDEX

A **boldfaced** page number indicates where a term is defined or a feature explained; an *italicized* page number indicates an illustration.